Education in the Truth

Education in the Truth

Norman De Jong

P&R
P U B L I S H I N G
P.O. BOX 817 • PHILLIPSBURG • NEW JERSEY 08865-0817

Dedicated to the King of the Church,
and to my parents, who have been
my most influential teachers.

CONTENTS

Acknowledgments 9

The Blind Men and the Elephant 10

Preface 13

PART I

I. The Role of Faith or Belief 19
   Faith versus Reason? 19
   The Limitations of Science 22

II. The Unity of Knowledge 37

III. The Organic Unity of Man 46

IV. The Dilemma of Analysis 51

V. The Philosophy Proposed 57

VI. The Only Firm Foundation 64
    Historical Foundations Considered 65
    Philosophical Foundations Considered 66
    Psychological Foundations Considered 67
    Social Foundations Considered 68
    The Word of God Considered 69

VII. What Is Man? 71
     The Original State 72
     The Unredeemed State 75
     The Child as Security-seeker 77

VIII. Goals toward Which 81
      The Ultimate Objective 83
      Criteria for Primary Goals 87
      Primary Goals 91
      Born to Be Free 97
      Summary of Primary Objectives 107
      Secondary Aims Considered 108
      Practical Suggestions for School Administrators . . . 112

IX. Definitions of Education Considered 114

X. The Responsible Institution 120

XI. Implementation of Goals and Objectives 131
    The End of Teaching 132
    The Multi-faceted Nature of Teaching 136
    Science, Art, or Commitment? 139
    The Means to the End 146

XII. Considerations of Learning 156
    Practical Suggestions for Teachers 166
    The Necessity of Frustration and Success 167

XIII. Evaluation of Education 179
    Contemporary Criteria 180
    The Normative Standard 185

Questions for Discussion 187

PART II. RELATED PROBLEMS

XIV. Is Teaching a Profession? 191

XV. Government Subsidy to Nonpublic Schools 197

XVI. Religion and Morality in Public Schools 204

Bibliography 210

LIST OF ILLUSTRATIONS

1. Psychological Strength of Beliefs 35

2. Misconception #1 41

3. Misconception #2 42

4. The Christian Conception 43

5. Man in His Organic Wholeness As He Is Related to God . . 53

6. Analysis of Man As Person 54

7. Analysis of the Personality 54

8. Man Seen, More Meaningfully, As a Whole 54

9. The Dual Demands Made on Finite Educators 55

10. The Philosophic Ladder 63

11. "From" "Through" "To" 69

12. Man Integrally Oriented to God 73

13. The Re-forming Direction 86

14. The Structural Pattern for Education 128

15. A Misconception of Sphere Sovereignty 129

16. The Inter-relatedness and the Distinctiveness of
    Primary Institutions 129

17. The Problem 175

18. The Answers 177

19. The Circular Route to Professionalism 194

ACKNOWLEDGMENTS

Numerous persons have assisted in the preparation of this manuscript. To them is due public recognition and personal thanks for their services. My faithful wife is to be commended for her long-suffering patience and consoling encouragement while I spent long evenings writing and rewriting. Rev. B. J. Haan and Dr. Douglas Ribbens, the administrative heads of Dordt College, deserve sincere appreciation for granting me the opportunity to devote much of my time to this project during the spring and summer of 1967.

Professor Merle Meeter of the Dordt College English Department contributed materially to the technical production. He read the entire manuscript in its rough draft and offered innumerable suggestions for improvement in diction and vocabulary. Other persons who labored over all or part of the manuscript were Rev. Richard De Ridder and Dr. Gordon Clark. Their suggestions and perceptive criticisms have been thoughtfully received and incorporated. If errors of logic, exegesis, or grammar are detected, these men should be absolved of all guilt. Finally, a word of thanks is also due Mrs. Donn Rubingh for her efficient and accurate typing service.

"In thy light shall we see light" (Psalm 36:9).

THE BLIND MEN AND THE ELEPHANT

John G. Saxe

It was six men of Indostan
   To learning much inclined,
Who went to see the Elephant
   (Though all of them were blind),
That each by observation
   Might satisfy his mind.

The First approached the Elephant,
   And happening to fall
Against his broad and sturdy side,
   At once began to bawl:
"God bless me! but the Elephant
   Is very like a wall!"

The Second, feeling of the tusk,
   Cried, "Ho! what have we here
So very round and smooth and sharp?
   To me 'tis mighty clear
This wonder of an Elephant
   Is very like a spear!"

The Third approached the animal,
   And happening to take
The squirming trunk within his hands,
   Thus boldly up and spake:
"I see," quoth he, "the Elephant
   Is very like a snake!"

The Fourth reached out his eager hand,
   And felt about the knee.
"What most this wondrous beast is like
   Is might plain," quoth he;
" 'Tis clear enough the Elephant
   Is very like a tree' "

The Fifth, who chanced to touch the ear
    Said, "E'en the blindest man
Can tell what this resembles most;
    Deny the fact who can,
This marvel of an Elephant
    Is very like a fan!"

The Sixth no sooner had begun
    About the beast to grope,
Than, seizing on the swinging tail
    That fell within his scope,
"I see," quoth he, "the Elephant
    Is very like a rope!"

And so these men of Indostan
    Disputed loud and long,
Each in his own opinion
    Exceeding stiff and strong.
Though each was partly in the right,
    And all were in the wrong!

*Reprinted by permission from Houghton Mifflin Company

PREFACE

Although it is the author's judgment that many prefaces would be more aptly titled "postludes" or "reviews," this one is being penned as a statement of intention. Whether the completed volume will bear any resemblance to that which is presently contemplated is a moot question, the answers to which may be varied and may prompt the reader to disregard entirely these opening thoughts.

American education is in intellectual ferment. Crucial issues appear with increasing rapidity. The status quo is neither static nor determinable, but can best be described as change. Many of these constantly shifting patterns in educational thought are the results of the even more rapid fluctuations in the scientific and technological dimensions of life. Our scientific and technological age, says Glenn Seaborg, chairman of the Atomic Energy Commission, may not only overwhelm us, but can easily make us a "civilization of drugged, purposeless people controlled by a small elite." In almost prophetic words he describes and forecasts the way by which American people must respond to this challenge by our own machinations. He says,

> There are indications that society is reacting to the "feed-back" of certain personal and social effects of technology. This feedback is coming from more and more people in all levels of society and all walks of life. It is expressing an increasing uneasiness about the state of our personal and community lives in a highly materialistic society, a concern over the individual's role in the growing complexity and impersonalization of that society, a groping for "national purpose," and a feeling that the unity of man, referred to by poets and philosophers throughout the ages, is becoming a reality with immense psychological and physical implications.

> To me, these feelings forecast the need for a huge re-evaluation of our goals and values, and it will be in our universities where such a re-evaluation will take place. Perhaps its seeds have already been sown in the current unrest on the campuses of many of our universities. From this re-evaluation, from the debates and soul-searching that take place, will evolve both a new understanding and reinforcement of those old ideals which are still valid, and new ideals and goals. Together they may provide us with something like a comprehensive philosophy of life to match the physical unity of mankind rapidly being fostered by today's science and technology.

> If we can use this new philosophy to guide the great scientific and technological forces we have created, we could witness, possibly within a few decades, the equivalent of a new "human breakthrough" — an

13

advance to a new stage of social development — one that was initiated by our reactions to today's trends.

In such a development the university, the greatest depository and dispenser of man's knowledge, should play a major role. In fact, I can see no other institution more logically equipped to be the central force in this evolutionary process, to develop, refine, and pass on to the new generations a new heritage of a higher level of mankind.

But if we are to carry out such a monumental task, many changes will probably have to take place in the universities and our educational system in general. One such change will involve reconciling the continuing importance of specialization with a growing need for interdisciplinary thinking — not only in science and technology, but in all areas of our economic, social and human development. Specialization has been giving us increasing amounts of knowledge, but the world cries out today for more of something beyond knowledge — for wisdom ("The Cybernetic Age: An Optimist's View," *Saturday Review,* July 15, 1967, p. 23).

With Seaborg's insistence on the need for total re-assessment I find myself in wholehearted agreement. He may not agree with me, however, when I insist that Christianity is the only source from which such an all-pervasive philosophy could ever spring.

For a number of years the author has heard discussion about the need for a statement of Christian philosophy for education. It has been asserted by many Christian school teachers that the one great need of Christian school workers and supporters is that of a distinctive, cogently stated, Biblically-based philosophy to serve as a guide for practice in Christian schools.

To formulate such a philosophy is the goal to which I have set myself. Whether the following statements will be accepted or acceptable is known best by God, whom I ask to forgive whatever departures from Truth I may slip into. For those issues and concepts that are harmonious with His will I ask Him to grant the reader's acceptance.

To the reader I make the following requests: First, don't expect this short volume to answer *all* the questions you may have already asked yourself about the necessity and nature of Christian education. Second, don't expect definitive answers to those new questions which may have been generated in your mind by the issues discussed on the following pages. If the book does nothing more than provoke a self-conscious Christian examination of existing thought patterns and educational practices, it will not have been a failure. Nevertheless, the aim is certainly not to leave a desperate sense of meaninglessness or an array of unanswered queries. The aim is, on the contrary, to structure our educational thought upon the Christian's Biblical basis of principle so that our religious beliefs become more than trite, and ignored, expressions. Hopefully these basic tenets of Biblically-attuned Christians will become reformationally relevant to our educational endeavor. God enlightening us, the reader will begin to see more clearly that educational principles, in order to be authentic, true, must not only avoid contradiction with Christian religious principles, but must be completely one with God's infallible and inspired Word, out of which all principles of life and education must be derived. Third, don't be surprised or angry if some of the definitions offered for common words cannot be found in your home or school dictionaries. Dictionaries are not only fallible, but are frequently structured by descriptive lexicographers to conform to contemporary usage. And since contemporary usage is often determined by the philosophic impact of a movement or a single man who is religiously non-Christian, it will be necessary to grant the author enough literary and philosophic license to formulate definitions for key words so that these definitions are in closer harmony with his ultimate criterion. To the reader who remains skeptical of the basic definitions herein offered, I make this additional plea: slow down, re-assess, and define for yourself. We live in an age that is characterized by dishearteningly rapid change. Most of us are willing to talk about this rapid pace, but few are willing to do much about it, to stop and seriously think and re-think. Finally, be gracious to the author if he inadvertently slips into the employment of technical and senseless jargon. I hope to avoid the specialized language of the academic disciplines because such terminology confuses as often as it clarifies. Also, its usage creates the impression that those who most often employ jargon are those who most jealously guard their little cluster of knowledge for the entertainment of their exclusive ring of professional initiates. To be in possession of jargon, for them, is to be in possession of the key that unlocks professional secrets. For these reasons jargon has no intended place in this volume.

If theologians, philosophers, psychologists, and educationists should find none of their pet terms or phrases included here, nothing much will have been lost, provided, of course, that this absence has not deterred them from reading. The intent is to cut across the lines so artfully and artificially constructed between the various disciplines, to write in such a way that both philosopher and farmer can understand, and to break down those barriers which exist between the layman and the professional.

Philosophy, education, psychology, theology — such disciplines need not have an aura of mystery or exclusiveness. On the contrary, those who best understand these areas of knowledge should be distinguishable by their very ability to discuss and explain them in language that is lucid and intelligible to the layman. Those who cannot divorce themselves from their specialized academic diction are on the one hand an annoyance because they often fail to communicate, but on the other hand ought to be considered a disguised blessing because their ideas may not be worth communicating and may even be destructive because of their ultimate falsity. For example, I am thankful that John Dewey's writings are not very readable or approachable by the average teacher, simply because more persons might knowingly promote his anti-Christian pragmatism if his teachings were clear. The modern mind, however, is of such a mold that it tends to deify or mythologize any author who appears to think more deeply than does the average man. Consequently, men like Dewey become intellectual leaders despite the irony that few people have ever read, understood, or evaluated their bases in principle.

Although the word "philosophy" is traditionally understood to mean love of wisdom, I intend to use it here with a somewhat different connotation. When we think of any specific philosophy such as pragmatism, existentialism, or positivism, we think of a systematic, presumably consistent arrangement or systematization of thought proceeding from a central principle or set of principles. These central principles usually are attempts to answer ultimate questions of origin, meaning, and destiny. On these central principles of faith or *a priori* beliefs no discussion is tolerated. Only if the protagonists in the discussion agree to these basic assertions can meaningful dialogue take place. Consequently, little worthwhile dialogue could develop between two persons or groups who start from differing foundational principles. A thorough-going pragmatist and a dedicated Christian, for example, would seldom engage in extended argument, simply because each rejects the other's core beliefs. For that reason the author is not writing with the purpose of winning arguments with non-Christians. He assumes that the non-Christian — as a consistent non-Christian — will reject this book simply because the central tenets of his faith will be principially hostile to those expressed here.

It is then primarily to the Christian that these words will be directed. More specifically, it is the Protestant Christian in the Reformation heritage. (Regrettably, the word Christian is no longer distinctive; this necessitates the qualifying adjectives.) Even more specifically, this book is meant for those Christians who concern themselves with the relationships between their "religion" and their "education." This philosophy of Christian education, is, then, an attempt to arrange systematically some thoughts on education as they are given their meaning by the Biblical teachings that constitute the orthodox Christian faith. By this Scriptural orientation, it is hoped that true relationships can be more clearly seen. At the same time, all the relationships will not be examined

16

or even hinted at, thus leaving the reader with a number of intellectual extensions to make on his own.

If this arranging and re-arranging of existing ideas sounds like an unexciting venture, the reader should question whether imperfect man can do more. Although we often delude ourselves into thinking that there is some great portion of knowledge yet to be created where no prior knowledge existed, such thinking is destined to remain a delusion. The extent of man's "creative" potential is to make new forms from previously existing things, to arrange new thought formations from age-old ideas.

It should not, then, be tragically disenchanting to discover that the component ideas are known already to many readers. As we find in Ecclesiastes: "There is no new thing under the sun. Is there anything whereof it may be said, See, this is new? it hath been already of old time, which was before us" (1:9b, 10). So it is with this attempt. Many, if not all, of the ideas may have been expressed before, but it is hoped that such reforming repetition will be considered as being meaningful re-dedication of our educational adventure to our Sovereign Triune God.

One final statement of intention. Although theoretical discussion may fill most of these pages, it is intended that theory and practical application never be far apart. If in any way this discussion bridges the gap between Christian theory and Christian practice, it will be partially successful. If this gap is not narrowed, then the only hope is that the theory be found in harmony with the Christian's only guide for faith and practice, namely, Scripture. Where even that cannot be said, the author requests of the reader that same forgiving spirit that he has been promised by the Judge of all mankind. Only because of His promised pardon for our sins do we dare to go forward in our fallenness, rejoicing in the Holy Spirit who has promised to guide us into *all* truth (John 16:13) and in our gracious covenant Father who will certainly establish the work of our hands when it is done to His glory.

CHAPTER I

THE ROLE OF FAITH OR BELIEF

Faith Versus Reason?

In the intellectual history of the Western world, the word "faith" is most often associated with the holding of religious beliefs, especially Christian beliefs. In common usage we talk of the Catholic faith, the Protestant faith, the Reformed faith, the Mormon faith, and countless other "faiths." When used in such a way, the word is used to imply that a distinction exists not only between the various "faiths," but also between those persons that profess a particular faith and those who do not profess a particular faith. Out of such usage an interesting and profitable question arises: What is included in the term faith?

In answering this question let us temporarily put aside the distinctions among the various denominations and focus on what is called the Christian faith. Those persons who hold to belief in God and to propositions based on the Bible are said, to have faith. Faith, with this connotation, explains the ability of the Christian to believe in something which is non-observable to the human senses. Faith, when so construed, is the possession of the Christian only and is considered antithetical to the "reasoned" belief of the non-Christian. A further implication of such usage is that faith is a relatively narrow, rather than comprehensive, possession. Just that segment of one's belief which is Biblical in origin or which is cultic in nature is thought to be included in the meaning of the word faith. For example, a person's affirmative beliefs about God and Christ and sin would legitimately (in contemporary usage) be included in the concept of faith, but one's beliefs about molecular theory and algebraic equations would not. But is that the way "faith" must be defined? Must faith merely denote a limited area of man's thought? If so, what are the lines of limitation? Must the term denote only that which is admittedly partisan, or must it denote the total thought and knowledge of man?

For those who would limit faith, an interesting challenge is presented: Where does faith stop and "neutral knowledge" begin? Does faith include all that might be contained in a typical Sunday worship service? Does it include the speaking, the listening, the singing? Does it include the reading of the Scriptural pages, the reading of chapter and verse numbers? If the answer should be negative, then what is included? If the answer is affirmative, what distinguishes the singing, reading, speaking, and listening of the worship service from those same human actions when exercised outside the church or within the school?

Nicholas Wolterstorff gives to the word faith a very comprehensive meaning. In a recent speech, since published by the National Union of Christian Schools, he used the term in the following way:

> The Christian life is . . . the life of faith; by which I mean, not that it is a life which *includes* faith, but that *as a whole* it is the life of faith. A curriculum for Christian education will aim at equipping the student for living the life of faith.

> Seen in the Biblical perspective, the situation of every man is a confrontation between God and man. Through His works and deeds God speaks to man. He sends forth His Word. And man, through his works and deeds, answers. God asks of man that there be fellowship between them — fellowship based on an honest and humble acknowledgement of the relative positions of both. To this call, man answers "yes" or "no," affirmatively or negatively. The Bible calls man's affirmative answer to God's call for fellowship, "faith," or "belief." His negative answer it calls "unbelief." It sees the issue of belief or unbelief as the basic issue in human life (*Curriculum: By What Standard*, p. 9).

Because of the various construals of the word, intellectual and philosophic history has often been disfigured by the "reason versus faith" controversy. Those who live by faith presumably wage ideological war with those who live by reason, with the implication that faith is the possession of one side and reason is the possession of the other. By many people who have reflected on this spurious faith-reason antithesis, reason is thought to be the superior possession and indicative of intellectual power, whereas faith is relegated to much lower human status and is considered a form of mental impotence and emotional immoderation. Because of this naive and invidious distinction, many young Christians become ashamed of their faith. And, since a high percentage of teachers are young people between the ages of twenty to thirty, it is important that this book begin with a discussion of faith. If teaching and education are thought to be intellectual endeavors and if reasonableness is thought to be a mark of intellectual stature, then it is quite normal for the novice Christian teacher to de-emphasize his faith, even if he does not go so far as to proclaim the deification of reason. When the Christian takes this apologetic stance, however, he is showing a culpable lack of intellectual and spiritual integrity or maturity.

A closer examination of this faith-versus-reason controversy will indicate that the controversy is mislabeled. When properly labeled and properly understood, the young Christian should be convinced that the possession of faith is not a sign of intellectual inferiority, but is actually an important characteristic not only of all men, but of all men at all times. Once it is fully accepted that "we [all] walk by faith, not by sight" (II Cor. 5:7), there will be no justification for neglecting to profess our faith. Once the role of faith in human life is understood, the faith-reason controversy can be interpreted correctly as faith in God versus faith in the rational ability of man. When understood this way, reason is no longer pre-eminent and capable of battling faith on equal ground. Rather, reason is subservient to faith and is only a name given to the method by which a person tries to make logical or consistent extensions of those ideas or assertions in which he believes, or to which he holds by faith.

In order to defend the above assertion, we must expose and recognize the limitations of logic, which is the science of rational principles. Logic deals not only with the validity of conclusions in arguments, but it also has to do with the truth or falsity of both the premises and conclusions. Many falsely assume that by following the right rules of reason or logic one can determine the *truth* or *falsity* of a conclusion as well as the *validity* of that conclusion. In symbolic and sentential logic the truth or falsity of all the argument statements must be agreed on or hypothesized in order to determine validity. In Aristotelian or propositional logic the truth or falsity of the premises is not stated but must be left for the person to decide for himself. In either case, the statements involved in any form of deductive reasoning are considered in two ways: (1) the truth or falsity of those statements, and (2) the validity or invalidity of the conclusions arrived at by consideration or extension of those statements. Of these two considerations, the first is of infinitely greater importance. If a conclusion is valid but false, the protagonists have engaged only in academic and useless debate, for only a fool would act on the basis of what he knows to be false. If beneficial action is to follow from an argument or discussion, it is obvious that the conclusion must be not only valid, but must also be accepted as true.

When using the truth table method of determining validity, an argument is considered valid if it cannot be shown to be invalid. In order to establish invalidity, the statements must be assigned truth values in such a way that the premises are true and the conclusion false. The following example will illustrate:

1. All men are good by nature.
2. My students are men.
3. Therefore, my students are good by nature.

In order to be judged invalid, the first and second statements would have to be considered true while the third were considered false. Unless one were grossly inconsistent in his thinking, such an assignment would not be made. If the premises were labelled as true, the conclusion would merit the same labelling. If they were judged to be false, one could not avoid the obvious falsity of the conclusion. The above argument would thus be considered valid, that is, the conclusion would logically follow from the premises.

If other methods or systems for determining validity were used, the determination of validity would not be altered. However, the designation of validity is inconsequential until the truth or falsity of the major premise is determined. Whether "all men are good by nature" is true or false, that is the prime and significant question. But, there is no device of logic or reason to determine whether "all men are good by nature" is true or false. In decision-making, the label "truth" or "falsity" is going to be assigned on the faith-basis of whether or not the persons *believe* it to be true or false. Reason, then, is confined to questions of validity and cannot begin to decide the essential and ultimate questions of truth or falsity.

If the crucial question of truth or falsity is going to be decided, some method other than reason must be used for such determination. At the same time, it should be recognized that mere belief in a statement or proposition does not make that statement or assertion true. The actual state of affairs, that is, the truth of the matter, is not determined by our belief. By what method, then, can the truth or falsity of our beliefs be ascertained? If the deductive method, the method of reason, cannot aid us, will the inductive?

Before we examine the inductive method, which is the method of science, one note of encouragement for the young Christian must be added. To reason consistently from one belief to another belief is not wrong or outside the Christian's domain. On the contrary, God created man as rational creature and requires that this function, too, be used for His praise and in His service. The warning of Scripures is not against reason, per se, but against faith in man's rational ability.

The Limitations of Science

Since we no longer live in an Age of Reason, but in an Age of Science, it is probable that the role of science in our thinking is of even greater importance than that of reason. Although contemporary times have been variously dubbed as the Space Age, the Technological Age, and the Scientific Age, it is generally agreed that space exploration, technological innovation, medicinal breakthroughs, and computerized products are all examples of scientific "progress." Theology, philosophy, and art have under the onslaughts of science receded to the point where these ventures must defend their very reasons for being. Naturally this onslaught of science is of concern to the Christian, if for no other reason than that prominent naturalistic biologists, chemists, archaeologists, and anthropologists are piting their "scientific discoveries" against the beliefs and traditions of Bible-believing Christians. Whereas the earlier churches fought the war of Reason versus Faith, today's Christians are fighting the war of Science versus Faith.

Harry Van Der Laan recognizes this conflict as one of the principal problems of the twentieth century. Concerning it, he says,

> In our humanistic society, men often turn to one of the causes of the urgency of our time, namely the contributions of the scientist, and also expect answers from the scientist to these fundamental problems. In other words, what we, and certainly many of those in positions of responsibility, expect is that the sciences, which have quickened the pace of our life, and have provided us with the technological apparatus, shall at the same time be a source of principal guidance and shall enable us also to set our priorities. Some people even think that, because we have science which can provide us with much information and insight into a particular state of affairs, we really no longer need principles because a great deal of information will always make it obvious which course we must take. That, of course, is itself a principle, although a very short-sighted one. But it is nevertheless a principle to expect that you can dispense with standards as to your fundamental orientation and direction, simply because the sciences now provide you with a great deal of information. Frequently things are expected of the sciences which by their very nature they cannot provide (*Science and Faith — Dualistic Paralysis or Scriptural Vigor*, p. 4).

Although there are many Christian scholars who are engaged in this battle of beliefs, many of us are taking sides without adequately understanding the relationships between science and faith. Many persons fail to thoroughly examine the insinuations and implications that are being bantered about. Many people choose blindly for one side against the other, hurling invectives as they go. Some of the chief accusations by the "science" faction are that faith is blind, dogmatic, closed-minded, and prejudiced. Those who live solely by "faith" blindly follow religious tradition and hold to pet misconceptions of reality promulgated by earlier scientists. The modern scientist, of course, has the facts and is in pursuit of objective truth. Moreover, the contemporary empirical scientist is the destroyer of old-wives' tales, myths, and dogma.

Because of these and similar indictments, many academic subjects that previously were not considered sciences are eager to share the certainty and invulnerability that the rubric "science" or "scientific" now confers. History is one example of this change in emphasis. In historiographical considerations, all predecessors are considered to have theorized out of biases and prejudices, thus making them inferior to the newly heralded "scientific historians" who are finally uncovering a true knowledge of the past. The same spirit can be observed on the elementary and secondary levels of schooling, where the term history is in disrepute, and is being replaced by the term "social science." Language studies is another academic area where the scientific impact has been felt. The new emphasis can be seen in the decline of grammar and the corresponding rise of structural linguistics, transformational grammar, phonetics (not to be confused with phonics), and scientifically structured alphabets. In their varied forms these are intended as replacements for the traditional grammar and phonics. The invasion of technology into the field of language may be even more obvious. Consider, for example, the introduction of language labs, speed-reading devices, and proof-reading machines. In all of this is the implication that the traditional approaches to language study are unscientific, and therefore based on mythical or prescientific assumptions.

Henry Zylstra, expanding on an observation of Frederick A. Pottle, has this to say about science and belief: "There is always an area of dogma, an area of things which we take for granted. For most people of our time this uncritically accepted area is the scientific one. 'Without being taught to do so, — we assign all 'truth' to the province of science. Whatever science cannot manipulate we feel to be unreal or untrue'" (*Testament of Vision*, p. 127).

Two other areas of academic life where the challenges of science have been keenly felt are teaching and educational psychology. Although the word "teaching" is seldom adequately defined by those who are most concerned with it, it is currently considered correct to think of teaching as a science.[1] In consequence, to be thought of as a good teacher, that is, a professional, one must act scientifically and be preoccupied with a scientific search for improved method. Education, also, as the occupation of teachers, is coming to be thought of as a science. Progress toward solving educational problems will come about only, it is believed, as education in general and teaching in particular, become more scientific, that is, as they gradually come to a greater control of the objective realities of teaching-learning situations. Psychology, which has been somewhat futilely heralded as such, is trying desperately to merit the appellation "science" in the same positivistic laboratory way that physics, biology, and chemistry have secured the title.

Other academic areas of interest could also be considered here, but the point is that the words "science" and "scientific" have become tremendously significant words in our culture. The intellectual climate

---

[1]For more complete discussion of this concept, turn to Chapter 11.

is such that the mere use of such charismatic words almost magically makes one deserving of high praise for having come into possession of objective truth, on the one hand, or condemns one as anti-Christian and anti-faith, on the other. To be unscientific is to be uninformed, at the best, and stupid or senseless, at the worst. To charge a person with not being scientific is to heap coals of condemnation on his head.

That many Christians should be fearful of science is not surprising. Science has been cast as the destroyer of faith, the force that corrupts youth, and the enemy of an almighty Creator. In some minds the fear exists that science is going to uncover information which will prove false our belief in God, in creation as a miraculous activity of God, and in miracles. Some Christians are afraid that science is going to corrupt our school children and lead them away from their historic Reformed faith. We submit, however, that science cannot destroy our faith and that science cannot corrupt our youth. Science cannot do this to the child or to the adult, simply because science is neither a person nor personal. People who call themselves scientists can destroy our faith, however, and people who call themselves scientists can lead our youth away from God. Those persons consciously or unconsciously in the employ of Satan can pervert the unwary when they try to make the Christian believe what they believe. The apostle Paul already encountered this "scientific" perversion in his day. In his concluding remarks to Timothy he warned, "Keep that which is committed to thy trust, avoiding profane and vain babblings, and oppositions of science falsely so called" (I Tim. 6:20).

It may sound somewhat ironical, but some of the most unscientific (by secular definition) men are the same ones who have been called great scientists. Charles Darwin is an eminent example. To anyone who has read his *The Origin of Species* it should be evident that the book is full of unwarranted assumptions and unverifiable hypotheses. The trouble with Darwin and his ilk is that they have pawned off as fact many unexamined assertions. These assertions, furthermore, are palatable to man who is "prone to hate God," and thus they become established, traditional beliefs. What happens as consequence is that one set of beliefs is replaced by another, often more-distorted set of beliefs. It is not an exchange of beliefs for facts, as the proponents of the newer theories would argue, but an exchange of beliefs for beliefs.

In order to make such a charge, however, it is imperative that we ask and answer two questions: (1) What is science? and (2) What are the limitations of science? If these questions can be satisfactorily answered, much of the mysticism and super-status that presently becloud science will be dispelled, and science can regain its proper place in men's lives.

Science needs to be considered on two, and only two, levels. First of all, science is a method of study. When we think of science as a method of study, we are thinking of the way by which legitimate scientists work. This is called the "scientific method" or the "inductive approach." When using this method, the scientist proceeds through the following generally stated steps:

(a) formulation of an hypothesis or theory to be proven;
(b) selection of events or phenomena to be examined;
(c) observation and categorization of the selections;
(d) generalization from these observations to all other similar events and phenomena;
(e) arriving at conclusions and formulating laws or theories on the basis of these observations.

Second, science has to be thought of as a systematic arrangement of what is known and available to man through his senses. When we consider science as a systematic arrangement, we are thinking of the classification of knowledge into organized patterns. Examples of science as classification and arrangement of knowledge are found in biology, chemistry, physics, and astronomy.

When science is considered as either methodology or arrangement, and we submit that science is nothing more, there is no reason to be afraid of science, per se. Also, by this dual definition, theology is a science. So, too, are mathematics, geography, history, philosophy, psychology, and linguistics. For those who expend their energies in a study of systematized information about the political dimension of life to label themselves "political scientists" is then legitimate. The same privilege, of course, should accrue to those who wish to be called "social scientists," "mathematical scientists," or "educational scientists." If and when such terminology becomes rightfully commonplace, the luster and gloss of "science" will be gone, but that forbodes no tragic consequence for the intellectual marketplace.

To think of ministers and seminary professors as "theological scientists" may seem unconventional, but such appellation is not unwarranted. Theology is, or should be, nothing more than a systematic arrangement of those propositional truths that God has incorporated in His Special Revelation. This is not to depreciate or de-emphasize theology or call into question the significance of the truths that have been observed, but merely to be honest about what theology is. If theology tries to become super-revelation, that is, super-Scripture, then it is bad theology. Also, if theology deliberately ignores or distorts part of what is observable in Scripture, it is again bad theology. When theology formulates hypotheses which are not corroborated by Scripture, and then tries to pawn off these hypotheses as being worthy of belief, it is guilty of devilish prevarication. So, too, with any other scientist. Anytime a scientist attempts to make his readers or listeners believe as truth a hypothetical assertion that is not verifiable by experience and in accord with Scripture, that scientist becomes a prevaricator and not worthy of belief.

Assuming for the sake of argument that this is an adequate definition of what science is and what it can do, we must now proceed to set down the limitations of science, or what it cannot do.

The first significant limitation of science is that it cannot deal with anything that is not observable to the human senses. Science can concern itself with the brain of man, but not with the mind. Although some early connectionist psychologists tried to equate the mind with the brain, it is usually acknowledged that these two terms are not synonymous. Simply because the mind is not observable through any of the human senses, science cannot begin to help us in understanding or knowing it. Other phenomena that are observable and amenable to the scientific method, along with related (and very real) metaphysical counterparts that are not observable, are as follows:

(a) The body but not the soul.
(b) Mental activity but not mental capacity.
(c) The physical heart of man, but not the Scripturally described heart of man.
(d) God's creation but not the creative act or the Creator.
(e) The activity of a living being but not its life.
(f) Emotional behavior but not emotion.
(g) The results of faith but not faith.
(h) Space but not infinity.
(i) Time but not eternity.
(j) Christ's human nature but not His divine nature.
(k) The commotion of a lover but not love.
(l) The eye but not the nature of sight.

Although all the things on the left side of the above column are legitimate concerns of science, it should appear obvious to the Christian that those super-sensuous realities on the right side are of equal and vital importance. If the educator hopes to build a worthwhile, Biblical philosophy of education, one that will portray the God-given nature of the child, it should be obvious that science will not be of much help in answering significant questions on the relationship of the seen to the unseen, of the physical to the spiritual. Thus, the educational psychologist, who purports to describe man accurately and completely by

27

trusting to the traditional scientific approach while ignoring the answers of Scripture, has no possibility of succeeding. Yet it is to science and to secular science alone that most educators and educational theorists are looking for the answers to the ills and dilemmas of education.

A second significant limitation of science is that it cannot make any value judgments, that is, it cannot ascribe quality to an observed event or thing. A scientist may be able to determine what cancer is, but, *merely as scientist*, he is not able to judge whether cancer is good or bad. Only as a *person* can be decide that cancer is good or bad, because that is a value judgment, and no systematic arrangement or method of study can make a value judgment. The same is true of an educational psychologist. As a scientific psychologist he can observe and describe youthful behavior, but only as a person can he determine whether that behavior is desirable and good or undesirable and bad. Again, it would seem that the work which is done as scientist pales into insignificance before that work done as a person. Christian faith, however, concerns itself with values and moral quality as an essential part of reality. Furthermore, we cannot expect help from the pure behaviorist because a norm or standard is needed to determine value and quality. Science lacks this. The description of behavior without the determination of that behavior's quality is worse than useless. Personal beliefs about goodness and badness are of far greater importance than is scientific study.

A third major limitation of science is that human beings can not trust the authenticity of human observations. For example, if I place a stick in a glass of water, the eye tells me that the stick is bent. But if I rub my finger along that stick, my sense of touch tells me that the stick is straight. Which sense do I trust?

My eye also tells me that railroad tracks converge in the distance. If I walk to that point, the convergence appears to take place farther down the track. Do I dare to believe my observations, or must my observations always be tempered by other theoretical considerations? My eyes tell me that the moon gives off light and changes shape. But scientists keep telling me that it neither gives off light nor changes shape. They have made observations with their eyes, but so have I! Are their observations more reliable than mine? The point here is not to engage in lunatic discussions, but simply to emphasize the role of belief. The scientist is asking for faith in his observations. When he makes his assertions about the sun or the moon, or the origin of man, he is asking for belief on my part. While he is asking me to have faith in his sensory observations, he is all the while implying that I should not have faith in my own sensory observations.

A fourth limitation of science is contained in the first step of the scientific method. No scientific observations or studies can be performed without the scientist's first setting up an hypothesis or theory. This hypothesis or theory is a statement of what the scientist tentatively and weakly believes to be true. The remaining steps in the scientific method are merely procedures for collecting and arranging sensory impressions so as to gather evidence on behalf of a belief. If the sensory observations corroborate the hypothesis, that belief is strengthened. If the observations do not support it, then additional observations must be made, or a new hypothesis must be posited. Since the human senses cannot be trusted for complete accuracy, and since persons have an egocentric tendency to look only for evidence that will support their beliefs, the scientific "proof" of the scientist is tentative rather than ultimate and final. The objectivity of the scientist disappears and he is again reduced to the level of finite, imperfect believer. With scientific "proof" being nothing more than evidence submitted on behalf of belief, the Christian finds himslf on the same finite plain as he gathers "proof," that is, Scriptural statements, on behalf of his beliefs. He selects and studies, not chemicals and cells and organisms, but words and verses and chapters. Love and sin and holiness, conveyed by the symbols of words and manifested in human examples, are just as real to him as are the proteins and neutrons and fluids with which the chemist works. The difference comes then, not in the false assertion that the scientist has proof while the Christian has belief, but in the quality and significance of the evidence submitted. The Biblical evidence is so superior to the non-Biblical sensory observations and interpretations of the non-Christian scientist, not only because the Bible is divinely inspired, but also because it has stood unchanged throughout the centuries while scientific formulations have undergone constant revision.

A fifth major limitation of science is that it cannot operate without the scientist's making at least three necessary assumptions. These three assumptions are as follows:

(a) There is reality outside oneself.
(b) This reality can be measured in an objective way.
(c) This reality in totality is orderly and consistent.

"In the beginning God created the heavens and the earth." Thus, the first assumption is true to Scripture and need not be further debated. But, the second of these assumptions is of extremely doubtful validity. In the history of educational psychology, for example, various conditioning, connectionist, and behaviorist theorists have observed animals for the sake of arriving at correct learning theories, but these men are notoriously disagreed on what they observed and on what interpretation should be given to their observations.

The third of these assumptions — that reality is orderly and consistent — is absolutely essential if one is to put his faith in science. For example, because of the assertions of natural scientists we have come to believe that no two snowflakes are alike. Scientists have observed the shapes and patterns of snowflakes, and have noted that among all the snowflakes observed there were no two alike. Being gracious to the scientists involved, we might suppose that they observed and recorded the patterns of ten thousand flakes. According to the scientists, these ten thousand observations would be sufficient proof. Skeptically, however, one could ask by what rule is it guaranteed that the ten thousand-first snowflake is not going to be a repeat of an earlier pattern? The same nagging situation prevails with the assertions about water always being made up of two parts hydrogen to one part oxygen. Scientists have tried to demonstrate by simple experiment that this is a true assertion and worthy of belief. That I am willing to believe this single experiment and to generalize from it to all available water is not important. That my believing this assertion about water is contingent on the prior assumption about the orderliness and consistency of nature, however, is important. Without this assumption, the scientist could do nothing. Even though this very assumption has been used by Christians as an apology for demonstrating the existence of God, the non-Christian scientist is constantly using it as a basis for destroying belief in God and His revelation.

Science, then, cannot objectively prove anything or establish the causes of events. Science can only show correlations and probability. It can only muster evidence on behalf of belief. The person who puts his faith in science and scientific progress is displaying ". . . faith in the intrinsic goodness of human nature and in the omnipotence of science. It is a defiant and blasphemous faith, not unlike that held by the men who set out to build 'a city and a tower, whose top may reach unto heaven' and who believed that 'nothing will be restrained from them, which they have imagined to do'" (Hoffer, *The True Believer*, p. 18).

Despite all that has been said in the foregoing pages, scientific endeavor nevertheless remains a legitimate activity of the Christian. Just because much of science is currently being used as a tool by Satan and those of his cohorts who take on the guises of objectivity and neutrality — for the sake of destroying belief in God and His Word — is no reason for the Christian's refusing to employ the method. This tool, too, must be brought into subjection to the King of kings.

To this point the role of belief or faith has only been partially characterized. In order to achieve a fuller and more accurate understanding of belief or faith, we must examine various avowedly Christian interpretations. Henry Zylstra, in his posthumous *Testament of Vision*, stated it as follows: "Belief is a basis of all learning, faith is inevitable in man, men are fundamentally dogmatic" (p. 98); "We believe in order that we may know, for belief is the condition of knowledge" (p. 101). To accept the truth of this definition is not difficult, but to accept it as an adequate explanation of the relationship between believing and knowing is another matter. For, to accept Zylstra's comments as final is to admit a basic dissimilarity between knowing and believing. Knowing, then, is merely an extension of, and different from, believing. To accept such a presumed difference is merely a first step to another question: Where does believing leave off and knowing begin? In my believing or knowing that all water is made up of H_2O, or that all snowflakes are dissimilar, what part is belief and what part is knowledge? Can I believe these assertions only, or can I know these assertions? If belief and knowledge are distinct, I am compelled to look for the distinctions.

In the history of Reformed Christendom it has been emphatically asserted that the Holy Bible is our "only rule [or guide] for faith and practice" (*Belgic Confession*, Art. VII). "Since it is forbidden to add unto or take away anything from the Word of God, it does thereby evidently appear that the doctrine thereof is most perfect and complete in all respects" (*ibid.*). In accepting this doctrinal statement as true and applicable to the problem of believing-knowing, Cornelius Van Til asserts, "The ontological trinity will be our interpretive concept everywhere. God is our concrete universal; in Him thought and being are coterminous, in Him the problem of knowledge is solved" (*Common Grace*, p. 64). Van Til also asserts, "The Reformed believer knows that he himself has been taken out of a world of misinterpretation and placed in the world of truth by the initiative of God" (*ibid.*, p. 7). With these theological admonitions to guide him, it becomes obvious that the Christian must go to the Bible for answers to his questions about the relationship between knowing and believing.

In II Corinthians 4:13-14 we read, "We, having the same spirit of faith, according as it is written, I believed, and therefore have I spoken; we also believe, and therefore speak; knowing that he which raised up the Lord Jesus shall raise up us also by Jesus. . . ." The implication here is that believing and knowing are not two distinct spiritual activities, but that the words can be used interchangeably. In the fifth chapter Paul says by the Holy Spirit: "For we walk by faith, not by sight" (II Cor. 5:7); and in Hebrews 4:2 we find this: "For unto us was the gospel preached, as well as unto them; but the word preached did not profit them, not being mixed with faith in them that heard it." Also consider Hebrews 11:1, 3: "Now faith is the substance of things hoped for, the evidence of things not seen . . . Through faith we understand that the

31

worlds were framed by the word of God, so that things which are seen were not made of things which do appear." And in James 1:5-6 the Apostle writes as follows: "If any of you lack wisdom, let him ask of God, that giveth to all men liberally, and unbraideth not; and it shall be given him. But let him ask in faith, nothing wavering, for he that wavereth is like a wave of the sea driven with the wind and tossed."

In Louis Berkhof's discussion of the Scriptural words for faith, he notes that three words are used in the Old Testament. "The most common word for 'to believe' (*he'emin*) stresses the intellectual element and signifies the acceptance of something as true on the testimony of another. The other two words (*batach* and *chasah*) emphasize rather the element of confident reliance on or of trust in someone else. The New Testament has one very important word for faith (*pistis*) which denotes (1) general confidence in a person, (2) the ready acceptance of his testimony on the basis of this confidence, and (3) the trust reposed in him for the future" (*Manual of Christian Doctrine*, p. 248).

The implications of Berkhof's comments on faith-words are at least twofold. First, it is implied that the phrases "to believe" and "to have faith" can be used interchangeably because they mean essentially the same thing. Second, it is implied that the concepts of faith and belief need not be restricted to faith in God or belief in religious doctrine, but can also be extended to intellectual apprehensions and to our personal relationships.

One of the serious mistakes being made by contemporary intellectuals, but also, and more surprisingly, by Reformed Christians, is that of limiting the role of faith to the acquisition of theological beliefs. Faith is still discussed as the means of justification, but seldom is faith discussed in relation to non-theological knowledge. That the non-Christian educational theorist would leave discussion of faith completely out of his considerations regarding the nature of learning is not surprising, but for a Christian educational theorist to ignore the concept of faith in his considerations of learning theory is both surprising and disconcerting. By what rationale can we assume that man's logical sense is autonomous when he learns geography, mathematics, or literature, but suddenly becomes dependent on God's generous gift of faith when studying Biblical doctrine? If God is sovereign even to the extent of knowing man's hair count and the welfare of the sparrow, by what rationale can we deny Him sovereignty in our learning of $2 + 2$? The same type of problem confronts the person who insists that knowing and believing are two distinct processes. To know that $x = y$ is to believe that $x = y$; and to know God is to believe God. The "whole contrast between facts and belief is completely false because, in order to deal with any kind of factuality, one always has certain basic beliefs and commitments, whether

32

one is dealing in one realm or the other. No matter what you are dealing with, a fact-belief contrast is a complete illusion" (Van Der Laan, *Science and Faith — Dualistic Paralysis or Scriptural Vigor* p. 8).

Any correct understanding of knowledge, then, is going to have to be fully integrated with an understanding of faith. "All facts are revelational of the true God. If facts may not be separated from faith, neither may faith be separated from facts. Every created fact must therefore be held to express, to some degree, the attitude of God to man. . . . Every manipulation of any created fact is, as long as man is not a sinner, a covenant-affirming activity. Every manipulation of any fact, as soon as man is a sinner, is a covenant-breaking activity" (Van Til, *Common Grace*, p. 70). Faith, or belief, or knowledge, must be understood as a gift from God Who "giveth to all men liberally" (James 1:5).[2] Only because "The Lord is good to all" (Ps. 145:9) can man believe or know the history of the United States and the plays of Shakespeare. Only if this total interrelatedness of knowledge and faith is kept thoroughly in mind will we be able to formulate a learning theory that approximates truth. To ignore this interrelatedness would be to make the same mistake as did such prominent learning theorists as B. F. Skinner, E. L. Thorndike, E. R. Guthrie, J. B. Watson, and W. Koehler. To repeat their basic mistake would be to divorce learning theory from God's revelation and to concoct learning theories as unsatisfactory as theirs.

Assuming that we have read Scripture correctly thus far, we must go on to other, related assertions. The first of these has its Scriptural proof in the passage already cited from II Corinthians 4: "I believed, and therefore have I spoken; we also believe, and therefore speak." The proposition is simply this: the purpose or intent of all our talking, and by implication also of our teaching and writing, is to establish belief. We communicate ideas and information expressly for the purpose of winning others to believe what we have tried to communicate. St. Augustine beautifully expresses this same concept in his book *Concerning the Nature of Good,* when he says, "For what is believing but consenting to the truth of what is said?" (*Basic Writings of St. Augustine,* p. 505).

The self-proclaimed neutralist, then, who lays out conflicting intellectual and philosophic fare in smorgasbord style, is actually trying to deceive. Neutrality, by Paul's words to the Corinthians, becomes impossible, even though temporary indecision, that is, partial acceptance and partial rejection of conflicting statements, remains a transitional characteristic of man as he moves from faith to faith.

---

[2] See also *Heidelberg Catechism,* Lord's Day VII, Q. 21 and Lord's Day XXV, Q. 65.

The second assertion is that faith or belief becomes the basis for all action. Man acts on the basis of his beliefs. His conduct, his attitude, and his thoughts are determined by his faith or belief. The apostle James puts it this way, "Even so faith, if it hath not works, is dead, being alone" (James 2:17). He later reiterates this idea when he asks, "But wilt thou know, O vain man, that faith without works is dead?" (vs. 20). It matters not whether beliefs are true or false, as far as action is concerned. A person will act on the basis of a false belief just as vigorously as he will act on the basis of a true belief. The child who believes that there is a ghost in his closet will cry just as loudly whether the belief is true or false. The important thing is the belief of the child, not the actual condition that prevails. Human action is based on belief, not on the actual state of affairs. Obviously, though, desired and correct action cannot take place unless desired and correct beliefs are held. If belief corresponds to the true state of affairs in God's creation order, correct and desirable action will then proceed from those beliefs.

Berkhof describes this volitional aspect of faith as follows, "Faith is not merely a matter of the intellect, not of the intellect and the emotions combined; it is also a matter of the will which determines the direction of life, an act of the soul by which it goes out to its object and embraces this. . . . It naturally carries with it a certain feeling of safety and security, of gratitude and joy. Faith, which is in itself certainty, tends to awaken a sense of security and a feeling of assurance in the soul" (*Manual of Christian Doctrine*, p. 252).

Quite obviously, the child who cries because of his belief in a ghost-inhabited closet does not possess a sense of safety, security, gratitude, or joy. If the parent merely tells him that his beliefs are false, the crying is apt to continue and will probably persist until the false belief is thoroughly eradicated. As long as any doubt remains, that is, until such time as the child firmly believes that the opposite of his original belief is true, he will experience little security or joy. In order to bring about this radical reversal in belief, the parent may find it necessary to "prove" the non-existence of ghosts by adducing sufficient evidence to establish the correct and desired belief. (For the sake of any empiricists who are still with us, the precocious child may adamantly reply that since ghosts are by very definition non-physical and therefore non-observable, the parent has not proven a thing. Mutual crying may result, and the disillusioned empiricist will have to resume his most despicable onus, namely, establishing belief on the basis of authority.)

Apart from this parenthetical poke at the greatest enemies of the faith concept, this leads to a third assertion: that beliefs are held with varying degrees of strength or conviction. Not all belief results in action. In the life of faith, not all faith results in works. In order for action to proceed from beliefs, those beliefs must be held with psychological strength. Beliefs that are productive of action must be held intellectually, emotionally, physiologically, and volitionally. If the belief could be adequately characterized as a cognitive awareness, that belief would not be likely to result in action. But, if intellectual, emotional, physiological, and volitional adjectives were all needed to characterize that belief fully, it could then be assumed that the belief would, of a certainty, result in corresponding action. Such deep-seated beliefs we will call core-beliefs. That faith which does not produce works we will call peripheral belief. This category of belief is not only unproductive, but also unreliable and most subject to change. The opposite is true of the core beliefs: despite vast collections of "proof" heaped up by antithetical factions, the belief remains intact and suitable action continues to result. In order to ensure continuing, desirable action, then, it is essential that the correct, desired beliefs be deeply imbedded, that the inculcating of doctrines penetrate to the emotional, physiological, and volitional fibers as well as to the intellectual. In short, those beliefs must become the heart commitment of that person.

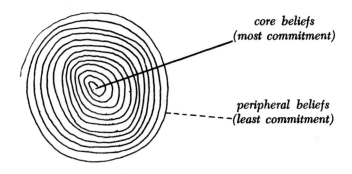

Fig. 1. Psychological Strength of Beliefs

It is easily recognizable that every person has underlying core beliefs to which he strongly holds, and which become the fountain of his life's activity. The skeptic, despite his assertion that nothing is fully believable and knowable, must violate his own conclusion by giving full, unquestioned assent to his original proclamation. The very assertion that nothing can be strongly held is strongly held, thus becoming a core belief.

The person to whom one's sympathies extend is the person who does not know what he believes. Led to believe that his previous belief patterns are no longer suitable, such a person has lost the stability of core beliefs confidently held; he now is insecure and intellectually uncertain. As Eric Hoffer explains, such a person is ripe for any proselytizing agent who seems to offer the sense of security and well-being that this idealogically-displaced person so urgently needs (*The True Believer,* p. 25).

For the Christian, knowledge and belief are not only synonymous, but also certain, although not yet perfect. For though the Christian can boldly proclaim, "I know in whom I have believed" and Faith is "a sure knowledge and a hearty confidence" (*Heidelberg Catechism,* Q. 21), that same Christian tempers his dogmatism with the words of I Corinthians 13:12: "For now we see through a glass, darkly; but then face to face: now I know in part; but then shall I know even as also I am known."

CHAPTER II

THE UNITY OF KNOWLEDGE

In his delightful but disjointed book, *Teacher in America*, Jacques Barzun makes the following statement:

> There is no such thing as separate, isolated "subjects." In Shakespeare's English are tags of Latin, allusions to medicine, elements of psychology, facts from history and so on ad infinitum. Nor is this true of fiction alone. The great philosophers and scientists are — or were until recently — universal minds, not in the sense that they knew everything, but in the sense that they sought to unite all they knew into a mental vision of the universe (p. 67).

Without offering explanation as to why there are no "separate, isolated 'subjects,'" and without suggesting a unifying set of principal truths around which the intellectuals may gather, Barzun has exposed the atomizing, incoherent tendency of twentieth-century education. With the blatant emphasis on specialization, with proficiency in limited areas of knowledge, educators have turned their attention to methodology, guidance, technological advances, and availability of financial resources. The earlier concern for developing the universal mind has all but disappeared from the stage, whereas the secular farce presents its superficial theme flippantly: "So what if a man is not philosophically bent? He knows his specialty and makes more money than you do. He is a genius in his practice and he even worships regularly on Sunday. What more can you want?"

The prevailing situation, and one which draws far too little attention, is that many young persons leave our schools thinking "in clusters." Their thoughts and beliefs are neatly arranged into separate little packages, variously called subjects, cores, specialties, or disciplines, including Science, Politics, Literature, Religion, History, Philosophy, Business, and Psychology.

These students and teachers, alienated from any unifying element, cannot see any relationship between the areas of thought, the "disciplines" to which they are subjected. Although they may recognize that there are no real contradictions between history and literature, or between science and religion, at the same time they are blind to the interrelationships of these different processes in the body of reality. Since the interrelationships are so often missed, the values of theology for art, of philosophy for business, and of Christian methodology for education are not appreciated. Christianity has nothing to say to education or to psychology, they say, because Christianity, education, and psychology are all separate. They readily admit that a person should be a Christian and an educator, but they fail to recognize the inextricable relationship that must exist if one is to be a truly Christian educator.

Knowledge is unified by nature. Knowledge is an organic oneness, but because of the ingenuously labeled "knowledge explosion," its unity is obscured by fragmentation. We fail to see its unified arrangement and we get lost in the shrapnel of detail without ever recognizing knowledge's essential character. In order to grasp and control knowledge, we fragment it, dissect it, and re-structure it into inanimate classifications called subjects or disciplines. We think "in clusters" partially because we are not big enough to grasp the magnitude of knowledge, but primarily because we have been taught to think that way. We seldom make conceptual relationships of those facts and responses that make up our perceptual fields because such conceptual relationships are seldom made for us. We talk about "faith" in connection with religion and "knowledge" in connection with science, as though faith has nothing to do with science and knowledge has nothing to do with religion. We talk about perceptual fields in connection with psychology and aesthetics in connection with philosophy of art, again as though perceptual fields have nothing to do with art, or aesthetics with science. We talk about "learning" in relation to schooling and "growing in grace" as associated with congregational worship; and we damn the man who teaches like a preacher or preaches like a teacher.

The greatest challenge facing Christian education today is that of discovering the unity of all that is known, of formulating for our children a single mental vision, of bringing every tidbit of interpreted fact and every theory of explanation into subjection to Christ. "For the weapons of our warfare are not carnal, but mighty through God to the pulling down of strong holds; casting down imaginations, and every high thing that exalteth itself against the knowledge of God, and bringing into captivity every thought to the obedience to Christ" (II Cor. 10:4, 5). This all-encompassing rule of the King is further expressed in Colossians 1:16-17 and 18b, where Paul writes, "For by him were all things created, that are in heaven, and that are in earth, visible and invisible, whether they be thrones, or dominions, or principalities, or powers: all things were created by him, and for him: And he is before all things, and by him all things consist . . . that in all things he might have the preeminence." This submission of all knowledge to the preeminent Christ, then, becomes the prime concern of the Christian educational theorist, for Holy Writ demands nothing less.

The Christian reader has probably heard this Scriptural command before, but he may have become insensitive to it and have taken the fatalistic attitude that since a Christian philosophic implementation of this mandate has been so slow in coming, education can wait no longer, and we had better get on with our job of teaching. The truth is that we can never get out of a philosophic position in education. If we are not now educating out of a Christian philosophy, we, by logical necessity, are educating out of a non-Christian philosophy. Whether we recognize it or not, and whether we are able to articulate it or not, everyone of us is teaching according to some educational philosophy. Our choice may not be dignified by either formal articulation or consistency, but it will, fundamentally and certainly, be either Christian or non-Christian. It cannot be neutral, for Christ has said, "He that is not with me is against me: and he that gathereth not with me scattereth" (Luke 11:23, see also Matt. 12:30).

For the Christian thinker, the foregoing Biblical demands are antithetical to the philosophy of specialized or "clustered" thinking. Being antithetical to the lordship of Christ, such idolatrous clustering of thoughts, such absolutizing of an aspect, must be renounced if "in all things He might have the preeminence." To the extent that the Christian community allows such secularistic thinking to persist, Christian orthodoxy will be dead orthodoxy.

Even apart from the Christian's recognition of the centrality of truth in Christ, such thinking in clusters is very unnatural in the same way that standard time zones are unnatural. Our time zones are neither inherent in nature nor are they direct constructs of God. Although some people have foolishly argued that standard time is God's time and daylight saving time is the devil's time, the standard time zones are human inventions ascribed to the railroad lords of the nineteenth century. God's time is unified, without gaps or joints or time boundaries; He marks time with events, with historical realities — Creation, the Fall, the Incarnation, the Resurrection, the Judgment — for the glory of His name and the salvation of His people.

The same is true of knowledge. Knowledge is not divided by nature; it is not made up of disciplines or subjects or studies. The dividing of knowledge into disciplines and subjects and studies is purely a human invention, a human construct. God's knowledge is one, and is characterized by no divisions.

Edgar B. Wesley alludes to this oneness of knowledge in his discussion of history teaching. Writing for a prominent national journal, he states, "History is past politics, past economics, past sociology, past geography, past anthropology, and past current events" ("Let's Abolish History Courses," *Phi Delta Kappan*, September 1967, p. 4). Others have recognized this fundamental characteristic too. Tyrus Hillway has based an entire volume on the correct assertion that "knowledge is a seamless whole" (*Introduction to Research*, second edition, p. x). Alfred North Whitehead, internationally famous philosopher and mathematician, emphatically asserts that we "may not divide the seamless coat of learning" and urges an eradication of "the fatal disconnection of subjects which kills the vitality of our modern curriculum" (*The Aims of Education*, p. 10).

Whitehead further elucidates this concept when he cognitively focuses on the quantitative aspects of the world. "Through and through the world is infected with quantity," he says. "To talk sense, is to talk in quantities. It is no use saying that the nation is large, — How large? It is no use saying that radium is scarce, — How scarce? You cannot evade quantity. You may fly to poetry and to music, and quantity and number will face you in your rhythms and your octaves" (*ibid.*, p. 11).

But what do we mean when we talk about the oneness of knowledge? In the first place, it means that in every instance or portion of knowledge, all of the so-called disciplines are represented. There are no distinctly historical facts or distinctly religious facts or distinctly biological facts or distinctly musical facts. Second, it means that every portion of knowledge is at one and the same time religious, economic, historical, aesthetic, philosophic, mathematical, educational, on to the end of our abstracted analytical categories. Barzun has already alluded to this with his references to Shakespearean plays. With little effort, literary, historical, economic, phychological, linguistic, religious, and political considerations can be found in the dramas of the famous Elizabethan humanist. With a Biblically-founded and -unified epistemology, one could use any of the bard's dramatic pieces for practical, Christ-centered study in mathematics, grammar, language development, economics, politics, and religion.

A very elementary and yet very practical example of the unity of knowledge was called to my attention recently by a teacher of handicapped children. In her morning class she began with a variation of "show and tell." After culling out the significant tales from the trivia, she had the authors of the worthy narratives write these on the chalkboard, emphasizing good penmanship with each one. The next step involved the correcting of mistakes in grammar, punctuation, and spelling. Next came a review of phonics rules for new words and unfamiliar sounds. The final step was that of oral and silent reading.

A third example that could be used would be the battle of Gettysburg. Although this parcel of knowledge usually shows up in history courses, the famous battle and its consequences are also fit subjects for speeches, military strategy, psychological study, literary research, political maneuvering, and religious zeal. Pursuing the quest further, the battle is a capsule of medical technique, chemical concoction, technological invention, and geographical revelation.

A final example involves current events. Using as subject matter a recent space flight by our astronauts, into which discipline shall this item of information be funneled? — Medicine, Engineering, History, Politics, Physics, Geography, Religion, Philosophy, or Astronomy. Because of the recency of such flights, the assignment of this knowledge to a discipline or subject is not yet computerized. Which discipline will get this delectable material? To which subject does it belong? Obviously no one has exclusive claim to it except Christ. It is His world and His knowledge. It belongs to Him, exists for Him, and occurs by Him.

For theoretical and practical consideration of knowledge, certain misconceptions must be revealed and eradicated. Figures 2 and 3 below are two of the more common misconceptions, whereas Figure 4 is intended to portray the conception that conforms to the reality of the created order and its position under God.

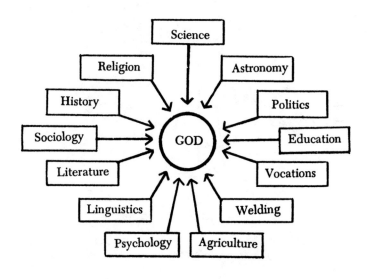

Fig. 2. Misconception No. 1

In this conception, knowledge does not originate with God, but comes into existence as new areas are formed and new classificatory terms are formed. Now, somehow, this humanly originated knowledge must be sacrificed on God's altar.

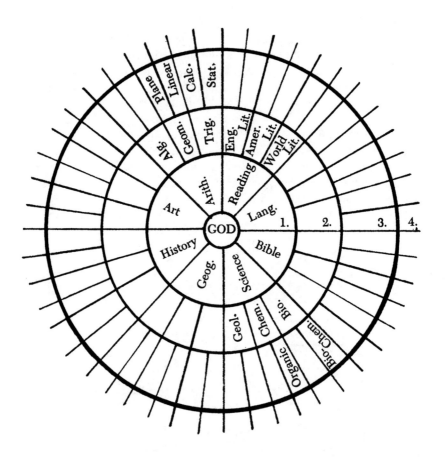

Fig. 3. Misconception No. 2

Designations of numbers: 1. elem. school level; 2. secondary school level; 3. college level; 4. post college. In this conception knowledge is not bounded and has no limits. Also, the further one moves from the center, the farther he is from God and the more alienatedly eccentric he becomes.

GOD

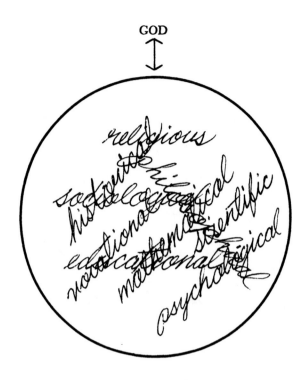

Fig. 4. The Christian Conception

In this conception, all knowledge comes from God and goes to Him. The disciplinary terms are now simply adjectives to describe and classify knowledge, to emphasize its various dimensions by orderly abstractions.

In Figure 4 above, the descriptive adjectives are intermingled to illustrate their indivisibility. Every portion of knowledge is rightly classified as being religious, just as every portion of knowledge is rightly classified as being psychological or historical or mathematical. Henry Zylstra alluded to this fact when he boldly asserted, "Whatever is human is religious" (*Testament of Vision*, p. 97). By maintaining that education is human, we would also have to correctly deduce that education is religious. Whether that education be of the liberal, vocational, or professional variety, logic would demand, and rightly so, that all these varieties be properly labeled religious. But Zylstra could easily have gone on to say that whatever is human is also mathematical, biological, economic, and literary. Because of God's authorship of all knowledge, however, Zylstra focuses on the religious characteristic. He goes on to argue that "There are no irreligious people. The question is one only of a false or of the true religion" (*ibid.*, p. 97). He goes on to state,

43

In the long run the liberal's effort at evading dogma is as futile as it is ill-disguised. He too is a man committed to religious decision, and he makes this decision. A dogma underneath the reason, a faith that informs it, is active in Pagan, liberal, Catholic, and fundamental Protestant alike. There is no such thing as irreligion. There is false religion, and retired religion. But irreligion? No! The liberal has his basic allegiance. It is as absolute as the Communist's, as active as the Catholic's. His refusal to say by what dogma he professes what he professes is a ruse. His crusade against dogma emerges from dogma. His neutrality is a pose. Watch him in crisis. He bristles like other authoritarians at what is opposed to his vindicating creed. In the end he will name his god (*ibid.*, p. 143).

Eric Hoffer makes the same judgment in the preface to *The True Believer*: "For though ours is a godless age, it is the very opposite of irreligious. The true believer is everywhere on the march, and both by converting and antagonizing he is shaping the world in his own image" (p. 10). With Louis Berkhof's earlier teaching that man is "incurably" or constitutionally religious, this truth is going to be of central concern in our formulation of educational principles (*Manual of Reformed Doctrine*, p. 1).

But simply to label all human endeavor and all knowledge as religious is not going to be sufficient. All that is human and religious must also be judged as to its spiritual quality, as to its truth or falsity. All that we are called to believe must be critically evaluated so as to determine whether it has its origin in the God of all Truth or in Satan, the father of lies. The Apostle John calls us to such critical examination when he cautions, "Brethren, believe not every spirit, but try the spirits whether they are of God: because many false prophets are gone out into the world" (I John 4:1). A similar admonition appears in the Apostle Paul's letter to the Thessalonian Christians, where he counsels, "Prove all things; hold fast that which is good. Abstain from all appearance of evil. And the very God of peace sanctify you wholly; and I pray God your whole spirit and soul and body be preserved blameless unto the coming of our Lord Jesus Christ" (I Thess. 5:21-23).

Concerning the extent of man's knowledge, one rein of caution must be applied. It is frequently thought that man's capacity for knowing has been constantly expanding since the beginning of time. Man, with his self-assumed autonomy, is gradually building on the previously discovered knowledge of earlier generations, pyramid fashion. With added resources, with unbounded academic license, and with enough incentive, man will someday break the last bands of ignorance and arrive at a full discovery of the truth. The limits that foolish, self-redemptive man has assigned himself are ever expanding, ever exploding. If beneficent legislatures would only release the purse string for more millions of dollars to escape, and if the miserly taxpayers would stop wallowing in their ignorant complacency, our great universities, high schools, and grade schools could intensify their search for truth, that most illusory object of pursuit.

Scripture, however, does not characterize man's knowledge in such Tower-of-Babel fashion. Knowledge, which is God's possession, is not accumulated pyramid fashion, by autonomy-assuming man. Knowledge is distributed, gift-fashion, by God to his people, according to their needs and according to His good pleasure. Jubal already had sufficient knowledge to be called "the father of all such as handle the harp and organ" (Gen. 4:21); and Tubal-cain had received sufficient knowledge to become a teacher of those who worked with brass and iron (Gen. 4:22). Yet, from suffering, God-fearing Job knowledge was withheld. Zophar rebukes (unjustly) Job while praising God thus: "But oh that God would speak, and open his lips to you, and that he would tell you the secrets of wisdom! For He is manifold in understanding" (Job 11:5, 6a, RSV). If man is ever to discover or know truth, he must know God, for God is not only the source of truth, but very Truth itself. But Zophar continues: "Canst thou by searching find out God? Canst thou find out the Almighty upon perfection? It is as high as heaven; what canst thou do? deeper than hell; what canst thou know? The measure thereof is longer than the earth and broader than the sea. If he cut off, and shut up, or gather together, then who can hinder him?" (Job 11:7-10).

CHAPTER III

THE ORGANIC UNITY OF MAN

One of the belief patterns with which the Christian should always find himself in conflict is that called "faculty psychology." In this European-originated approach to the understanding of man, the person is not regarded as an organic unity, but as a collection of various faculties or functions, each of which can be studied as a separate entity. In this tradition, the person is divided between mind, body, soul, and will. Each of these functions can be cared for and developed without serious consideration for the other parts. The mind is to be developed and trained in school, the body is to be nurtured in the home, and the soul is to be nourished in the church. Since the mind can be further divided into the reasoning, memorizing, aesthetic, and analytic faculties, it is consistent with this psychological approach to believe that these separate mental faculties can all be developed independently of the others.

In order to develop the aesthetic faculty, for example, separate appreciation courses in art and literature are included in the curriculum. Courses with large accumulations of factual material, such as history and biology, are intended to develop the memory capacity, with little concern for the fact that most students are unable to recall even a small portion once the final tests have been taken. In order to train the thinking and analytic functions, the school may require courses in mathematics and foreign languages, again with little interest in aesthetic attitudes or spiritual values that a student may be holding. If the student's values, emotions, or attitudes are observed as deviating from that which is socially acceptable, a separate, differently constructed course can always be recommended for him, or a special counselor can always be employed to bring about the correction.

In most educational circles this psychological approach is officially labelled taboo and outdated. The practice of it, however, continues relatively unhindered. In order to curb this practice and reverse current trends, we will have to examine carefully the concept of organic unity, which is antithetical to that of faculty psychology.

Cornelius Jaarsma, late professor of educational psychology at Calvin College, gives extensive although not sufficient treatment to this matter in his book, *Human Development, Learning and Teaching*. Relying primarily on Scripture, he also draws from the writings of such Reformed thinkers as Abraham Kuyper, Anthony Hoekema, and H. R. Wyngaarden.

Jaarsma states that although the word "person" has been given various meanings in different cultures, "in modern usage the word generally designates the total subject. You are a person. I am a person" (p. 23). The person, or the self, "manifests itself psychically, in the soul-life, and physiologically, in the life of the body. To show the intimate unity of this manifestation, we often say that it functions psycho-physically. The person, then, is the single psycho-physical life of the self" (p. 23).

In further illustrating the organic oneness of the person, we can isolate any instance or event in the life of a person, and use it to show that the total person is involved in each event. In the following quotations, Jaarsma illustrates both the unity and the complexity of the person:

> Suppose that you see a house. The you that does the seeing is your person as a psycho-physical unity. Yet we may distinguish the various processes that go on: light rays act physically and chemically on your retina; other physical and chemical processes carry an electrical message through your body to your brain; the image is perceived and related to your memories, concepts, and feelings; and all the while you recognize that this is an activity of your own peculiar self. Seeing a house is, in a sense, one act performed by one individual (pp. 23-24).

Continuing this discussion in another chapter, Jaarsma says,

> Every function, both mental and physical — to use a common distinction among functions — is an activity of the self. The light waves upon the retina, the sound waves upon the ear drum, etc. set up a physiological activity in the nervous system. These are experienced by the person as a part of himself and are translated into personal experience. In the activity of seeing, I identify a house as my residence. As person I call it my home. All that home stands for, love, security, rest, good food, etc. enters into the total activity of the person. The whole person is involved in the process from the first stimuli to the final self-conscious act of identification and acceptance.

> We have become accustomed to grouping the functions of the person as mental and physical. The distinction is helpful as long as we do not sharply differentiate the two. We do not know where the one ends and the other begins. The morning grapefruit has a bitter taste about it which one has come to like. Because of the taste, the grapefruit has acquired personal value as a breakfast food. . . . Mother's act of selecting grapefruit with careful discrimination is based upon the experience of tasting and valuing grapefruit according to the symptoms that suggest this taste. Psychic functions and body functions interact, flow into one another, but one cannot point out the point of transition (p. 42).

When Jesus summarized the Ten Commandments with the words, "Thou shalt love the Lord thy God with all thy heart, and with all thy soul, and with all thy strength, and with all thy mind" (Luke 10:27), He was not implying that man is composed of separate faculties. As Matthew Henry points out, these distinctions are meant to illustrate the necessity of loving with our complete persons, our total selves. Henry says, "Our love to him must be sincere, hearty, and fervent; it must be a superlative love, a love that is as strong as death, but an intelligent love. It must be an entire love; he must have our whole souls, and must be served with all that is within us" (*Commentary*, p. 1448).

Although Henry does not dogmatically assert the oneness of the person when he treats the parallel passage in Matthew 22:37, there are numerous other Scriptural passages which give credence to the idea of personal organic unity. When the Psalmist says, "Thy word have I hid in mine heart, that I might not sin against thee" (Ps. 119:11), he is describing the heart as the center of his feeling. In Exodus 25:2, Joshua 24:23, and Luke 21:14 the volitional facet of man's being is also attributed to the heart. When Mary kept all those things which she had seen and heard concerning her Son "and pondered them in her heart" (Luke 2:19), the heart is characterized as the seat of understanding, thinking, and memory. The same idea is expressed in Proverbs 2:2 with the words, "Incline thine ear unto wisdom, and apply thine heart to understanding." In verses 10 and 11 of that same chapter, the concept is even more elaborately expressed: "When wisdom entereth into thine heart, and knowledge is pleasant unto thy soul; discretion shall preserve thee, understanding shall keep thee."

As Jaarsma again points out. "The Bible clearly indicates the unity of the person. He is a living being of whom the Bible speaks as heart, soul, mind, body, blood, and the like. In each concept the whole is represented. These are not technical terms to label parts in an analytical fashion, as we do when we study human anatomy. Each points to the whole in its functional relationship. The organic unity of the person is clearly established in Scripture. The Bible does not confront us with man in his component parts, nor with the comparison of human existence over against that of animals. Rather, it gives us the compelling aspect of man's existence in his relationship to God" (p. 47).

Whenever a person is involved in any human encounter, the total person is involved. When a person is engaged in the hearing of a joke, that person is using the physical ear for the receiving of auditory stimuli, the mind for the interpretation of the sound waves, the emotional response for indicating pleasure or displeasure, the vocal structure for emitting laughter, and the heart for making moral judgments about the joke. In his laughter, all of these are involved simultaneously, and the observer cannot begin to separate the laughter from the facial muscles, the cognitive understandings, the values, the attitudes, or the vibrations on the ear drum.

Whenever a person enters the classroom, he enters in his organic oneness. Not only will his posture indicate his attitudes and emotional involvement, but it will also be influential in determining the rate and ease with which he evaluates and assimilates the meanings and interpretations being presented. Not only will the functional abilities of his ears, eyes, and throat be instrumental in determining the rate of learning, but so will the amount of love he has received from his parents and the tensions he has encountered on the playground. All human behavior is permeated with feelings, emotions, attitudes, values, understandings, and physiological activity, and not in ordered succession, but simultaneously. The person does not make value judgments and engage in attitude formation only after he cognitively encounters information about the Civil War, but already — and often determinatively — *while* he makes the encounter.

Because the child functions as organic unity in every situation, those who seek to instruct him and mold him must concern themselves with all the facets or dimensions of his personality. The teacher may not ignore the emotional aspect of the child, thinking that no emotion is present. Rather, the teacher must be continually educating so that the desired emotion, the desired value judgment, and the desired attitude will be produced in each curricular encounter. The development of correct attitudes and correct values and correct emotions in the student must be of just as great concern to the teacher as the student's acquisition of true information, for all of these are inseparable.

The development of attitudes, values, and beliefs will not wait until the child finishes a year or a phase of his schooling. This development will be going on continuously and may have evolved into a set pattern before the instructor or the parent has realized what has occurred.

What has been said of the child in his school life must also be said for the child in his church life. When a child enters the church sanctuary and the catechism classes, he does not leave his emotions, his values, and his attitudes outside. Neither does he leave behind the knowledge that he has acquired at school, at home, or in the street. He takes his total self with him wherever he goes. The minister, just like the school teacher, must have a Christian commitment to advancing knowledge, establishing belief, developing correct attitudes, and producing desired emotions. Just as in any school or home situation, there is never a question as to whether emotions, attitudes, and values are involved. The only question is whether the desired, Christian ones are being established, or whether undesired, non-Christian ones are.

That all life becomes education in Christ should not be disconcerting.

49

The only disturbing situation is that in which the beliefs, the values, and the attitudes that the child has absorbed in one place of instruction come into conflict with those beliefs and values that have been established in other places of instruction. When such a situation develops, not only does the child experience disturbing internal conflict, but he will choose one source of instruction as his reference point and reject the rest. No child can give allegiance to antithetical instructors anymore than a man can serve two masters. Either he will accept the values and beliefs and attitudes of the one and act according to them, or else he will accept the values and attitudes and beliefs of the other and act consistently with them. The important thing, whenever such undesirable conflict occurs, is that the child accept the true and Biblically-correct reference point. The only other options are to have the child accept a false reference point or to encourage multiple acceptance and thus produce schizophrenic tendencies.

In addition to the above evidences for the organic unity of man, two terms from the area of psychiatry will help to illustrate the point. The first word, schizophrenic, has already been used. It is a term used to describe a disintegrated or dichotomized personality, with the connotation that such a condition is both unnatural and extremely unhealthy. The second term is psychosomatic, a word used to describe the functional interrelatedness of mind or soul and body. Although one can infer from this second term that the person acts as a unity, the connotation here is an undesirable one, with the implication being that such close interaction is unnatural.

Although the connotations of "psychosomatic" deny organic unity, and are at odds with the connotations attached to "schizophrenic," the unavoidable conclusion to all that has been said is that the person is not a collection of parts, but a unified whole. It is precisely such a conclusion that must be recognized and accepted if we are to remain in agreement with the organic unity of knowledge. To envision knowledge as being unified while at the same time designating the human knower as being composed of separate parts, or vice versa, would be to invite the charge of inconsistency from those who recognize the common origin of both.

Chapter IV

THE DILEMMA OF ANALYSIS

To be caught on the horns of a dilemma is to be pulled in opposite directions at the same time by seemingly conflicting demands. To analyze is to extract component parts from a whole so as to gain a better understanding or conception of the whole. As analysis is carried on, the parts are not only pulled out for examination under more favorable light, but the parts must be seen in relationship to each other and in relationship to the whole that they form.

If a man were called upon to know, understand, and appreciate a forest, it could be assumed that no worthwhile intimacy of knowledge or appreciation could be achieved from the vantage point of an airplane flying overhead. In order for knowledge and deep appreciation to result, the person of whom such knowledge and appreciation is required would be expected to make frequent, detailed study of the trees, brush, soil, and streams which make up that forest. Such detailed study might involve research on the ages of trees, the types of trees, the mineral content of the parent soil, and the availability of seasonal moisture. This intensive study might result in a prodigious accumulation of knowledge about the existing forest, but the extent to which the researcher becomes engrossed in the components of the forest would also be the extent to which the total vision of the forest would be diminished. For such a person we would allow that "he can't see the forest for the trees." To know the forest means to see it as a whole, but to know it as a whole requires that we see it as parts or pieces. To carry on both functions simultaneously is impossible for limited, finite man, but it is precisely the execution of such seemingly conflicting demands that constitutes the dilemma of analysis for man's sin-warped mind.

As man confronts the expansive knowledge that God has made available, both of Himself and His cosmos, it immediately becomes obvious that such knowledge cannot be apprehended in its oneness or unified form. Division, classification, and systematization become essential. If man is to "take fast hold of instruction; let her not go; [and] keep her for she is thy *life*" (Prov. 4:13), while at the same time "be filled with the knowledge of his [God's] will in all wisdom and spiritual understanding" (Col. 1:9), then man is forced into systematic division and unification at the same time. Artfully and artifically to construct subject-matter or disciplinary boundaries is as necessary as to divide time into standard or daylight saving zones; but to argue that such constructions take on the sanctity of divine mandate is to be as foolish as those who argue for God's standard time versus the devil's daylight saving time. Obviously such artful divisions must be considered as human expedients, as means to the comprehension of unity.

Throughout history such division and systematization has taken place. The schools of the Medieval Era were known for their trivium and quadrivium. The schools of today are known for their reading, writing, history, literature, mathematics, and science. The schools of tomorrow will probably be better known for their calculus, linguistics, phonetics, and apologetics. The sin of the educational establishment, however, is not in the abstraction or division of God's knowledge, but in its failure to unify this knowledge in the lives of students and teachers who are alike commanded to "present [their] bodies a living sacrifice, holy, acceptable unto God, which is [their) reasonable service" (Rom. 12:1). If the student is allowed to conform to the secularistic thought clustering of an atomized, incoherent world, rather than being transformed by the renewing of his mind into proving "what is that good, and acceptable, and perfect, will of God" (Rom. 12:2), the school and the teachers responsible for such Christ-denying conformity will not hear the Eternal Judge's "well done."

This dilemma is not a new one and it is not something which exists only in theory. Anyone who has tried to instruct someone else even in the simplest lesson has encountered the problem although no label may have been attached to it: In the explanation of a reading story, for example, the problem is always present and unavoidable. Although the story probably has one central message which the author wishes to convey, the only way by which this message can be grasped is by having the reader dissect the story through a series of steps. In the initial encounter, the entire story is placed before the reader. He sees it as a whole, but the whole is meaningless. The only proper thing to do is to take it apart, looking at individual words, single sentences, and paragraphs. Since this is seldom sufficient for complete understanding, the characters, the setting, the plot, the conflict, and the climax must also be examined and understood. Once all these components have been examined in isolation, they must again be fitted so as to form the whole. As we say, all the pieces then form a completed puzzle. The process of analysis moves from the whole to the parts and back to the whole, giving us the phrase "whole-part-whole" which is currently in vogue with many educational psychologists.

The same procedure must be applied to the study of words or poems. When a new word is introduced, the student's initial experience is with the whole word. Unable to use it, however, that student is directed to break it down into syllables and finally into letters and letter sounds. Once all these steps have been completed, the word must again be reconstructed, for the whole is what is desired and not a collection of parts. In memorization of poems the same procedure must be followed. Given a poem which is too long to memorize in one attempt, the student is directed to learn phrases or lines or stanzas separately. If all the lines and stanzas were memorized separately, but could not be recited as a single unit, as the complete poem, the work would be considered as unacceptable and incomplete.

On a grander and far more significant scale, this is the situation that exists with respect to God's knowledge. He has given us a whole creation and has commanded us to come to know it, enjoy it, and use it for His praise. Yet we rarely get beyond an unintegrated awareness of its component parts.

If the beginning reader insisted on remaining with the letters and sounds of a word while refusing to recognize its intended wholeness, both student and teacher would soon be desperately frustrated. When God's students, learned men who bear His image, do exactly the same thing with the assignments He has given them, we applaud them and call them specialists.

What has been said about the analysis and reconstruction of knowledge must also be said about the person. Having previously demonstrated the unity of the person, we must now proceed to the necessary dissection or analysis. In order to do so, however, we must remind ourselves of the whole that we will be attempting to analyze. The following diagrams, studied in the sequence given, will illustrate the line of thought that must be followed.

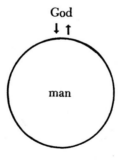

Fig. 5. Man in His Organic Wholeness As He Is Related to God

53

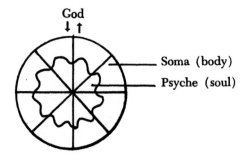

Fig 6. *Analysis of Man As Person*

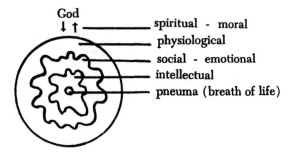

Fig. 7. *Analysis of the Personality (projection of the person into his environment)*

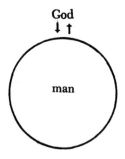

Fig. 8. *Man Seen, More Meaningfully, As a Whole*

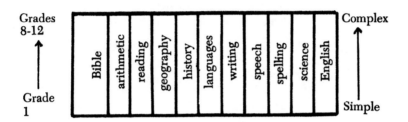

Logical, systematic development within subjects.

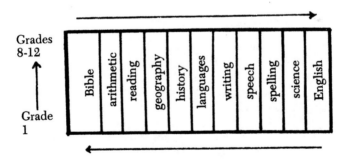

"Cross-referencing," "re-unifying," or "on-going inter-disciplinary discussion." Showing the interrelatedness of all subjects, the unity of all knowledge.

Fig. 9. The Dual Demands Made on Finite Educators

Practical administrative suggestions derived from these principles:

1. Emphasize to your teachers that they are never objective, but are always interpreting according to some criterion. Insist that the Word of God be their criterion for all judgments.

2. In the employing of new teachers for your school, try to hire those who have a broad academic background rather than a very narrow, specialized one.

3. In making financial reimbursement for teachers' summer school attendance, make provision for those who take worthwhile course work even though that study may not be credited toward a degree.

4. Encourage teachers to change subject and grade-level assignments periodically. For the narrow subject matter specialist, it will even be beneficial if he is forced to teach outside his field.

5. Avoid overspecialization by not having one person teach more than two sections of any one course. Three or four preparations per day will force the teacher to expand his interests horizontally, thus allowing him to relate more effectively his subjects to each other.

6. Ask all your teachers to teach at least one class of Bible. Bible is not meant to be an isolated, specialized subject capable of being handled only by the clergy. Its influence and content must extend to every course in the school curriculum, and every teacher should increase his own knowledge of it by having the opportunity to teach it. The current shortage of specialized Bible teachers is probably a result of our own errors in educational thinking, and should not be corrected by drafting ministers for work that should be within the capability of most mature Christians.

7. Be certain that all your teachers continually enhance their interests in the courses taught by teachers in other departments. Every teacher, for example, should take an active role in the teaching of correct spoken and written language as these forms of communication appear in their courses.

8. Encourage your teachers to spend less time in their classes with developing the systematic material that can be gotten very easily by the student from textbooks, and more time with developing the horizontal relationships between subjects, as well as the meaning of their specific subjects for the child of God, the servant of the Savior-King. Interdisciplinary discussion will do much to enliven the material for the students and will also serve as motivation for them to study the textual materials.

56

CHAPTER V

THE PHILOSOPHY PROPOSED

In Chapter II it was asserted that whatever is human is religious. It was further affirmed that, since education is human, education is also religious. Now it can be further deduced that whatever is human is educational since all life and all knowledge is characterized by unity or oneness. Assuming the truth of this assertion, it should be noted that the Progressives in education (John Dewey, Kilpatrick, Bode, *et al.*) were not far off the mark when they said that "education is life." Before such remarks are misconstrued as approval of the Progressives, it should be quickly noted that their conception of life is basically wrong. Central to their philosophy is the pragmatic existence of man, rather than the sovereignty of the Creator-Provider God. Although these men were right in extending their conception of education to the totality of man's living, they were damnably wrong in failing to give God the central place in man's life. Using Zylstra's and Hoffer's statements, these men were not irreligious; rather, they were engaged in either true or false religion. In religion there is no place for neutrality, for Jesus said, "So then because thou art lukewarm, and neither cold nor hot, I will spew thee out of my mouth" (Rev. 3:15-16).

Since formal education is also comprehended in God's unified knowledge, it, too, is humanly related properly or improperly to the Author of all knowledge. As previously stated, education is by logical necessity either Christian or non-Christian. Also, because there is no such human being as an irreligious person, since all persons fall into either the true-religion or false-religion category, we can now go on to assert that there is no such thing as an uneducated person. This may sound strange because of the all-too-common usage of this word in describing persons who have not been enrolled in our schools. However, it may help to clear away misconceptions if we used the term "unschooled" where we now erroneously use the word "uneducated." The point that needs to be made is that all men are educated, not only to greater or lesser degrees, but most significantly along either true or false lines. Consequently, it becomes of great importance that we distinguish between Christian and non-Christian, between true and false (pseudo- or mis-) education rather than between the educated and the uneducated. The child whose life God ended after three years of schooling was educated, not to the same extent as the person who graduated from high school, but nevertheless he was educated, as a Christian or as a non-Christian. Since God calls people out of this temporal life at varying age levels, we know from the Bible ("Choose ye this day whom ye will serve") that the Righteous Judge is going to be far more concerned with the Christian truth or the anti-Christian falsity of our education than with its extent, quantity, or sophistication.

A popular assumption is that only the ecclesiastically or liturgically religious mode of life is in a positive or negative relationship to God, whereas the educational and vocational modes are neutral. In this popular tradition, education is the same for all persons. It, apart from religion, is objective. For education in this tradition to be made Christian, we simply have to add Christianity to education in order to make it Christian education. Sprinkle a few delicacies of grace over the plain bread of nature: the old but still persevering, Aristotle-Aquinas, Roman Catholic dichotomy that glorifies natural man and promotes the lie of the undepraved, still-reliable human reason. With this kind of humanistic recipe, education will never become fully Christian, and Christianity will never become more than an additive. Henry Zylstra, devoted Christian that he was, made this mistake when he said, "Christian education must be both education and Christian if it is to justify itself and successfully meet the secular challenge." "Our Schools must be schools — that for one thing. And then they must be Christian — that for another thing. And in making these two points I shall want to insist, of course, that they must be both at once" (p. 90). With this insistence we do not wish to disagree. Obviously schools must be schools. If they should pre-empt the sacramental work of the church or the legislative work of the state, they would not only lose their distinctiveness, but also should no longer be called schools.

But as Zylstra puts it, education, by the very fact of its existence apart from Christianity, must be labeled as non-Christian or pseudo-education. This compromising, man-made marriage of Christianity and education is actually a divorce of partners who were married by God, who were created one. Such a marriage is not going to be productive of a philosophy for Christian education unless that education is already Christian, in which case the marriage is unnecessary and redundant. Zylstra's proposed marriage was thought necessary because of the obviously non-Christian character of contemporary education but we must look elsewhere if we are to formulate a distinctively Biblical and integrated Christian philosophy for education.

Another, probably clearer, way of demonstrating the foregoing problem is to use the term "quality education." This term as used today implies that there is now a great concern among educators for the improvement of the quality of education. Simply to call for quality education implies that the adjectives good, bad, inferior, superior, for example, can be attached to the word education. European education is considered to be better than American education, suburban education is considered to be better than inner-city education, and Northern education is considered to be better than Southern education. In fact, since the Russians sent their Sputnik aloft in 1957, the whole matter of evaluating education — for its utilitarian and technological worth primarily — has been as much a matter of discussion as death, war, sex, and taxes.

This excited evaluation of teachers, curriculums, buildings, libraries, and finances is quite often, however, shallow and blind criticism. Not only do those making the evaluations fail to explain what are their criteria for evaluation, but they often try to compare and evaluate on the same bases, schools, teachers, and systems that are working for avowedly different goals. For example, it is still a *Time-Life-Post* fad to criticize American schools for not doing as good a job as the European or Russian schools. Seldom, if ever, do these critics stop to consider the fact that the American schools may be trying to do something quite different from that intended by the Europeans and Russians. If the aim of the European secondary school is to produce highly knowledgeable candidates for university entrance, and the aim of the American secondary school is to produce vocationally adapted citizens of a democracy, it would be grossly unfair to criticize sharply the American school for not turning out the highly knowledgeable high-powered candidates for university entrance, simply because they never intended to produce such creatures. The same criticism should be made of those who attempt to compare private, Christian schools with public, secular schools. If the aim of the Christian school differs from that of the public school, again, it would be an injustice to condemn the Christian school for not turning out the same products as the public schools.

Using an analogy from transportation, let us imagine that two people are setting out on a journey. One chooses to go to Chicago, and the other chooses to go to New York. If the one who chose as his destination Chicago does not arrive in New York, it would be ridiculous to condemn him as a failure. The same would be true if the New York-bound traveler did not arrive in Chicago. The only valid criticism that could be offered to either of these travelers involves their choice of destination and the means used for arriving at that destination. Why did the travelers choose the destinations that they did? Suppose that they wanted to see the most beautiful, the most cultured city in the country. Then by what standard did they decide that New York or Chicago was superior?

Was the criterion used a valid, authoritative one, or was it a constantly shifting, personal whim, or fancy?

Much of the criticizing and evaluating that is going on in education today fluctuates on the level of personal predilection, rather than revealing a clearly-articulated, principial base. Discussion in education about goodness or badness, about high quality or low quality is carried on with little or no concern for defining the central term — education, for stating its purposes and goals, or for examining the validity and authority of the bases that support the whole educational superstructure. In short, the number of blind assumptions that supposedly objective educators make is enough to stagger the imagination.

One of the most ludicrous and yet most tragic situations that obtains in education today is the oft-heard attempt of a school or superintendent to devise a rationale for the existence of school courses and programs that have been in existence for years. After a program has been in operation for some time, those involved in teaching the courses and in structuring the curriculum finally decide that it is time to sit down and determine why they teach that course and whether they hope to accomplish anything specific with each unexamined course presently being offered. This is comparable to a person's buying an automobile, filling it with gas, driving for dreary hours on the tollways from Detroit to Chicago, and then sitting down in his Chicago hotel room to concoct a reason for his trip. But the analogy must be extended. If he is unable to establish a sufficient reason for his journey, he will fly back to Detroit and repeat the same ritual the next day — with a new car, probably the same gimmicks, but still no purpose. Then confronting the need to explain his considerable expense and trouble, he must either decide, stubbornly, to continue the hopeless and futile cycle, or he may simply decide that he should stay home until he knows not only *where* he is going, but *why* he is going there.

Such purposeless, follow-the-crowd wandering is precisely what characterizes secular education today, whether that education goes under the additional adjective Christian or public. The majority of the persons who are supposedly educating have never even asked themselves or their colleagues to define the term that they use so glibly to indicate their profession.

> Of the actions that human beings perform, one would surely expect teaching to be among those done most reflectively and with the clearest perception of goals. But what a deluded expectation. For vast numbers of teachers *just teach*, teaching as they were taught, unreflectively exercising their ingrained habits, enslaved to custom, no more deciding what to teach and what to emphasize than the crow decides what song to sing (Wolterstorff, *ibid.*, p. 4).

Those who most loudly clamor for "quality education" have not even bothered to name their criteria for judging quality, much less have they tried to establish a certain meaning for the word education.

If a sense of direction and a sense of purpose is ever going to be aroused in our currently fluid and highly chaotic education-minded society, it should be undeniable by now that some basic questions must be asked and answered, but also that some order, some sequence must be given to the asking of these questions. Remembering the meaning applied to the word philosophy in the preface to this book, such ordering, such sequencing of questions is essential to the formulation of a worthwhile philosophy for education. Also recalling that education is either good or bad, true or false, ultimately Christian or non-Christian, in the same sense that all religion is either true or false, Christological or Diabolical, it should be evident that our purpose in formulating a Christian philosophic system for education is to determine that which is good and true and Christian education, rather than that which is bad and false and non-Christian education.

Proceeding immediately to the basic question, we must first ask, "What is the basis upon which all our thinking rests?" Only after that question has been satisfactorily answered can we go on to the next one. Before that first answer can be formulated, however, we must reflect on the whole process that we normally call education. Since we send children and young people to school and since we expend much time and money on them in those schools, we may rightly conclude that education is an attempt to do something with or to children and young people.

If this assertion is agreeable, we ought then to ask what it is that we are trying to do with or to our youth. If, on the one hand, we decided that we wished to effect no change in them, we would not only find ourselves engaged in a foolish expenditure of money, time, and effort, but it would also be mandatory that we come to understand thoroughly their condition and characteristics prior to their coming to school so that we could properly preserve them unchanged while they were under the jurisdiction of the schools. In this case, the whole purpose of education would be to prevent change and to preserve the status quo. But such an impractical program of at once distorting and preserving unchanged the child would be a goal acceptable to no one.

If, on the other hand, we decided that we send children and young persons to school for the sake of bringing about some change in them, it becomes imperative that those engaged in the execution of this process not only know the *desired* condition, but also the *existing* condition. Change involves a movement from one state of affairs that is existing to another state of affairs that is desired. Quite obviously, the latter choice for controlled change will be far more acceptable, and since the above alternatives are the only ones possible, the option for change is compelling and unimpeachable.

We can now proceed to ask the second question in our philosophy. The question is simply, What is man? Stated in other terms, we could ask, "What is the nature of the child at birth?" or "What is the unsatisfactory condition that exists and from which that child must be changed?" Keeping in mind the first question, What is man?, we must remember that this question and all succeeding questions must be answered on the basis of the foundation that we have previously accepted. Failure to do so will necessitate the changing of the basis and will make useless any subsequent discussion.

The third question in our philosophy follows immediately from the second. It is simply this: "What is the desired condition for man?" Paraphrasing it slightly, we could ask, "What are the goals, aims, and objectives that we desire for the students who experience the process that we call education?" When addressed directly to the educator, the question is put with parental forthrightness: "What changes do you have in mind for my child whom I am placing in your charge?"

The fourth question that should be asked is, "In what kind of structural setting and by what agent are you going to effect the changes that we have previously discussed and agreed upon?" "Is the church going to bring about these changes?" "Is the government going to make these changes?" "Or are the parents going to produce these changes?"

The fifth question is this: "With what tools or implements, and by what methods are the agents in charge going to bring about these desired changes?" "To what kinds of experience are you going to expose my child so that the desired results will be obtained?" "By the use of what media are you going to implement the objectives and purposes that we agreed on in answer to question three?"

These five questions necessitate a sixth. Having decided on such things as the basis, the nature of man, the goals for man, the structural setup, and the means of implementation, we can now proceed to an evaluation of that which was done. Only with such preliminary answers can we legitimately ask the final questions, "How well is the job being done?" or "Are our schools doing what is expected of them?" or "Are we getting true quality education?"

The above set of questions, then, outlines by suggestion the system, the philosophy that must be followed if we are to arrive at a true understanding of education. In ladder form (Fig. 10) the system must be followed from the bottom to the top, and must be consistent at all points with the underlying foundation.

62

Evaluation

↑

Implementation

↑

Structural Organization

↑

Objectives or goals

↑

Nature of man

↑

Basis or Authority

Fig. 10. The Philosophic Ladder

Before we proceed to a detailed discussion of the above points, it will be helpful to consider a few implications of the proposed system. The first implication is that considerable theoretic discussion must precede practice. A second implication is that theory and practice may not be divorced from each other, but practice must always be assiduously crafted from the blueprint of theory. A third implication is that the six-step system is essentially nothing more than a structuring of questions which have repeatedly been asked in education, although not always in the above sequence. A final implication is that the choice of basis or foundation for education is the most important decision to be made. Once the choice is made, all future considerations will have to be made in relation to that foundation and in its strength. The following chapter will deal with that first all-important question.

CHAPTER VI

THE ONLY FIRM FOUNDATION

> Christianity has not been tried and found wanting. It has been found
> difficult and never sufficiently tried. — G. K. Chesterton

Probably the most important, the most difficult, and yet in one sense
the easiest task confronting the educational theoretician is that of choosing the foundation on which to build his educational edifice. Since all
future discussion is going to rise from this presuppositional basis of belief, the choice must be wisely made and examined carefully as to its
soundness and validity.

When one examines the current situation in education by perusing the
catalogs of American universities, one notes that many undergraduate
programs in education offer no "foundation courses." The reader of these
catalogs could conclude that undergraduate education courses either
have no foundation or that the foundation is so universally accepted
and understood that no further instruction is required. However, when
the reader examines the graduate-level entries, he is likely to find a
slight but concentrated emphasis on "foundation courses." The puzzling
question, then, is why such courses are needed on the graduate level
after the student has already been subjected to the methods, curriculum,
and evaluation courses on the undergraduate level. Among the graduate-level offerings, one discovers such entries as "historical foundations,"
"social foundations," "philosophical foundations," and "psychological
foundations."

About these graduate-level entries we should make a few observations: first, if we would make the seemingly warranted assumption that
these "foundation courses" are basic, would it not be reasonable to insist
that they be required of (or at least offered to) everyone at the *beginning* of the educational studies program rather than at the *end* for
those few that select them? Second, it seems paradoxical that the state
public-school system, which tries with signal diligence on the elementary
and secondary levels to achieve uniformity and conformity, should offer
on the graduate level where leaders are trained a smorgasbord of
"foundation" courses. To recommend for acceptance the notion that an
educational leader can build simultaneously on several foundations is
nonsense. To attempt such would be analogous to asking a carpenter
to build a house on two or three foundations at once. To present all
the historical, social, philosophical, psychological foundations (with their

64

many sub-groups) as being of equal value would be to invite the student to become eclectic with conflicting and diametrically opposed fare as his diet.

If the purpose of all man's talking and writing is to establish belief, it is evident that the various academic departments of a school must come to agreement as to which foundation is the correct or desired one, and then to employ only those teachers who are in intellectual and spiritual conformity with that faith-determined foundation. Deliberately to recommend for belief conflicting positions and foundations would be tantamount to admission that the department neither knows what it believes nor does it know what it wants the student to believe. To speak with many tongues results in confusion and doubt. But, even worse, for educators to speak without knowing what they believe requires the student to believe what the professors themselves do not self-consciously know.

Confusing as the above situation may sound, this is precisely the chaotic state of affairs that perplexes and enervates American education today. In the language of Rushdoony, there is "a radical rootlessness in the intelligentsia" (*Intellectual Schizophrenia*, p. 4). But how does that presumably intelligent person, the American teacher, justify his capitulation to principial relativism? He rationalizes by dealing with trivial, peripheral beliefs that can not be productive of right conduct; by forcing students to absorb lists of names, dates, places, events, formulae, and related minutiae that will give them the illusion of being educated, but which cannot give sufficient basis (and the only basis) for right and desirable conduct.

Historical Foundations Considered

After the preceding discussion the reader should be willing to acknowledge that a single basis or foundation for education must be chosen. Beginning with the most popular choice, namely, history, we shall start by examining the firmness of that foundation.

In that study called "historical foundations of education" it is customary to consider the educational programs of ancient Greece. Because of tradition and availability of materials, the educational systems of Athens and Sparta are given almost exclusive attention. Athens had a private-school system that was philosophically conditioned by the fatalistic worship of the Greek gods, such as Zeus, Hera, Appollo, and Athena. This private education was available only to boys, and then only to those boys from the citizen class. Sparta, however, had a public, that is, state-directed and state-controlled system that was determinatively influenced by the worship of power and the state. Again, the Spartan educational system was open only to boys from the Spartiate or citizen class.

If we are to learn *from history,* as many assert that we can, whose history shall we learn from? Sparta's or Athen's? If we accept Sparta's history as normative, we would be consistent only by supporting an educational program comparable to that of Hitler's Nazi Germany which was a logical extention of Spartan totalitarianism. If we accept Athen's history as normative, however, we would be compelled to advocate a private, Zeus-oriented system. Obviously if one is to use history as his guide, some prior criteria must govern his choice as to which historical form of education will be normative for him or will most nearly objectify his own theoretical standard. To make a choice of this sort, with the use of prior criteria, is to admit that the prior criteria and not the historical situation is the basis or foundation of choice.

Many well-meaning Christians, nevertheless, foolishly argue for private Christian schools on this basis of historical precedent. They aver that we must have private Christian schools because the New England Puritans had a system of private Christian schools. This form of argument breaks down for two reasons: first, a careful study of the Massachusetts education Laws of 1642 and 1647 (The Old Deluder Satan laws) indicates that education was not private, but quasi-public. Schools were set up and taxes were levied for their support by edict of the state government. The second reason involves the same question asked about the Greek educational systems: On what basis can one justify the choice of the early colonial period as an educational model? Why not choose the academy or the contemporary public school as models? They are also historical, are they not?

Philosophical Foundations Considered

Since history is clearly an inadequate foundation or basis on which to build, do educational philosophies supply our starting point? In those studies that are traditionally called "philosophical foundations of education," it is common to read and digest the philosophic systems of such men as Plato, Aristotle, Quintillian, Aquinas, Comenius, Rousseau, and Dewey. Each of these philosophies differs markedly from all others. If the student were to choose one of these philosophic systems as his model, and thereby reject all others including Biblical revelation, by what standard of judgment again is the choice made? If the choice were made by so arbitrary a method as drawing lots, what rule or regulation denies others the same method and the resultantly frequent acceptance of alternate, conflicting systems? But, if those engaged in choosing an educational foundation were to practice the art of eclecticism and select only those parts of each philosophy that they considered good, by what standard have they differentiated the good elements from the bad?

Such pseudo-philosophical nut-picking is obviously no more than fancy-satisfaction and irresponsible whimsicality. But even in this kind of philosophical window-shopping, no man can avoid making value judgments. If he extracts some ideas that he considers to be good, he is by virtue of his choices declaring all those not chosen to be inferior and of poorer quality. In so doing he is making value judgments on the basis of some standard, some criterion that he held before his encounter with the supermarket philosophies. Even if the educational eclectics were to act so preposterously as to decide that all philosophies were of equal quality, they would still be making qualitative judgments about each separate philosophy when they decide that each is equal to every other one. In such a system it makes no difference which one is chosen; all are of equal worth or worthlessness. No moral or spiritual criticism may then be adduced against any educational philosophy, whether it be Nazi, Communist, Secular Humanist, or Calvinist. To some persons, such an environment might seem ideal. Would that not be complete freedom, perfect pluralism? Would it not be wonderful to shield the Neo-Nazi in his philosophic determination to annihilate all Jewry, and the Ku Klux Klan in their determination to terrorize all opposition? Obviously not! Some choice, some differentiation must be made. To that even the most comfirmed liberal will agree.

Psychological Foundations Considered

We shall now consider the "Psychological Foundations of Education." One of the first things that the reader should note is that the same arguments which have just been applied to philosophy will apply equally to psychology. Psychology, like philosophy, is not a monolith but a collection of models. Some of the more famous models (theoretical positions or schools) are the psychoanalytic school, the classical conditioning school, the behaviorist school, and the Gestalt school. Some of their human progenitors are Freud, Pavlov, Watson, Jung, Thorndike, and Wertheimer. Again, the student who hopes to disinter a foundation here is going to make value choices on the basis of prior criteria.

But there is another reason that psychology cannot be accepted as our foundation for true education. Psychologists have struggled to make their discipline a positive science like the natural sciences (as they are considered today). Therefore, they, by their own choice, have excluded all consideration of the very reality that they purport to study. Psychology is a study of the psyche or soul, but the soul of man is not

67

observable by the human senses. Since science as a *method* of study depends completely on observation, "scientific" psychologists have thrown out the child they had hoped to wash and watch. To study the material, physical shell which houses the soul is no great or new accomplishment; anatomists and physiologists have already dominated that study. Psychology, therefore, cannot provide a foundation either; it has abdicated by renouncing its realm, the psyche, and has handed over its crown to be analyzed by the empiricists.

Social Foundations Considered

Becoming increasingly popular with American students is the study called "social foundations of education." Sociology is currently thought a way of salvation and the sociologist modestly dispenses his homilies of self-redemption through the communal brotherhood. His function, he feels, is to examine contemporary society so as to determine how people think, how people act, and what people want.

If it can systematically be determined what people want, then we can proceed from there to decide what should be. In other words, by deciding what humans desire (what the current direction for self-gratification is) we discover our standard for what ought to be. By this reasoning, we would conclude that public secular education is what people want and, therefore, ought to be. In other quarters we would observe that "black power" is what people want and, therefore, ought to be. In still other quarters, communistic atheistic education is desired by some people and therefore ought to be. In many areas of the Deep South systematic study would show that segregated school systems are still desired by sizeable majorities. By sociological reasoning, a return to such segregation would be in order.

Obviously sociologists approach their studies with a set of (often unexamined or undisclosed) criteria by which to judge what is good and what is bad in their world. To have no *a priori* standards is impossible — though it is what the existentialist innanely asserts about his presumed freedom. For any sociologist to pretend that no *a priori* standard governs his choice of study area or his conclusions and recommendations is to be guilty of fraud and deception. Some principle, some standard always guides and directs him.

For the Christian, especially, but also for any man that values his life and property, existentialist sociology that makes human desire the basis of morality and is committed to the lawlessness of situational ethics becomes anathema. When God's absolute standard of conduct, his moral law, is flouted and ignored, then "social foundations" is synonymous with anarchy, with the abolition of man, and with the idolatry of animalization.

68

The Word of God Considered

As educators searching for a true and reliable foundation, we must reject all the quicksand foundations that have been exposed. We can learn nothing *from* them; at best we can learn *through* them. We learn *from* that set of heart-commitment criteria which enlightens our study of history, philosophy, sociology, psychology, literature, or whatever other subject might be considered. That body of prior beliefs determines the starting point, the foundation from which. For the Christian this foundation can be none other than the Word of God, the sacred Scriptures. The Christian accepts the Bible as the divinely inspired, infallible, and inerrant revelation of God on the authority of that Word itself. When the Christian reads that crucial New Testament passage in which the Holy Spirit assures us that "All Scripture is given by inspiration of God" (II Tim. 3:16a), he knows that it is true. And by referring to the preceding verse, he finds that these "holy scriptures . . . are able to make [him] wise unto salvation through faith which is in Christ Jesus" (vs. 15).

Scripture itself becomes the basis for all belief, for all knowing, and thus the basis for all thoughts concerning education. It is *from* the Bible, God's Word to man, that the Christian will learn.

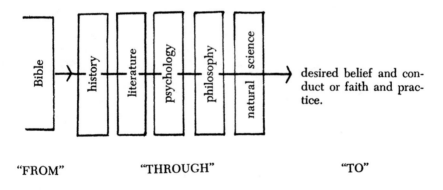

desired belief and conduct or faith and practice.

"FROM"   "THROUGH"   "TO"

Fig. 11

It is precisely this God-centered view of life that the Psalmist is presenting when he writes, "For with thee is the fountain of life: in thy light shall we see light" (Ps. 36:9). As the Bible reveals Christ the Incarnate Word, He as the Way, Truth, and Life gives all reality, all education, its meaning. Alienated from Him, we can do nothing, know nothing: we are blind, lost in the darkness of our sin and estrangement.

But in His Word He consoles those who repent: "I am the light of the world" (John 8:12). Furthermore, the sufficiency of that Word to shed light for all belief, all behavior, and all practice is witnessed in II Timothy 3:16-17: "All scripture . . . is profitable for doctrine, for reproof, for correction, for instruction in righteousness: that the man of God may be perfect, thoroughly furnished unto all good works."

CHAPTER VII

WHAT IS MAN?

What is man, that thou art mindful of him? and the son of man, that thou visitest him? (Psalm 8:4)

The above question, as asked by the Psalmist David, is a fundamental one. It must be asked and answered by all who purport to engage in education. Not to ask oneself this question seriously and then to proceed uncritically with the process of schooling — which, by previous definition, is an attempt to bring about some form of change in the student — would be like a carpenter's remodeling a house without knowledge of, or concern for, its existing structure. Such thoughtlessness would not only result in an unstable and monstrous edifice, but the very attempt would be denounced as folly. Equally foolish would be the carpenter who, in his search for knowledge about the house-to-be-altered, would scrutinize and analyze the pigeon cote, the chicken coop, or the dog house. Even though these backyard buildings might contain elements in common with the house, perusal of them would soon prove of minimal value and would probably also prove misleading if exact correspondences were thereby concluded to exist in the house.

But such a muddled approach is sadly characteristic of many educational psychologists. Those who practice this art of imagining correspondences are the conditioning, connectionist, and behaviorist psychologists, the psyche-denying naturalists who examine pigeons, chickens, dogs, and rats as their models for understanding the nature of the child created a rational-moral religious being in the image of God.

Another brand of educational psychologist operates from an equally non-Christian assumption. In this attempt to examine the structure of the house the carpenter stands outside the house and merely watches all those that enter and leave the house, computing the number and variation of the entrants and departees, thus producing cunningly devised tables. In current psychological jargon such industrious statisticians bear the name "stimulus-response psychologists." One professor in the author's academic experience idolized the S-R method and cheerfully referred to the child (house) as the "little black box." Unaware of the superficiality of his own technique, he was content to tabulate the entering stimuli and the departing responses, all the while leaving the child as an unexamined mystery on which no light from Scripture might shine.

By rejecting the Scriptural explanation at the outset, "It follows that

71

non-Christian psychologists and educators cannot have an adequate perspective on the nature of man, and therefore cannot understand the child adequately either. In the blindness of their immanence they raise one phase of their observation to a general perspective and judge the whole thereby. The inadequate definitions of psychology which the student meets in current readings and texts have their source in this limited perspective" (Jaarsma, p. 39). By not allowing Scripture to flood-light their studies, these blind men of Indostan have absolutized sensory perceptions and stimuli, conflicts and tensions.

Having already chosen the Bible as the only firm foundation for any educational philosophy, it is to this God-gift basis that we must turn for a correct understanding of the nature of man. It is in Scripture that we must first look for answers to the questions that David raised in Psalm 8:4. Only after that divinely-illumined source has been carefully studied, and after its answers have been accepted as true, may the educational theorist proceed to logically extend from them and elaborate, always Christocentrically, upon those answers. The opposite direction of thought, namely, beginning with a non-Biblical exposition of psychology and then reverting to Scripture for substantiation, will not only prove sinfully hypocritical but will relegate the Bible to the status of check-point rather than preserving its God-ordained role as "only guide."

The Original State

For those who are already familiar with Scripture, it need only be repeated that God's Word presents man in three different states. Taken chronologically, the first state is the one of perfection, the pre-fallen state of Adam and Eve in the Garden of Eden, the state in which God could look upon the world and the man He had created and pronounce them "very good" (Gen. 1:31). The second state of man is the fallen or outcast state (Gen. 3:23-24), the state of sin occasioned by the deliberate disobedience of Adam and Eve, but consequently (in Adam, our representative, federal, and familial head) the lot of all men, "For all have sinned, and come short of the glory of God" (Rom. 3:23). The universality of this second state is further enunciated by Paul when he writes, "Therefore, as through one man sin entered the world, and death through sin; and so death passed unto all men, for that all sinned" (Rom. 5:12). The third state of man that the Bible describes is the state of the regenerate man, the condition of those who "through the obedience of the one (Christ) shall . . . be made righteous" (Rom. 5:19).

The first state that has been described can be called the original or intended state of man. Although the Biblical narrative on this state is very brief (Gen. 1 and 2), there is sufficient information there, and in subsequent passages, that can be found and made applicable to the process we call education. The first thing that the Bible tells us about man is that he is created, which means that he is dependent. He is most evidently dependent on God for life and strength and daily nourishment. All men, through the historical Adam, who is the father of the whole human race, are also spiritually dependent on God, constantly needing Him for well-being, for security, for purpose, for happiness, for the hope of blessed immortality in Christ who destroyed the power of sin and death.

A second characteristic of man in the Garden of Eden is that he was created in the image of God and was, therefore, good: "And God saw everything that he had made, and behold, it was very good" (Gen. 1:31). *The Heidelberg Catechism* describes this characteristic as follows: "But God created man good, and after His own image: that is, in true righteousness and holiness, that he might rightly know God his Creator, heartily love Him, and live with Him in eternal blessedness to praise and glorify Him" (Lord's Day III, Ans. 6). *The Canons of Dort* in a parallel explanation says that "His understanding was adorned with a true and saving knowledge of his Creator, and of spiritual things; his heart and will were upright, all his affections pure, and the whole man was holy" ("Third Head of Doctrine," Art. 1). Cornelius Jaarsma, relying upon an earlier illustration from Dr. H. R. Wyngaarden, graphically describes this harmony existing between God and Adam through the following figure:

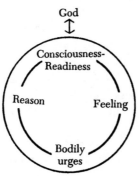

Fig. 12. Man Integrally Oriented to God (Jaarsma, *Human Development, Learning and Teaching*, p. 54)

In traditional Reformed language, man was, through God's creative act, ordained as prophet, priest, and king. As prophet, he was ordained to proclaim to all the sovereignty of God over the whole created cosmos. As priest, he was in direct and personal communion with the Creator, for God walked and talked with Adam and Eve in the Garden (Gen.

3:8-19). As king, man (the crown of creation) was designated as the regent of the created order, ruling it, developing it, and glorifying his Maker through it. Not only does the Genesis account inform us that "the Lord God took the man, and put him into the garden of Eden to dress it and to keep it" (Gen. 2:15), but the Psalmist answers his own question with the following beautiful verses:

> For thou hast made him a little lower than the angels, and hast crowned him with glory and honor. Thou madest him to have dominion over the works of thy hands; thou hast put all things under his feet: all sheep and oxen, yea, and the beasts of the field; the fowl of the air, and the fish of the sea, and whatsoever passeth through the paths of the seas (Ps. 8:5-8).

A third characteristic of man in the original state was that he was created rational and communicative, thus capable of conceptualizing and transmitting ideas. Although already alluded to in the previous paragraphs, this function of man is more clearly described in Genesis 2: 19-20: "The Lord God formed every beast of the field, and every fowl of the air; and brought them unto Adam to see what he would call them: and whatsoever Adam called every living creature, that was the name thereof. And Adam gave names to all cattle, and to the fowl of the air, and to every beast of the field."

A fourth attribute of unfallen man was his social or communal character. Because it was not good that man should be alone, God created Eve, the first woman, as a partner for Adam, thus allowing the communal and social qualities of man to find fulfillment. "Then the Lord God said, " 'It is not good that the man should be alone; I will make him a helper fit for him' " (Gen. 2:18, RSV).

A fifth quality of man in the pre-sinful (prelapsarian) state can best be explained by the word "free." "And the Lord God commanded man, saying, Of every tree of the garden thou mayest freely eat" (Gen. 2: 16). Adam and Eve were at complete liberty to move in the garden, to eat the fruit, to live with each other unashamedly, and to rejoice in each other's perfect fellowship. Only one restriction was placed upon them, namely, to obey God. So long as their compliance with God's law was complete, they were free to use and occupy the Paradise that He had provided. Although this concept of freedom-to-obey may be difficult to understand, the author requests the reader be patient enough to wait for a fuller explanation of this seeming dilemma until Chapter VIII.

A sixth characteristic, suggested by Jaarsma's figure, and more implied than stated in the opening chapters of Scripture, is the organic oneness of man. In this early description there is no distinction made between the various facets of man's personality that are commonly discussed in contemporary psychology. No divisions are made between heart, mind, will, emotion, and physical body. The implication seems rather to be that Adam, in his totality, was properly oriented and attuned to all that he encountered. This totally perfect, God-related man is what Jaarsma and Wyngaarden attempt to describe by their phrases "integrated person" and "organic unity of the person."

A seventh important characteristic of the nature of man is that all men were created equal and remain equal (even in the fallen state) before God. Although God has elected some from eternity for salvation and has justly passed the impenitent unto reprobation, "God is no respecter of persons" (Acts 10:34). For though God has endowed men with varying talents, and has called some to be apostles, and some to be prophets, and some to be teachers, before his bar of justice "there is none that doeth good, no, not so much as one" (Rom. 3:12). This recognition of the equality of all men as depraved sinners needing cleansing in the blood of Christ is important, not only in the granting of admission to our schools, but also in the treatment accorded to the students once they enter. Children are quick to become concerned with fairness and equal treatment by the teacher. This innate desire for equality and justice is especially exhibited in children's disapproval of teacher's "pets," which frequently expresses itself in attempts to blacklist and to downgrade the pet so as to re-establish equality.

In summarizing this original state of man, the Genesis account testifies that while Adam occupied the Garden, he enjoyed and understood the perfect relationship existing between himself and God, between himself and fellow man, and between himself and the natural world.

The Unredeemed State

"Through one man sin entered into the world, and death through sin; and so death passed unto all men, for that all sinned" (Rom. 5:12). Man, because of disobedience, is characterized by the adjectives "sinful" and "dead." By cutting himself off from his source of life, strength, and truth, man is not only cast out of the perfect Garden, but has set himself adrift from meaning in time and space. Man is now a transient, wandering from delusion to delusion, from idol to idol, always repressing the truth in unrighteousness (Rom. 1:18), forever flouting the law of God written upon his heart (Rom. 2:14-15), hopelessly condemned to indecision, spiritual torment, and lovelessness. He is no longer God-centered, God-serving, God-enjoying, or God-obeying, but is now self-centered, self-serving, self-enjoying, and self-obeying. His entire person and all the facets of his personality function imperfectly. He is now a "fractured person" not only prone to hate God and his neighbor, but experi-

75

encing continuous internal conflict, so that the Apostle Paul confesses, "For the good that I would I do not: but the evil which I would not, that I do" (Rom. 7:19). Paul continues this description of the internally-warring man when he adds, "But I see another law in my members, warring against the law of my mind, and bringing me into captivity to the law of sin which is in my members. O wretched man that I am! who shall deliver me from the body of this death?" (Rom. 7:23-24).

Because man listened to Satan and chose to sin, he has lost his true righteousness, knowledge, and holiness. He is no longer perfect king and priest and prophet, but is now characterized by ignorance, prejudice, and inability to know or reason perfectly. He is still a creature of faith and trust, but now becomes an idol-maker and idol-worshipper so as to have a lodging place for that faith and trust. He still feels his dependence sharply and he becomes a frenetic security-seeker. He is no longer a joyful, willing servant of God, but now he must work by the sweat of his brow: he has become the slave of sin.

When Adam and Eve sinned, God immediately asserted His claim on both His creature and His creation. For God said to Satan, "I will put enmity between thee and the woman, and between thy seed and her seed; it shall bruise thy head, and thou shall bruise his heel" (Gen. 3:15). Man becomes the battleground between the arch enemies — Satan and the Savior. This battle between Satan's host and the army of Christ is fought within the lives of persons, within the lives of children in school. This is not a Sunday battle, but a seven-day-a-week battle, in which Satan, today, insidiously employs the myth of objectivity and neutrality. In its sinful state, the heart of man becomes the cleavage line of the antithesis; but finally the choice must be made: for Christ or against Him. If, through the grace of God, a person chooses *for* Christ and *against* sin, carnality, the world-hostile-to-God, and Satan, then his direction becomes clear. Every thought, every decision, every deed is dedicated in love to his Savior, and Christ becomes all and in all for him in his living, in his learning, and in his teaching.

The devil would have us forget his presence in the school environment. He would prefer that we perceive the school as neutral ground and the child as a non-combatant. But such deception is a key weapon in his arsenal. The conflict between the Truth and the father of lies is part of every school day. The choice of weapons may be the choice of textbooks or the choice of curricular experiences. Although the teacher may elect *Huck Finn* and intend it for edification, the crafty devil may readily concur and intend it for damnation. The athletic coach may choose for basketball and intend it for human cooperation, but the father of lies may use it for establishing pride. The medium of warfare, the tool of battle, may be the curriculum, but those who wish to redeem are not the only ones who desire to use it. Satan, using the myriad of human agents at his beck and call, seeks to turn and twist every curricular experience, every idea, and every action to his own rebellious end. He is even not averse to using saintly Christian teachers as his mouthpiece. The Apostle Peter (unsuspectingly used by Satan) had to experience Christ's rebuke: "Get thee behind me, Satan: thou art an offence unto me" (Matt. 16:23). Unable to avoid his insidious and subtle doing, the Christian teacher rises in opposition, selecting, guiding, and interpreting for the student.

In C. S. Lewis' *Screwtape Letters,* Screwtape reminds Wormwood that even seemingly insignificant encounters can be beneficial to their ruler Satan. Warning Wormwood to intensify his activity, Screwtape says, "While they are young we find them always shooting off at a tangent. Even if we contrive to keep them ignorant of explicit religion, the incalculable winds of fancy and music and poetry — the mere face of a girl, the song of a bird, or the sight of a horizon — are always blowing our whole structure away. They will not apply themselves steadily to worldly advancement, prudent connections, and the policy of safety first. So inveterate is their appetite for Heaven that our best method, at this stage, of attaching them to earth is to make them believe that earth can be turned into Heaven at some future date by politics or eugenics or "science" or psychology, or what not" (p. 144).

In *Mere Christianity* Lewis discusses the whole subject of the antithesis from a different viewpoint. There he writes, "Christianity agrees with Dualism that this universe is at war. But it does not think this is a war between independent powers. It thinks it is a civil war, a rebellion, and that we are living in a part of the universe occupied by the rebel. Enemy-occupied territory — that is what this world is. Christianity is the story of how the rightful king has landed, you might say landed in disguise, and is calling us all to take part in a great campaign of sabotage" (p. 36).

In his unregenerate state, man is not only at war with his God and slavishly attached to the natural world, he is also at war with his fellowman. Those beautiful, harmonious relationships which man once experienced are no longer enjoyed or rightly understood.

The Child as Security-seeker

The first characteristic that we used in describing man is of sufficient importance to warrant elaboration. Parents and teachers will constantly be concerned with this trait in children, whether they recognize it or not; and psychologists have given much attention to it. Although a perfect sense of security will not be the possession of the child until he is fully re-united with his Creator, there is much that parents, teachers, and psychologists can do so as to establish partial security.

In addition to the parental responsibilities of providing food, clothing, and shelter, much also has to be done by whoever is dealing with the child. In order to fill this basic need, however, teachers and parents ought to know how this quest for security is evinced in school situations. The following list will give examples not only of the ways by which the child displays his need for security, but also of the ways by which the child may try to satisfy his own basic need. The child:

1. Will show desire for peer approval.
2. Will desire attention from both peers and adults.
3. Will desire success and teacher approval in those studies and activities wherein he has a good chance of achieving.
4. Will crave the love of parents and teachers.
5. May test the mettle of a teacher to determine how firm or reliable that teacher will be. Will be disappointed if the teacher is of weak character and bends to pressure.
6. Will usually display a lack of trust in any thing or person with whom he is not familiar.
7. May display braggadocio (outward display of strength to cover inner weaknesses and insecurity).
8. May try to disrupt those activities in which he has no chance of success.
9. May deliberately violate rules so as to determine whether the rules are firmly enforced.
10. May deliberately destroy or damage property so as to get the attention and concern of adults.

Just as the need for security may be observed in many different ways, so, too, the meeting of that need may be accomplished in different ways. Teachers may promote security by rewarding right conduct. A word of praise, a brief written compliment at the end of a test, a smile of approval — these all promote that feeling of well-being that children need. But this kind of loving action is not our only concern; in fact, most teachers today are made well aware of these responsibilities. What is harder to do, but just as necessary, is to promote security by punishing wrong conduct. Only the Christian teacher who knows that his own authority derives from a just and merciful Lord can consciously and logically punish the child firmly, yet in love, as God loves His children.

Any correct understanding of the need of the human being for security must be intimately related to a correct understanding of discipline. If there is no discipline, there will be no security. Children not only need discipline, but they want it. Their security system is based on the certainty that they have parents and teachers who will keep them in control if they are unable to do so themselves. One of the best ways to provide security is to set limits or boundaries to human conduct, and then firmly to enforce those boundaries. It is precisely on this point that the old vogue of permissiveness has failed. When those in authority set limits, they inevitably give the child something against which he can rebel. And having limits set for him, the child exercises his sinful urge to rebel by pushing and stretching the limits. If no enforcement of rules results from such rebellion — or if there are no rules against which to rebel — children will push on farther and farther until they either become delinquents or criminals, or autonomously establish their own boundaries.

But the injunction of Christ to "Love God above all and neighbor as self" provides the child with his rock of security when parents and teachers, out of gratitude for their salvation, keep God's law of love. But not only does Jesus command us to love our children and our neighbors (students) as ourselves, He also tells us to love our enemies and those that treat us spitefully. Paul appears to complicate the matter, however, when he includes discipline and chastisement in his discussion of love. Contrary to many current notions in the field of educational psychology, and contrary to the Hollywood propaganda, love and discipline are inextricably linked in Scripture, and thus must also be in our educational programs. If a Christian parent or teacher loves a child, he will set Biblical boundaries to human conduct, and violation of rules will be enforced by justly consequent penalties. Guided by the Holy Spirit, Paul could write with authority, "For whom the Lord loveth he chasteneth, and scourgeth every son whom he receiveth" (Heb. 12:6) because he correctly understood love. The writer knew that love is a godly concern for the temporal and eternal well-being of others. He correctly distinguished it from "liking" and infatuation, which is not necessary of teachers for pupils. He correctly understood that parents and those that stand in place of parents must discipline their children if they are to deal with them as their own offspring, rather than as illegitimates: "For what son is he whom the father chasteneth not? But if ye be without chastisement, whereof all are partakers, then are ye bastards and not sons" (Heb. 12:8).

Harry Blamires, in his highly recommended book, *The Christian Mind*, emphasized this relationship when he wrote,

> As a result of historical developments and changes of psychological habit the idea of authority has been totally severed from the idea of love. There is an iron curtain between them. They now belong to two

different modes of thinking. Yet it was not always so. There was a time when these two concepts were blended together in the embracing idea of Fatherhood, which has provided the richest summing-up of God's significance for us. The father was the loving provider and defender whose hand was open in liberality and raised in protection: he was also, at the very same time, the awesome ruler to whom implicit obedience was due (p. 137).

Commanded by Christ's summary of the law, teachers must love their pupils. It is a hard command and must be worked at. It is not an easy emotional relationship in which one becomes involuntarily ensnared when least expected or when the defenses are relaxed. But, rather, it is the foremost duty that God has laid upon all men, teachers not excepted. As Cornelius Jaarsma appropriately observed, "For a classroom to be genuinely Christian, the atmosphere must be one where love is supreme" (*Human Development*, p. 127). If that law is obeyed, tranquility will not be the mood of every classroom day, for "no chastening for the present seemeth to be joyous, but grievous: nevertheless afterward it yieldeth the peaceable fruit of righteousness unto them which are exercised thereby" (Heb. 12:11).

By this we know that we love the children of God, when we love God and obey his commandments. For this is the love of God, that we keep his commandments. And his commandments are not burdensome. For whatever is born of God overcomes the world; and this is the victory that overcomes the world, our faith (I John 5:2-4).

Security, discipline, and love are not separate entities which can be administered or acquired apart from each other. If the child is loved, he will be disciplined; and, if he is disciplined in love, he will be secure.

CHAPTER VIII

GOALS TOWARD WHICH

Teach us what we shall do unto the child that shall be born. (Judges 13:8b)

Question 1. What is the chief end of man?
Answer.   Man's chief end is to glorify God, and to enjoy him forever. — *Westminster Shorter Catechism*

Before anyone can answer the question how anything should be done, it is imperative that such a person know what needs to be done. Similarly, before a teacher can properly determine how a school subject or a graded concept should be taught, that teacher must know what needs to be taught and why. Correct educational procedure demands that purposes determine the choice of materials and methods.

To assume that such reflective, critical thinking precedes the teaching that goes on in the majority of classrooms would be intellectual generosity. However, in current educational practice it is accepted, and in many schools required, that teachers have their daily purposes and objectives carefully delineated before proceeding to choose materials and methods for the accomplishment of those purposes. Primarily for administrative reasons, similar demands are not applied to the larger choices of selecting courses and extra-curricular experiences. If such a procedural sequence is mandatory on a daily or weekly basis, and certainly it ought to be, it would be equally justifiable to require such articulation of purposes and objectives before a unit, a course, or an entire curriculum is planned.

In contrast to the ideal of establishing a preliminary, guiding rationale, many of the schools and teachers in the author's experience have been tradition-bound rather than thoughtfully purposive. But, as long as this tradition-bound approach is followed, distinctive Christian education will occur only despite, not because of the teaching, schooling process.

Since all processes must lead to some end, goal, or objective, and since the contemporary American educational position is not truthfully characterized as Christian, any student who arrives at the Scripturally designated goals while under the direction and influence of the secularized American tradition must have broken with, or rebelled against that tradition. Of course, if the philosophic system currently in vogue should have the same goals and purposes as those laid down in Scripture, the need for a distinctive Christian philosophy of education will be considerably lessened. Judging from current educational trends, however, this agreement on ultimate and primary goals is not only improbable, but on a national scale in our pluralistic society is impossible.

The goals and objectives of the secular educational establishment are not in accord with those of Christianity. Having already discussed the humanistic foundations upon which secular education attempts to find footing and having rejected all of them as unsatisfactory, we can not now expect the humanist to build sound superstructures on those unstable foundations. The humanist will neither curtail nor reverse his tendencies, nor will he look to Scripture for statements of purpose. Since the Bible is the only valid, reliable guide for practice and planning in education, any direction offered by antithetical sources must be rejected.

Although there is a great deal of diversity within the secular community, R. J. Rushdoony succinctly summarizes current educational philosophy when he says, "Behind much of the production and consumption of . . . information stands . . . a highly respectable theory, one which has become an unconscious article of faith: 'Knowledge is power.' For Francis Bacon, as he expounded it in his 'Aphorisms Concerning the Interpretation of Nature and the Kingdom of Man' in *Novum Organum*, man is 'the servant and interpreter of nature' rather than of God. This is in radical departure from the Biblical concept of Psalm 8, affirming man to be king over creation under God" (*Intellectual Schizophrenia*, p. 12).

Within this "knowledge is power" concept we find that the quality of education is determined by the quantity of knowledge acquired. That man is best educated who has attended the best school for the longest time. And that school is best which has accumulated and is capable of disseminating the greatest amount of knowledge. That teacher is best who has the most advanced degrees, because degrees are badges that people wear to indicate how long they have remained in school and how much knowledge they have acquired. In this tradition, which dates back at least to Francis Bacon, little concern is shown for the attitudes and emotions that knowledge evokes. No attempt is made to unite this conglomerate of mental acquisitions into a single, unified vision. No source outside the human mind is given credit for this knowledge, and its use is confined to man, for man. The ultimate purpose of teaching, in this tradition, is to dispense knowledge so as to give man power, power over himself and over his environment so that he may adjust to it and control it for his own ends. In sharp contrast to this we hear the paraphrase of Psalm 1: "That man is best, who, fearing God, from sin restrains his feet."

The Ultimate Objective

Having already insisted that our total educational philosophy must be consistent with our educational foundation, it is to Scripture that we must turn for statements of purpose. Because of Scripture's expansiveness, however, it is expedient first to review the various Scriptural summations, that is, the doctrinal creeds and catechisms. In the *Westminster Shorter Catechism*, previously quoted, man's chief end or purpose "is to glorify God, and to enjoy him forever." In John Calvin's *Genevan Catechism*, the first question and answer is almost identical: "What is the chief end of man? To know God and enjoy him forever."

The *Heidelberg Catechism*, in agreement with the Westminster and Genevan Catechisms, defines the goal or objective for man in the following statements:

Question.   What is your only comfort in life and death?

Answer.   That I, with body and soul, both in life and death, am not my own, but belong unto my faithful Savior Jesus Christ: who with His precious blood has fully satisfied for all my sins, and delivered me from all the power of the devil, and so preserves me that without the will of my heavenly Father not a hair can fall from my head; yea, that all things must be subservient to my salvation, wherefore by His Holy Spirit He also assures me of eternal life, and makes me heartily willing and ready, henceforth, to live unto Him.

The apostle Paul, writing to the Ephesian Christians, summarizes the required work of God's earthly servants in the following words, "And his [God's] gifts were that some should be apostles, some prophets, some evangelists, some pastors and *teachers, for the equipment of the saints, for the work of ministry, for building up the body of Christ, until we all attain to the unity of the faith and of the knowledge of the Son of God, to mature manhood, to the measure of the stature of the fullness of Christ; so that we may no longer be children, tossed to and fro and carried about with every wind of doctrine, by the cunning of men, by their craftiness in deceitful wiles. Rather, speaking the truth in love, we are to grow up in every way unto him* who is the head, *into Christ*, from whom the whole body, joined and knit together by every joint with which it is supplied, when each part is working properly, makes bodily growth and upbuilds itself in love" (Eph. 4:11-16, RSV).

In Paul's summarization it should be noted that no radical distinctions are made between the work of teachers and the other Kingdom functionaries. Teachers, as well as pastors, evangelists, prophets, and apostles, are called to equip the saints and build up the body of Christ. Teachers are called to direct children so that they may "grow up in every way into Christ."

Jesus Himself summarized God's law for men when He rebuked the Pharisees with the words, "Thou shalt love the Lord thy God with all thy heart, and with all thy soul, and with all thy mind. This is the first and great commandment. And the second is like unto it. Thou shalt love thy neighbor as thyself. On these two commandments hang all the law and the prophets" (Matt. 22:37-40).

These statements express the commonly accepted aim for all of education in the Christian community. In fact, their recitation has been so common that they frequently sound trite. The only difficulty with this ultimate Godward aim is that very few (even Christian) educators have been able to translate it into workable, functionally-stated objectives for parents and teachers. It is precisely at this point of translation or transmission that the ties between the church and the school become tenuous or are severed. Lack of understanding results in lack of common purpose, with church, home, and school pulling the child in different directions educationally, religiously.

In the churches of the Reformation heritage, an oft repeated admonition is that the members be Reformed. Especially in the autumn of the year clarion reminders are issued: "Be Reformed." Regrettably, the meaning of the term has narrowed to include only the labelling of a tradition, ignited in 1517 by a radical monk, but dying a gradual and certain death under the onslaughts of scientism, secularism, and humanism. If the term takes on no added life and meaning, the demise will be definite. Parents and teachers and ministers and school board members must awaken to the fact that the word, in its original and fuller sense, means "formed again" or "formed over." The very tradition and its symbolizing word demand change. It cannot demand a preservation of the status quo. It cannot be limited to Sunday sermons and October rallies.

The child is not so constituted that he can be formed-over on Sunday and preserved intact on Monday. In the words of Scripture, the child, as well as the adult, must not be "conformed to this world," but "transformed *by the renewing of his mind*" (Rom. 12:2).

Such an educational emphasis will probably stir the classification instinct of philosophers. Theodore Brameld, one of those gaining notoriety for his classificatory schemes, has his compartments pre-labelled. In *Education as Power* he writes,

By and large, the contention can be made that four major philosophies prevail in American educational theory today.

The terms that are frequently applied to these major views are (1) *essentialism,* which is the educational philosophy concerned chiefly with the conservation of culture; (2) *perennialism,* which centers its attention in the kind of educational guidance provided by the classical thought of ancient Greece and medieval Europe; (3) *progressivism,* which is the philosophy of liberal, experimental education; and (4) *reconstructionism,* which believes that the contemporary crisis can be effectively attacked only by a radical educational policy and program of action (p. 25).

In further examining Brameld's philosophic categories, the following additional characteristics should be noted. The essentialists are those who believe that there are certain essential truths which must be transmitted to each generation. By making these essential truths central in their educational program, these persons have inherited the added label of reactionary. The perennialists are those who believe that there are certain truths which perennially appear throughout culture and time. By pedagogically focusing on these reappearing truths, the perennialists have been equated with conservatives. The progressivists believe that schools are instruments for solving future and often unspecified problems. Such philosophic position-holders Brameld has encamped with the liberals. Finally, the reconstructionists hold to the notion that education is a tool which must be used to rebuild or reconstruct society. Because of this philosophic bent, they have been equated with the radical liberals.

Such categorizations may be tantalizing if one wishes to pidgeon-hole his educational opponents, but Brameld is wrong. The labels are too neat and fit nobody, especially not the Christian. The Christian is an essentialist, but he is more than that. The Christian is also a perennialist, but he is also more than that. The Christian is a progressivist, but he is also a reconstructionist. The Christian is all of these at once. He uses essential truths which perennially appear to solve future problems and thus rebuild or reform society.

The Christian is a radically conservative liberal. He is not afraid to call his school a "reform school," for he has recognized that the reforming, the renewing, the transforming of his children from the condition of depravity into "the unity of the faith" and unto the "measure of the stature of the fullness of Christ" (Eph. 4:13) is his most challenging and ennobling task.

To accept this reforming emphasis does not imply that school leaders must scour the jails, alleys, and detention centers for the foulest prospective students. Rather, the reforming task must be directed to all existing clientele, from the most suave to the most grubby. All must be "transformed by the renewing of their minds," some to greater and some to lesser degrees.

The Old Man		The New Man
self-loving	————————————→	God and neighbor loving
self-obeying	————————————→	God and authority obeying
self-centered	————————————→	God centered
self-serving	————————————→	God and neighbor serving

Fig. 13. The Re-forming Direction

If the church, home, and school are to work cooperatively toward the goal of Christ-commitment, a number of lessons must be learned. The first of these lessons can be learned through an examination of the way by which John Dewey resolved a similar difficulty. Dewey's philosophic aim for education was to produce democratic citizens. This aim is radically opposed to the ultimate purpose of Christian education. Having defined the aim of education in these terms, Dewey then had to face formulating workable objectives that would realize this aim. After expending considerable verbiage about ends, means, and ends-in-view, Dewey and his followers concluded that the process by which the student would move toward that goal must be democratic at every point if the ultimate goal were ever to be reached.[1] In trying to conform the child to that democratic citizenship which he wished all men to emulate, Dewey recognized that the authoritarian classroom and home atmospheres were working at cross purposes with his purpose.

The same important lesson must be learned by the Christian. If the Christian student is to "know God and enjoy him forever" or to love God with all his heart and soul and mind, the educational process must foster that knowledge and love at every point. In every subject, in every classroom, in every hallway, and in every gymnasium the students must be reminded of the importance of this God-given goal. As Deuteronomy 6 enjoins: "Thou shalt teach them [God's laws] diligently unto thy children, and shalt talk of them when thou sittest in thine house, and when thou walkest by the way, and when thou liest down, and when thou risest up. And thou shalt bind them for a sign upon thine hand, and they shall be as frontlets between thine

---

[1]For more detailed consideration of Dewey's discussion on this point, read "Theory of Valuation." *International Encyclopedia of Unified Science*, II, 4. University of Chicago Press: Chicago, 1939.

eyes. And thou shalt write them upon the posts of thy house, and on thy gates" (vss. 7-9).

A second important lesson that must be learned by the Christian involves the delineation of derived or primary aims.[2] Once a person has been rejoined to God through the recreative and redemptive work of Christ, not only is he given the desire and potential to live out that relationship, but he is also commanded to develop that relationship toward perfection. "The school," says Henry Zylstra, "addresses itself to the task of taking the Christian pupil and making his profession of Christianity a significant profession. The school, in short, teaches the pupil how he can express and gives him the means to express a responsible human citizenship in the kingdom of Christ" (*Testament of Vision*, p. 94).

Criteria for Primary Goals

This expansion of objectives becomes crucial in the Christian schools. At this point we must lay down some ground rules, some additional criteria, so that the school does not err in the formulating of primary aims. The following rules are hopefully in conformity with the foregoing Scriptural and Reformed confessional basis; therefore, they should prove helpful to school boards, parents, and teachers. In order to qualify as legitimate primary aims of education, those aims or objectives:

1. Must be in complete harmony with the Biblical basis for education.

2. Must be in harmony with the ultimate objective at all times. If an articulated purpose or aim does not contribute to the students' knowledge, enjoyment, and praise of God, that purpose or aim should not be allowed to stand.

3. Must be consistent with all other stated primary aims. If two or more purposes are in principial or practical conflict with each other, one, both, or possibly all of these purposes must be repudiated. Since God's revelation is not contradictory, educational purposes which are extrapolated from it can not be in conflict with each other. Although it may appear on the surface that the previously-mentioned goals of obedience and freedom are contradictory, a closer examination will reveal them to be complementary.

4. Must be based on a Scriptural conception of the nature of man. Any objective that is formulated without consideration for the ba-

_____

[2]Consistent with the terminology of the educational community (but outrageous to the philosophic community), the word *primary* is used to denote those objectives that derive from the ultimate objective.

sic Biblical doctrines about man will not be acceptable as a primary objective. In the United States of the 1960's it is common to hear educators argue that one of the primary functions or purposes of the school is to prepare or train young persons for their vocational choices. If such functions are defined without consideration of the truth that man is a dependent, totally sinful (that is, imperfect in all his functions) creature, created by God for His own glory, then those functions may not be classified as primary. Whether such functions may still be kept as a secondary or tertiary objective will depend largely on the criteria that are established for those subsequent, more-specialized functions.

Although this regulation may seem too narrow and too arbitrary, it must stand. Having previously asserted that schools and educational processes are intended to bring about some change in children, and having also asserted that any correct understanding of the child's nature must be rooted in Scripture, it becomes not only reasonable, but absolutely essential that any statement of intended change (of educational aim or objective) be made with Biblical knowledge of the subject's nature.

5. Must be based on a Scriptural conception of what man is to become. Any attempt to bring about change implies that there are two conditions, one existing and one desired. In criterion four above we asserted that objectives must be made in light of the sinful and depraved or existing condition. With this criterion we are also urgent that primary objectives be made in the light of the desired conditions, namely, the regenerated and sanctified condition.

6. Must be directed to the total person. Recognizing that the person is an organic oneness, and that any attempt to subdivide man may only be done for the purposes of temporary analysis, it again follows that all objectives of the first rank must be consistent with man's unified being, his essential wholeness. If the school personnel should decide that one of the school's primary functions should be the improvement of manual dexterity, such decision would have to be vetoed for failure to comply with this criterion of man's organic unity.

7. Must be applicable to all facets of, or steps in, the educational process. If properly understood, the ultimate and primary objectives of the school will be equally applicable to all levels of education, whether they be on the elementary, secondary, or on a higher level. Also, it should make no difference whether the activities be called extra-curricular or curricular. The primary

and secondary goals should be the same in all situations. Only when the educational planner is thinking on the level of tertiary or incidental aims will the purposes and objectives become distinct for the various levels or activities.

8. Must be applicable to all students within the school. Since Scripture emphasizes the commonality and equality of all men before God, any educational purpose which seeks to benefit only a portion of the student body to the neglect of others may not be elevated to the rank of primary objectives. For example, musical, speech, and athletic activities which seek to benefit only a percentage of the students in that case may not be considered of primary importance or be given primary consideration in educational planning.

9. Must be capable of attainment. When this rule is applied, the interpreters of it must not consider it either as an invasion of pragmatism or as an alienation from the other rules. In addition, two explanatory clauses must be appended so as to give the full meaning of the rule. The first of these is that man is not, nor can be, an autonomous or independent individual. Through the special and common grace that God extends to man, men are capable of doing things that they could not possibly do by themselves. If man were to limit 'his aspirations to those things that he can do by himself, nothing would ever be accomplished. In fact, man could not exist without God. By relying on God in faith, the Christian can not only move mountains (I Cor. 13:2), but "can do all things through Christ who strengthens him" (Phil. 4: 13). By pondering these promises, some of the objectives that will shortly be given will not only seem possible, but will be credible.

The importance of this divine assistance should not be underestimated. Often teachers set up high ideals and noble objectives but find themselves frustrated and despondent because of apparent failure to accomplish those goals. In times of such frustration one's response should not be to denounce the ideals or resign from the profession. Rather, the correct response would be to re-examine those goals in the light of Scripture and then to plead for assistance from the Father through the Son. For Christ has promised, "Whatsoever ye shall ask the Father in my name, he will give it you. Hitherto have ye asked nothing in my name: ask, and ye shall receive, that your joy may be full" (John 16:23-24).

The second corollary is that the objective need not be attainable in the span of one's temporal life. The ultimate goal of education is an obvious analogy. When we state that the over-arching purpose of all education is to "know God and enjoy him forever," it should be readily apparent that such a goal can not be fully accomplished within the framework of this life. In eternity "the Lord will perfect that which concerneth me" (Ps. 138: 8a). Teachers voice distress over unfinished tasks. Having set for themselves goals that were attainable, and then seeing students leave their realm of responsibility without having arrived at those goals, teachers are apt to bemoan their inadequacy. Understandable though such distress may be, such teachers have made the mistake of thinking that Christ will immediately perfect that which they set out to do.

The purpose of this rule is twofold. On the one hand it is intended to remind those involved in the educational process that there is an omniscient, omnipresent God assisting them in their pursuits. On the other hand, it is intended to discourage the formulation of man-centered, utopian ideals that God will not bless.

10. Must be intrinsically valuable as well as instrumentally valuable. In order to qualify as primary rather than secondary or tertiary, the goals that the school articulates must be worthwhile ends in themselves and not merely means to an end. Using this criterion, it should become evident that the teaching of the basic skills such as reading, writing, and arithmetic can not be considered as primary in importance. None of these skills has intrinsic value: they only begin to demonstrate their value as they are utilized for the attainment of something beyond. Their value is purely instrumental, that is, they have value only as a means to an end.

This criterion may seem strikingly strange because of the traditionalist emphasis on the teaching of the three R's as the school's prime function. The following illustration may demonstrate the necessity of this rule, however. Suppose that some student, disturbed by the teacher's just demands, inserts into the reading lesson a phrase or word that is blatantly derogatory of God. If the teacher is of any worth at all, she will, or at least should, halt the reading lesson immediately so as to correct the misconduct and urge penitence. By so doing, the teacher is implying that the use of God-honoring language and the presence of humble contrition are of higher rank and of more significance than the skill development. This is not to say that the development of skills does not deserve classification on the secondary level, for certainly the skills must be taught. The purpose of the example is, explicitly, to remind the teacher that other, more significant concerns, must take precedence over the mastery of skill. Without this regulation, the teaching of the skills may pre-empt significant psychological, spiritual considerations in the teacher's mind.

11. Must be definitely and functionally stated. In order to prevent ambiguity, this rule must also apply to all primary objectives. If an objective does not conform to this requirement, but does not violate any of the other rules, reformulation may be necessary. The purpose of this rule is simply to remind the educational theorist, and the author included, of the importance of clearly translating the ultimate objective into functional statements that teachers and parents can implement.

Primary Goals

Using Christ's summary of the law again, we conclude that the most important command given to man is to love. Since this command, this summary of the law, is intended for all of life, it must follow that the requirement also holds for education, which is part and parcel of life.

In seeking to understand this command, the reader must not look at the law simplistically. As Cornelius Jaarsma points out, "Love is not simply an emotion and not even a virtue in the ordinary sense, but rather a summary description of what every person ideally ought to be. Love is the fulfillment of the divine creation ordinance; . . . When love is perfect, the man is perfect. . . . The ability to love is the measure of maturity" (*Human Development*, p. 126).

Love for God and love for fellowman is not something innate in post-lapsarian man, else why would Christ command it. Also, growth in love is not something which the child will "fall into." Consequently, growth in love may not be left to chance, or assigned exclusively to either the church or the home. If man is to love God and his fellowman, he must develop in this love intellectually, emotionally, psychologically, and even physiologically. His total self must grow in this concern to the extent that his total behavior becomes God-directed and man-serving. In his devotion to serving fellow humans he must be made ready to give willingly of time, ability, and finances so that the welfare of others may be advanced and so that God's Kingdom may expand. Harry van der Laan has stated, "To love our neighbor as ourself means simply to attempt to change the conditions of his life in such a way that he will profit as we do from the regeneration of Christ which we already experience" (from "Science and Faith: Dualistic Paralysis or Scriptural Vigor," lecture delivered at Dordt College on April 20, 1967).

The supremacy of the command to love is further emphasized by Paul in I Corinthians 13:8, "Charity [love] never faileth: but whether there be prophecies, they shall fail; whether there be tongues, they shall cease; whether there be knowledge, it shall vanish away." And verse 13 concludes as follows: "And now abideth faith, hope, charity, these three; but the greatest of these is charity."

But the key to understanding Christ's summary is not to be found in the word love. Rather, the correct interpretation can only be gained through a focusing on the total and parallel phrases, "love the Lord thy God" and "love thy neighbor." The significance lies not in man's loving, but in his loving the proper object. Further examination will substantiate such emphasis, for Jesus concluded the second commandment with the words, "as thyself." The implication is then obvious: parents and teachers must not primarily be concerned with instruction in *how to love;* rather, the emphasis must be on *whom and what to love.*

Remembering that the primary purposes of the school may not be contradictory to its foundation-source, one sees that the school may not seek to instill, nor even condone, selfishness and egocentrism. The child, self-loving and egocentric creature that he is, must be redirected, reformed so that his God and his fellowman become the objects of his love.

The recent campaign of the National Education Association, in which that organization sought to combat the drop-out problem by emphasizing the financial rewards of increased schooling, is repugnant to the Christian. If greater remuneration should accrue to those who remain in school longer, such compensation should be considered only incidentally and should not be elevated to the status of primary aim.

A second objective or purpose of the school is to teach obedience. In any serious perusal of Scripture it will be noticed that the one command which is most often directed to children is the command to obey. In the fifth commandment God gives a special mandate to children in the words, "Honour thy father and thy mother, as the LORD thy God hath commanded thee; that thy days may be prolonged, and that it may go well with thee, in the land which the LORD thy God giveth thee" (Deut. 5:16). When Paul instructed Titus as to what and how he should teach, Paul also emphasized obedience: "Put them in mind to be subject to principalities and powers, to obey magistrates, to be ready to every good work" (Titus 3:1).

In considering this requirement for the school, it is important to be reminded that obedience and instruction are not separate. For those teachers and parents who attempt to separate them, discipline becomes a disrupting evil in the school environment, and disobedience soon becomes an impediment to teaching where discipline is considered extraneous. For such permissive persons, teaching becomes essentially the dissemination of knowledge, with obedience being relegated to the lower, less important position of being merely one unpleasant means to that end. Such teachers not only become quickly frustrated in their teaching function, but they are guilty of distortion whenever such un-Biblical abstraction of discipline from instruction is considered an educational ideal. In the classic passage from Proverbs, Solomon does not divide obedience and knowledge, but intimately relates them: "The fear of the LORD is the beginning of knowledge: fools despise wisdom and instruction. Hear, my son, your father's instruction, and reject not your mother's teaching" (Prov. 1:7-8, RSV).

In connection with this objective one other misconception must be corrected. In traditional humanistic thinking, obedience is considered almost exclusively as response to persons. A child is obedient when he submits to the demands of another human being. However, the correct conception of obedience must also be extended to include a person's responses to the laws and commands of the personal covenant God, and to truth which we may know through Christ *the* Truth. Even when no other persons are present, a child must be obedient to the truth which is in him through the Holy Spirit. Made aware of laws and truth, the child must conform to them even in his most private life. Failure to obey the truth, as Paul says, is really being obedient to the lie, to unrighteousness, and to Satan (Rom. 2:8).

A third goal that Scripture holds before man involves the acquisition of knowledge. Emphasizing man's responsibility in life, Solomon commands, "Take fast hold of instruction; let her not go: keep her; for she is thy life" (Prov. 4:13). The Christian cannot and may not ignore such an imperative. For the Christian, the acquisition of knowledge is not a social expedient or man-made possibility that should be sought for the sake of speeding up the child's adjustment to society or for ameliorating societal ills. It is a God-given mandate in the same sense that loving and obeying are demanded by Him.

Since the acquisition of knowledge is a God-given command already in His creation ordinance, it is imperative that God direct us in our use of that knowledge which He generously bestows. Is knowledge its own end? Should we acquire knowledge for the sake of knowledge? Should knowledge be sought mainly for the sake of meeting vocational requirements? Should knowledge be desired simply to help one attain higher income in his professional field? Obviously not.

Having previously noted that primary objectives are not only to be consistent with, but also to be delineations and derivations of our ultimate objective, we must conclude that the function of man in his role as knowledge-acquirer and knowledge-examiner is to enjoy and praise God. In coming to know about the cosmic creation in which he resides, man must see the coherence, the cohesiveness of that universe in Christ (see Col. 1:16-17). But to see the coherence of the creation in Christ is also to become aware of its cosmic complexity. This amazing variety, along with its total cohesiveness in Christ, must in every individual provoke the praise and awe that David uttered. When students consider the heavens, the work of God's fingers, the moon, the stars, and the earth, their first and best response should be one of humility. To abstract correctly from the cosmic unity is to realize how ignorant one truly is, because each abstraction opens unexplored vistas. To know properly is to become increasingly humble.

Although awe and fear of God are right responses to God's generous distribution of knowledge, such response may not mesmerize the believer into inactivity. Whole-being praise and whole-hearted work must flow out of that God-implanted faith. Man still stands as vice-gerent, and, unlike Milton's poetic rationalization, can not adequately serve by standing and waiting ("On His Blindness"). Obedience, then, not only precedes the acquisition of knowledge, but follows it and entirely controls it. If a person is not wholly obedient in returning all knowledge, all belief, in homage to God from whence it came, such a person would be better off not having such knowledge. Knowledge received from God, but not used for God, will only intensify eternal damnation. Jesus strongly warns us of the significance of false instruction with the words, "But whoso shall offend one of these little ones which believe in me, it were better for him that a millstone were hanged about his neck, and that he were drowned in the depth of the sea" (Matt.. 18:6).

In the God-denying, scientific humanism of the twentieth century, knowledge has been idolized in Indostani fashion. In elephant-grabbing blindness, the mind of modernity looks to its presumptive autonomy for the salvation of the educational process.

In Christian perspective, the acquisition and transmission of knowledge remain essential and primary purposes of schools. But, in theoretical considerations, this transmission and acquisition may not take precedence over the commands to love and obey. Even though a student "have the gift of prophecy, and understand all mysteries, and all knowledge" but have not love, he is nothing (I Cor. 13:2).

In educational discussion, especially on the secondary and higher levels, the idea is frequently stated that the search for truth (or Truth) is education's most noble function. In the name of this noble function, fantastically large research grants are justified. Professorial nonconformity is explained away and allowed to continue, no matter how blasphemous a direction such professing and researching may take. Research grants and sabbaticals for counting and correlating "facts" become the mark of distinction and educational excellence; for, say the truth-seek-

94

ers, truth exists "out there" in the objective world. One must leave the ivory tower of the classical humanists. Only by ridding oneself of all biases and preconceived notions can the objective, that is, the scientific, search be carried on. Only by utilizing this means can truth ever be discovered.

In almost every culture it would be readily agreed that those who call themselves teachers or educators desire to impart truth to their students. Anyone who would make a practice of imparting falsehoods would quickly be judged as not deserving the appellation of either teacher or educator. Mis-educator would be a more appropriate title. Only a Satanically inspired teacher would deliberately try to foist a false mathematical equation on his students' minds. If such a teacher tried to convince his class that $2 + 2 = 9$, or that George Washington was a Communist, that person would summarily (in most schools, thanks be to God) be discharged for propagating falsehoods. Presumably, matters of truth and falsehood are of great important even to agnostic educators on this elementary level.

Proceeding to the secondary and higher levels of schooling, one encounters analogous false teachings. On these levels one finds teachers encouraging and cajoling students to believe that man evolved from apes or sea-side amoebae. Again, such a statement of belief must be either true or false. Either man did evolve from animals or man did not. Another belief, strongly implied and subtly advocated by secular teachers, is that the universe and man's role in it can be correctly understood without reference to God. Once again, such a naturalistic assumption must be either true or false. Either the universe with all its physical, biotic, and spiritual activity can be correctly understood apart from God, or it can not.

For the Christian as well as for the non-Christian, the search for truth is accepted as a foundational and *necessary* function in education. For the Christian, however, the solution is disarmingly simple and already within his power as he is filled with the light and power of the Holy Spirit who leads us into all truth. Accepting the deity and authority of Christ, the Christian also accepts Christ's claim to being Truth personified. Christ's claim that "I am the way, the truth, and the life: no man cometh unto the Father, but by me" takes on cosmic significance (John 14:6). The Gospel writer's further statement that "the Word was made flesh, and dwelt among us, . . . full of grace and truth" expands the believer's vision of truth so that the inscripturated Word as well as Jesus as God Incarnate is included. Since Jesus Christ — the Word of God in Flesh — existed from the beginning, and since "all things were made by him; and without him was not anything made that was made," no man can defend the charge that this concept of truth is too small or

95

too limited (John 1:2-3). "For by him were all things created, that are in heaven, and that are in earth, visible and invisible, whether they be thrones, or dominions, or principalities, or powers: all things were created by him, and for him: And he is before all things, and by him all things consist" (Col. 1:16-17). With all things cohering in Christ, only those things which are examined in the light of that Incarnate Word as we study His Scriptures can be correctly and truly understood. Only when the Christian accepts the truth of that promise, "In thy light shall we see light," does the knowledge that is transmitted in the educational process become true knowledge, worthy of belief.

When True knowledge and obedience are considered conjunctively, a third element comes into focus. This is what the Scriptures call wisdom. Neither True knowledge by itself nor obedience by itself can be productive of right conduct and attitude. Only if a person has the two in firm conjunction will he be worthy of being characterized as "wise." Being in possession of false knowledge or being disobedient to true knowledge can only produce unwise thoughts and unwise behavior. Remembering that "wisdom is the principal thing" (Prov. 4:7), teachers must seek to intensify the student's commitment to the truth. Mere cognitive awareness of the truth will not suffice. Neither will an increase in the amount of knowledge, for knowledge apart from obedience is not power. It is rather, a flamboyant cloak of hypocrisy that is assumed so as to dazzle the simple with a meretricious show of wisdom.

Since all learning is essentially a search for truth, the pupil's proximity to truth is determined by his proximity to Christ and His Holy Word. Does that mean that theology is the only legitimate subject in the school curriculum? Emphatically no! The whole world belongs to our Father and must be redeemed, reclaimed, reconstructed for Him. The world of nature, the world of literature, the world of economics, the world of politics, all must be made subject to the law of God. In order for this to be done, all the dimensions of man's existence must be examined in the light of Scripture.

One other consideration deserves the educator's attention: not all men seek truth. The unregenerate teacher and the unregenerate textbook author, but for God's restraining grace in some details, perpetuate lies and falsehoods because their father is the devil. "For every one that doeth evil hateth the light, neither cometh to the light, lest his deeds should be reproved. But he that doeth truth cometh to the light, that his deeds may be made manifest, that they are wrought in God" (John 3: 20-21).

If there is any one mark of unrighteousness that characterizes the secular educator, it is that he refuses to let the light of Scripture illuminate the concepts of history, jurisprudence, medicine, chemistry, and every other so-called secular subject. Even the designation of these studies as secular, that is, outside the influence of God, is an indication of the devil's devious working. For the Christian, no subject is or may be secular.

The last primary objective that we wish to consider is one that has been so badly distorted as to merit separate, more extensive discussion.

Born to Be Free

For those who are familiar with the liberal-arts tradition, it will be anticipated that a discussion of freedom enter our consideration of the school's primary objectives. In the liberal-arts tradition, attention has rightly been focused on the word "liberal." The original Latin phrase was *artes liberales,* meaning those higher arts that only the Roman freemen were allowed to pursue. With the rebirth of this phrase in the Italian Renaissance, the word *liberare* became focal. The meaning then was to liberate or to free. The purpose of the liberal arts, consequently, was to liberate or free the student. The educational philosophy which incorporated this liberal-arts emphasis has since been known as the classical humanist movement.

Pier Vergerius, an influential Italian writer during the Renaissance, has given us a classic definition of a liberal-arts education: "We call those studies liberal," he wrote, "which are worthy of a free man; those studies by which we attain and practice virtue and wisdom; that education which calls forth, trains, and develops those highest gifts of body and mind which ennoble men and which are rightly judged to rank next in dignity to virtue only, for to a vulgar temper gain and pleasure are the one aim of existence, to a lofty nature, moral worth and fame" (Good, *A History of Western Education,* p. 126).

Such a definition may seem completely acceptable and invulnerable. But, as soon as its philosophic import is understood, the entire expression becomes indefensible and spurious. The liberal-arts concept is based on a Platonic idea which ascribed two natures to man: a higher nature and a lower nature. The lower nature was characterized by physical urges, needs, and appetites. This was the nature of the laborer and the professional. It was considered to be vulgar, mundane, and practical. The higher nature was characterized by wisdom and reason. The purpose of the liberal-arts education was to free the student from this lower nature to the higher nature. Reason and intellectual power were applauded, whereas the vocational, practical interests were depreciated because of the vulgarity attached to them.

One of the evils resulting from this tradition is the large gap that schools allow to exist between theory and practical application. The ivory towers, because of their classical-humanist leanings, have not only condoned their lack of respect for the world in which they live, but have encouraged such denigratory idealism by their full and erroneous assurance of the laboring man's spiritual inferiority. Such Platonic idealism is completely unchristian. Moreover, the concept becomes utterly repulsive when one remembers that Jesus and His apostles were carpenters, fishermen, and tent-makers by choice. To hold to the liberal-arts tradition would cause one to cast aspersions on their occupational endeavors.

Regretably, the Christian community has long been enamoured of the classical-humanist movement. Conservative Christian colleges have long complimented themselves on being liberal-arts schools. Because of their adulterous infatuation with this tradition, Christians have allowed the non-Christian mind to dictate curricula and teaching emphases. If a serious examination of classical-humanism's philosophic base and intent were made, however, such enchangment would quickly be dispelled. Essential to the success of such scrutiny would be the willingness to ask at least three questions: (1) What is a suitable definition of freedom? (2) By what means can freedom be attained? and (3) How does the liberal-arts tradition answer the foregoing questions? When these questions have been asked and answered, we can again concern ourselves with the question whether the primary purposes of the school should include the freeing of the child.

What is freedom? What does it mean to be free?

In the intellectual heritage of eighteeneth-century rationalism and the French Revolution, the word freedom has come to mean absence of restraint. Also, judging from the types of litigation the American Civil Liberties Union (the ACLU) has endorsed, it would appear that this organization, among many, has accepted this definition and translated it to mean individual autonomy or release from law. According to the ACLU, the imposition of law on the behavior of individuals is unnatural and even criminal because it prohibits and restrains freedom. Oddly enough, a diametrically opposed and yet principially analagous movement, the radically conservative political right, evinces an almost identical concept of freedom. The radically conservative groups have released their broadsides not so much *for* the autonomy of the individual as they have *against* the government. According to them, each new law passed by the government further erodes our freedom, with the obvious implication that the fewer laws we have and the fewer restrictions the government places on us, the more freedom we have.

Using the above definitions, full and complete freedom could not be enjoyed until all laws and restraints were removed. For the Christian, freedom would be impossible so long as the Ten Commandments remain.

In a more plausible but basically similar approach, Adam Smith incorporated a concept of freedom in his laissez faire capitalism. In the economic domain every person should be free to do as he sees fit. Since the natural laws of supply and demand will prevent the economic tub from tipping, the government is not to interfere. In this tradition, that government is best which governs least. Again the implication is that freedom is absence of restraint. Governmental non-interference will allow freedom to flourish.

The implications seem clear enough, but it should quickly become apparent that wholesale elimination of law is not the intent of the above groups. The ACLU does not contest every law, and the radical right has even encouraged the passage of many. Flushed with an unexamined allegiance to the democratic ideal, these persons elevate themselves to a level equal to the law. Rather than seeking contentment in equality *before* the law, they earnestly desire equality *with* the law. Deluding themselves into believing that their goal has been attained, they elevate personal law (self-obedience) to the highest level. Whichever statute does not conform to their individualistic whims and fancies they seek to strike down. But, unable to change the immutable laws inherent in a falling apple, an icy sidewalk, or the sun's blinding rays, they damn the God who made them and curse the restrictions on their freedom.

In God's providence, these concepts of freedom have been tempered. Christian and non-Christian alike were led to see that adherence to such definitions could produce only chaos and anarchy.

Within the Christian community of the twentieth century, there has been, nevertheless, a general unwillingness to disavow this concept of freedom. Harry Blamires, in his book *The Christian Mind*, discusses this intellectual trauma. He says,

> A living dialogue is carried on in our midst on this obsessive issue of totalitarianism. But it is not a Christian dialogue. It is almost wholly dominated by a concept of freedom whose roots are deep in pagan naturalism. The Christian concept of freedom, rooted as it is in the notion of total self-surrender within the family of God, and accompanied as it is by a code of disciplines rigorous in their check upon self-indulgence or self-assertive individualism, is a virtually contradictory concept to that humanist notion of freedom as residing in an unfettered autonomous individualism, which plagues current thinking today (*The Christian Mind*, p. 12).

Holding to the basic definition that freedom is absence of restraint, Christian thinkers have tried to modulate the concept by arguing that

99

freedom must be exercised responsibly. In other words, the free man must be mature enough to put his own restraint on his personal liberty. Since children are not mature, they must still live under laws and rules. When they marry or reach the chronological mark of maturity (age 21), they can then be given freedom. They can then be released from the laws and regulations of home and school, but the parents' sincere wish is that they will not rashly exploit their sudden freedom.

As long as adults hold to such a concept, it can be expected that children will continue to refer to schools as jails and prisons. Schools, in the minds of such youth, are concentrations of rules which prevent the full enjoyment of the freedom to which young persons are entitled.

R. J. Rushdooney gives inadvertent support to such a conception of freedom in his book *Intellectual Schizophrenia* when he says, "The freedom of the creature is real only because of God's eternal decree, and it is never real except in terms of limitation and responsibility" (p. 116). In an explanatory passage he goes on to assert, "True political liberty establishes the restraint of law, insists on liability, cannot tolerate any creed which works to overthrow it, and will not confuse freedom of the press, for example, with freedom to libel or slander, but will impose restrictions to guarantee freedom with responsibility" (p. 116).

Although Rushdooney's conception of freedom with responsibility is certainly an improvement over the eighteenth-century idea of freedom as absence of restriction, the basic term remains unsatisfactorily defined. Freedom with responsibility based on restriction can not be a final or satisfying concept. Given such a concept, the urge will always be present to whittle down or diminish the restrictions so that one can enjoy full freedom.

In order to solve the problem, a new, basic definition of the word freedom must be offered. Although this term usually remains undefined by those who shout about it the loudest, we should shun their error. For the term is definable, and that, we think, in a distinctively Christian, Biblical way.

In trying to understand the concept of freedom, we can proceed from different viewponts. Let us begin with a reference to the Vietnam war as an attempt to preserve or gain freedom. Has it ever occurred to you as being somewhat paradoxical that those military men who are sent to secure freedom must undergo the most rigorous discipline and be continually subject to the strictest rules of conduct? Undisciplined conduct in the military inevitably leads to loss of freedom; only highly disciplined armed forces can defend and maintain freedom. Does the analogy hold for education? Can a teacher ever hope to make his students free if that teacher is not highly disciplined?

Without forgetting this approach, let us move on to another viewpoint.

When is a person free to drive a car? You would have to conclude that he is free only so long as he obeys all the rules of the road. He is free if he stops for every red light, obeys the speed limit, stays on the right side of the road, passes only when traffic clears, and otherwise adheres to the many regulations for the highway. As soon as he begins to disobey any of these regulations, he loses his freedom, either through an emotional disturbance brought on by his innate sense of right and wrong (see Rom. 2:14-16) or through the actions of the arresting officer.

A second illustration may clarify this point. Let us now use a baseball player for our example. Again we observe that a person is free to be a ballplayer only so long as he follows the rules of the game. Stop to think of the many rules for just a minute: you have to stand in a narrow batter's box; you have to run in a certain direction; you have to obey the umpires. Now, in baseball as soon as you violate the rules of the game or make indiscreet remarks to the umpire, you are no longer free to be a ballplayer.

A third and final example will suffice, and for this one let us use Adam and Eve. These two persons were placed by God in the garden (Eden) which God had prepared for them. They had work to do, and they had to obey the law of God precisely. The law was simple, but very exact. As long as they obeyed God's law, they were free, free to live as God intended, free to be truly human. As soon as they flouted this one, all-pervasive law of obedience to God, they lost their freedom. They lost it even before God talked to them or sent them from the Garden. They lost their freedom as soon as they violated the law under which they had been created to live.

Freedom, then, involves living within a framework of law and ceases to exist, either emotionally, spiritually, or politically, whenever we try to step outside that framework. In fact, freedom can not exist apart from rules or regulations.

Secondly, freedom involves a willing or joyful compliance with law. The ballplayer does not chafe because of the rules or because he must obey as many as six umpires in a World Series ballgame. He, in fact, is now more free to play the game than if there were very few rules and only one or two umpires. Neither does the driver of the car feel the restraint of the traffic laws as he engages in normal driving. It is only when he breaks the law or attempts to stretch the law that he begins to feel its restraining influence. We are sure, too, that Adam and Eve felt no restrictions or hampering of activity because of God's law. They were free until they chose to listen to Satan, and until they repudiated their freedom by violating God's command.

A necessary third element in any consideration of freedom involves the matter of release. It is not accidental or coincidental that modern man thinks of freedom as absence of restraint or release from law. Any analysis of freedom must address itself to this question of release. When Lincoln freed the slaves with the Emancipation Proclamation, he attempted to release them from slavery to something else. What was this something else? To what did he release them? Obviously, we will not be making any progress if we say that he released (that is, freed) them from slavery to freedom, for we have not yet defined freedom. Also, he did not release them from the laws of the United States government. On the contrary, it was considered necessary to set up Freedmen's Schools for the Negroes so that they might learn to read and write and become increasingly aware of the government under which they were to live. Such education was essential to the fulfillment of the freedom promise, for the freeing process was to release the Negroes from slavery to responsible citizenship, to a level of equality with other human beings. When the campus rebels of the present decade demonstrate for freedom, they are also seeking release. The sham and falsity of a crassly materialistic, income-gauged society that seeks its own salvation in scientific "progress" are damming and stifling to these academic dissenters. They seek release from such a society's demands, but, knowing nothing better, their only response is rebellion.

In the classical-humanist or liberal-arts tradition the release is presumably from man's lower nature to his higher nature. The liberal-arts curriculum is devised to release man from the practical, mundane concerns of the vocational life to the lofty, praiseworthy concerns of reason and philosophy. Because this tradition does not conform to our Scriptural base, such a concept can not be acceptable to the Christian even though it may contain an appealing element of truth woven into it.

The Heidelberg Catechism, as a summary of Biblical teaching, offers the Christian the only satisfying Scriptural answer to this question of release. In its succinct divisions of thought: sin, salvation, and service, we notice that sin summarizes man's unregenerate state. Salvation is both a definitive act and the process of releasing from sin, whereas service characterizes man in his redeemed condition. Using this very Biblically correct summary, we see that man is saved from a life of sin to a life of service. Defining sin Scripturally as disobedience to God's law, and service as compliance with God's law, salvation in Christ (Who obeyed the law perfectly) becomes a release from disobedience to obedience.

In Scriptural and in vernacular usage, the word free is used as a synonym for the word save. Paul speaks thus. when he writes, "For he who has died [to sin through Christ's death] is freed from sin" (Rom. 6:7). Jesus Himself makes this transition in usage with the words, "If ye continue in my word, then are ye my disciples [learners] indeed; and ye shall know the truth, and the truth shall make you free" (John

8:31, 32). In reply to a subsequent question from the Pharisees, Jesus reaffirms this teaching as follows: "So if the Son makes you free, you will be free indeed" (John 8:36 RSV).

To be freed, then, is not to be released from the requirements of the law. It is to be released from the curse of the law to a willing and joyful compliance with the law. The laws of the highway and the laws of the ball game all remain when free people participate in corresponding activities; and the laws of God are in effect over all life. The curse and the sense of restraint, however, are gone, for free men do not seek to break the law. They strive to conform to its demands.

In the light of these remarks, what is the function of the law? Is it to curse? Certainly not, "since through the law comes knowledge of sin" (Rom. 3:20). In the language of the book of Galatians, "the law was our schoolmaster to bring us unto Christ, that we might be justified by faith" (Gal. 3:24). Accepting this as the function of the law, it becomes easily understandable why modern man wants to define freedom as release from law or absence of restraint. Not wanting to be made aware of his sinful condition, he has no desire to confront the law which will expose his disobedience. As Paul puts it, "The law worketh wrath: for where no law is, there is no transgression" (Rom. 4:15). In schools, too, laws and rules frequently make children angry. But without laws and rules there can be no freedom. If schools never subject children to laws, there will probably be little anger and certainly no law-breaking. But neither will there be any freedom.

Summarizing this aspect of freedom, we can say that true freedom allows man to become what he was intended by God to become. The Negro was not intended to become sub-human chattel, so he needed release from slavery. God's divinely created man was not intended to be a slave to disobedience; rather, he was created for obedient and joyful service and praise.

One final aspect of freedom remains to be considered. In the contemporary humanistic thought that we have been analyzing, freedom is approached in two distinct ways. In one of these approaches, freedom is considered to be an individual possession. Those persons who have apparently succeeded in finding release from the presumably foolish demands of law are thought to enjoy personal freedom. Also, those persons who have never had strict regulations imposed on them by their parents or by their schools are thought to be enjoying freedom. Although such freedom may be shared by many persons at once, the relationship to the law is still singular and personal, thus making freedom individual.

In the second approach, which is far more nebulous and naive, freedom is considered as an objective state of affairs existing apart from individual persons. In this mode of thought, for example, the United States is called the land of freedom. Persons become free by affiliating themselves with a country, for freedom is an objective characteristic of a nation. This same form of reasoning is applied to academic institutions. Some schools are considered to be free, that is, without restraints, whereas other schools are thought to be tightly bound by law. Those persons who are affiliated with the school that is tightly bound by law, say these libertarians, cannot possibly be considered free, because freedom is not a characteristic of such a school.

For those who naively accept this latter definition, only those persons who live in the United States or in countries with very similar political structures can be free. Thus, our neighbors in Communist Cuba cannot be free and must be released. Because they are not free, they will desire to be released from their bondage, for it is believed that all men seek to be free. To the great chagrin of the Central Intelligence Agency and the late President Kennedy, most Cubans failed to support the Bay of Pigs invasion, which was our attempt to free them. Why? Did they already possess freedom? Is the idea that freedom exists only in democratic societies nothing more than a myth? Can people be free to the extent that they willingly comply with the Satanically-inspired laws of Godless Communism?

Or when teachers readily accept teaching appointments in Christian schools that admittedly have more restrictions on the content and the manner of instruction than do the public schools and universities, are those teachers depriving themselves of freedom? These two examples represent the type of problem that must be solved by those who believe in freedom as an objective state of affairs.

A second situation that needs understanding can be typical of any home or school. Given two children who live in the same country, state, and town, one may claim to have freedom, whereas the other clamors loudly for the freedom that has been denied him. Intensify the relationships to the point where the children also come from the same home, attend the same church, and are under the tutelage of the same teacher. A disparity between their freedom-concepts will still probably exist. Why? The framework of laws for both children is identical. If freedom were an objective state of affairs, both would obviously be in possession of it, yet one makes claims to the contrary.

A second example of this type of problem can be seen in most election campaigns. Members of one party will issue charges that their freedom has been eroded by the men in office. Members of the other party will proudly and vociferously announce that the same office-holders have given a new measure of freedom. Is one party guilty of perpetrating falsehoods? Or is freedom an individual matter?

Turning again to the Bible for answers to these questions, we are reminded that only Christ makes us free. Those who adhere to the Truth shall be free indeed. Since Christ does not save or free men en masse, and since every person has a unique, individual relationship to Christ, it follows that freedom is also individual. Man is individually freed from disobedience to obedience. Even unregenerate man, through the common grace extended by God in Christ, is individually made to comply with the rules and laws of the governments under which he has been consigned by the Father to live. Because of this, freedom is not an objective state of affairs, but a subjective condition that is displayed in man's psychic dimension. Freedom is a condition that characterizes some but not all persons. Speaking analytically and as Christians, it is the spiritual and moral relationship of man in his total being to God and all the laws that He has instituted.

Summing up all the elements just discussed, we can now formulate a definition of freedom. Freedom is the psychological condition of those persons who willingly and joyfully comply with that framework of laws under which they have been consigned to live in order that they may become what they believe they were intended to become. True freedom, that is, freedom in Christ, is the spiritual condition of regenerated man as he willingly and joyfully obeys God's laws in order that he may become a worshipful servant in the Kingdom of Christ. For those who do not possess such freedom, there is only one direction to turn. Only by asking God through Christ for a new heart of obedience to His laws can one receive the blessing of freedom.

Recognizing that all men are mandated to live under God's all-pervasive law, those who inexcusably claim ignorance of that law or belligerently defy that law cannot experience full freedom. Neither can they become truly human, for, to be truly human is to be restored to the humanity that Adam and Eve enjoyed in the prelapsarian state. Such restoration can take place only through Christ. Depraved, disobedient man becomes human and free to the extent that he becomes completely united to and one with Christ. Paradoxical as it may seem, man becomes free when he becomes a slave to Christ.

Obviously, there is radical disagreement between the classical-humanist and the Christian conception of freedom. It should also be obvious that the Christian definition of freedom offered here is not only consistent with those primary objectives of love, obedience, knowledge, and truth, but greatly complements them. Although the Christian will recognize that freedom can not be accomplished apart from the working of the Triune God, the Christ-believer should also be reminded that God works through His vicegerents, His human servants. The freeing process is God-ordained, but one in which man can and must engage. By acquainting the child with the law of the Scriptures, the laws that God has established in nature, and the laws that emanate from divinely instituted governments, homes, and churches, man can aid in the redevelopment of True obedience, True knowledge, True freedom, and True love under Christ. Why is it, then, that obedient Christian persons, to the human eye regenerated and sanctified in Christ, still search for freedom? Why is that saintly Christians find it difficult to obey certain laws and regulations? Various answers could be offered for such crucial questions. One answer, which certainly deserves consideration, is that Satan continues his insidious warfare, encouraging disobedience at every turn. Unwilling to concede defeat until death mercifully translates the Christian from temporal to eternal, the Satanic host persists in tempting to sin. A second answer is that the Christian, in the temporal state, imperfectly interprets the laws that God has ordained and permitted his earthly agents to formulate. Unable, and sometimes unwilling, to interpret these laws correctly, the Christian fosters an attitude of rebellion for which he, alone, is responsible. A third answer can be found, not within individuals as such, but within society as a whole.

Within the framework that we call American society one can find a wide array of laws and law-making institutions. The child, as he matures, is made aware of the rules and regulations of the home, the church, the school, the city, the peer groups of which he is a member, the state, and the nation. Each of these agencies and each of these institutions formulates laws for the regulation of the person's life, and each demands obedience. As the child becomes familiar with all these laws and regulations, he recognizes something with which all adults should be aware: these laws very often are out of harmony; these laws and regulations are often inconsistent with each other.

Within the home, the rules laid down by father may be inconsistent with those laid down by mother. Within the school, the regulations articulated by a classroom teacher may lack conformity with those articulated by the playground supervisor or the principal. The regulations of the church may be out of harmony with those of the state, and the laws of the state may be inconsistent with those of the federal government. All of them may lack conformity to God's divine law. Naturally the child experiences conflict. Naturally he wonders at the personal application of "Children, obey your parents in the Lord, for this is right" (Eph. 6:1). So, too, with the mature Christian. How can he enjoy his God-given freedom when such freedom demands obedience to conflicting or disparate laws?

The answer to such disparity lies not in disobedience. The child who finds his parents and his teachers guilty of formulating conflicting rules is not thereby excused from obedience. Neither is the mature citizen who discovers, or thinks he discovers, disparity between the laws of state and nation. The answer lies in continued obedience, for the eternal, immutable Law of God still stands. The failure of civil, school, church, and home authorities to make their laws and regulations conform to God's Law does not constitute excuse for the one who is to be obedient, unless, of course, those humanly formulated regulations directly and flagrantly violate Biblical mandate. Even then, established and legitimate procedure for correction must be followed. If such procedure is non-existent or ineffective, obedience to God's law must take precedence. In such situations the Christian must, like Daniel, be willing to endure persecution and to place his trust in the care of the Almighty.

The answer also lies, at least in part, in the removal of the disparities or inequalities. This much God's earthly creatures can and must attempt. Parents and teachers must seek conformity in their rules; not mere conformity of one set to the other, but conformity of both sets to the will of God revealed in Scripture. Those who have been given positions of responsibility in civil government, ecclesiastical government, and educational administration must also strive for conformity to the Scriptural model.

To the extent that the laws of America conform to the Law of God, and to the extent that the citizens of America willingly obey those laws, to that same extent will America be the land of the free. The responsibility is jointly shared, by those designated to make the laws and by all those to whom the laws apply. The same must be said of schools. To the extent that God's law is ignored or flouted by teachers, parents, or students, freedom in education is impossible.

Summary of Primary Objectives

Only when the child has learned to love, to obey, to serve, to know, and to be free in the manner prescribed by Scripture, have the goals of true education been realized. These goals, because they are all-comprehensive are applicable to all persons and to all situations. If followed in all of their ramifications by every student, each student will be restored to his correct relationship with God, his correct relationship with his fellow-man, and his correct relationship to the physical universe. The Christ-believing student will know, serve, and love his God and his fellow-man in obedience to God's law. In his appreciation and use of the physical universe, he will strive to honor God above all, which, at the same time, will promote man's well-being.

If these basic demands were all met perfectly, nothing more would be needed, for the student would then have been restored to the original state enjoyed by Adam and Eve. Also, if these demands could be fully met, the student would be a perfect member of temporal society, for by attaining these goals he would have become a perfect member of the Kingdom of Christ. Nothing more could be expected; for God makes no greater demands. Yet more *must* be said, and that for two reasons. The first reason is that man is imperfect: he continually falls short of perfect love, perfect knowledge, and perfect obedience. Not being able to meet these requirements of God perfectly, the teacher and the student alike need short-range objectives which serve as guide posts on the way of sanctification, but which do not demand *complete* sanctity (which is not found in this life) for their accomplishment. They need daily objectives which are quickly attainable and in the fulfillment of which they can find satisfaction. The second reason lies in the very comprehensiveness of the primary objectives. Because of their comprehensiveness, further analysis and articulation become necessary. But the analysis of these primary objectives must not result in a dimming of the total vision. Ideally speaking, abstraction from these primary goals should intensify their original significance and should give new meaning to the ultimate goal of praising God in all of life. At the same time that we become increasingly aware of our potentialities and responsibilities, we must become increasingly childlike in our faith and in our allegiance to God. This temptation to subordinate our faith to our intellectualizing confronts us as we seek to define the secondary aims of the educational process.

Secondary Aims Considered

In order to formulate adequate secondary aims or goals for education, it will be necessary to reconsider the criteria that were used in discovering and formulating our primary aims. These criteria are summarized below.

Criteria for formulation of primary aims:

Primary aims:
1. Must be in harmony with the Biblical basis for education.
2. Must be in harmony with the ultimate objective for life.
3. Must be consistent with all other stated primary aims.
4. Must be based on a Scriptural conception of the nature of man.
5. Must be based on a Scriptural conception of what man is to become.
6. Must be directed to the total person.
7. Must be applicable to all facets of, or steps in, the educational process.
8. Must be applicable to all students within the school.

9. Must be capable of attainment.
10. Must be intrinsically valuable as well as instrumentally valuable.
11. Must be definitely and functionally stated.

As attempts are made to formulate legitimate secondary aims, it will become obvious that not all the criteria listed above can be satisfied. Cursory examination of the school program, for example, will show that such necessary duties as the teaching of reading skills can not be carried on in all facets of the educational process. It will also become evident that the training of vocal talents is directed at some persons, but not at others. The accepted fact that children vary in the abilities with which they have been endowed prevents the development of those differentiating abilities from becoming a primary objective of the school. If such development is to be considered as a secondary objective, criterion six above must be deleted. The deletion of some and the retention of other criteria then become a practical necessity. In doing so, however, consistency must be maintained. Although *some* of the previously established criteria may be removed for the formulation of secondary and subsequent goals, the primacy of Scripture as a guide to such choices may not be neglected. Even though the Bible does not specifically demand the teaching of the communication skills, such objectives are implied in the demands for knowledge and obedience to the Truth. Such implication should be considered as sufficient cause for the instruction in those skills.

Secondary aims may vary with the level of education being considered and with the particular needs and characteristics of the student body. Consequently, it is more important for the educational theorist to outline the criteria that apply to these less-important aims than to define all the aims that might legitimately be considered. By removing the sixth, seventh, eight and tenth criteria from the list, allowance will be made for the delineation of additional aims without in any way violating the consistency that is desired. In doing so, however, it must be remembered that the remaining guidelines for choice should be given as serious attention as when they were applied in the articulation of primary aims. It must also be remembered that all the primary objectives remain in full force even though students and teachers are temporarily concentrating on a goal of lower value. For example, temporary attention to the development of a peculiar artistic talent may not negate the greater goal of learning to love, to know, to be free, and to obey. On the contrary, the striving for secondary goals should enlarge and enrich the person's capacity for reaching the primary goals. Thus, the secondary aims become the means to the fuller accomplishment of the primary and ultimate aims. Recognizing this means-end relationship, the third criterion in the foregoing list can now be reworded so as to be a logical stepping-stone to the second and first criteria.

Criteria for formulation of secondary aims:
Secondary aims:

1. Must be in harmony with the Biblical basis for education.
2. Must be in harmony with the ultimate objective for life.
3. Must be in harmony with the stated primary aims.
4. Must be based on a Scriptural conception of the nature of man.
5. Must be based on a Scriptural conception of what man is to become.
6. Must be capable of attainment.
7. Must be definitely and functionally stated.

Using these criteria, what are some of the secondary objectives to be met? By the implications already cited, it is apparent that the skills of communication and measurement must be developed. Since man is called by Scripture to be both a disciple[1] and a prophet, not only the skills of truth-acquisition, but also the skills of truth-proclamation must be exercised. As disciple the child is placed under instruction and is in need of the skills of listening, reading, computing, writing, and questioning. By the use of such skills the child absorbs; he acquires for himself the knowledge that is offered. But every child is also called to be a prophet, thus requiring him to proclaim the truth that has been given to him. As one called to declare the truth, the child requires speaking, writing, and singing skills. In conjunction with this objective, it would be well for teachers to consider the fallacious implications of the old adage that "children should be seen but not heard." To carry this precept, which can be wisely applied in certain situations, to its mistaken conclusion would be to ignore the child's role as prophet.

Because this type of cliché has been erroneously applied, as well as for other reasons, schools have often neglected training in the skill of oral communication and have reserved it for the extra-curricular volunteers. Such relegating of this skill to the area of non-essentials does an injustice to the student's office as prophet. A similar, but more serious, kind of (anti-Christian) omission deprives those children who are never taught to pray, for the believer's role as priest is a role of prayer. The individual's communication with God is, again, a skill that may not be

---

[1]Jesus illustrates the relationship between the function of disciple (learner) and *knowledge* in John 8:31, 32; disciple and *love* in John 13:34-35; disciple and *service* in John 15:8.

110

expected to blossom by itself, but must be directed by conscientious instruction in the same way that reading and speaking must.

In the Apostle Paul's first letter to the Corinthian church he makes us aware of the diversity of functions and capabilities of persons. People are given peculiar talents by God, for "God hath set some in the church, first apostles, secondarily prophets, thirdly teachers, after that miracles, then gifts of healing, helps, governments, diversities of tongues" (I Cor. 12:28). A parallel teaching of Scripture is found in Jesus' parable of the talents (Matt. 25:14-30). Although the word talent referred specifically to an amount of money in Bible times, the meaning of the parable has been rightly extended to include the twentieth century meaning of talent; namely, personal abilities. Whatever opportunities, whatever financial or personal abilities God has given to men, He expects the recipients to develop in thankful obedience. In the development of physical, intellectual, social, and emotional talents, then, the school finds numerous objectives or goals.

Again, caution must be used. In the development of these varying capacities the child must repeatedly be reminded that he always stands in a spiritual-moral relationship to God and to his fellowman. These talents are God's gifts and must be used in His service.

One of the gifts of God is the physical body. Interestingly, it is Paul alone, of all the Scriptural writers, who gives specific attention to the development of the body. It was he that was given "a thorn in the flesh" but could "take pleasure in infirmities" and consider himself to be strong when he was weak (II Cor. 12:7, 10). Out of his concern for the physical body and by the leading of the Holy Spirit, whose temple he was — as is every Christian, he gives the following Scriptural counsel for physical development in his image-of-God unity:

> I beseech you therefore, brethren, by the mercies of God, that ye present your bodies a living sacrifice, holy, acceptable unto God, which is your reasonable service. And be not conformed to this world; but be ye transformed by the renewing of your mind, that ye may prove what is that good, and acceptable, and perfect will of God (Romans 12:1-2).

> Know ye not that ye are the temple of God, and that the spirit of God dwelleth in you? If any man defile the temple of God, him shall God destroy, for the temple of God is holy, which temple ye are (I Corinthians 3:16-17).

> What? know ye not that your body is the temple of the Holy Ghost which is in you, which ye have of God, and ye are not your own? For ye are bought with a price: therefore glorify God in your body, and in your spirit, which are God's (I Corinthians 6:19-20).
> For bodily exercise profiteth little; but godliness is profitable unto all things, having promise of the life that now is, and of that which is to come (I Timothy 4:8).

> Wherefore God also gave them up to uncleanness through the lusts of their own hearts, to dishonour their own bodies between themselves: who changed the truth of God into a lie, and worshipped and served the creature more than the Creator, who is blessed forever (Romans 1:24-25).

When all the admonitions and implications of these verses are accepted as God's truth, Christian educators will have recognized and effected another series of important goals for the educational process.

Other secondary objectives could be articulated, but additional delineation can be accomplished by the reader if the relationship between the secondary and primary goals is correctly understood. These two groups are not to be considered as distinct or separate from each other, but must be integrally related. The commands to develop the talents and the bodies of students, for example, are not separate from the commands to obey and to love, but are specific examples where obedience is required. So, too, with the development of communication skills. These skills are not ends in themselves, but are means of effectuating the calling of the believer in his discipleship as prophet, king, and priest.

In summary, secondary and subsequent objectives are extensions of the primary, while the primary are extensions of the ultimate. Whether the educator works inductively from the specific to the general, or deductively from the general to the specific, the Biblical vision of life's wholeness in relationship to God must be continually present. If this vision is lost, teaching will be void of significance. It will then degenerate into an exercise in methodology.

Practical Suggestions for School Administrators

1. Request the Board of Education and the faculty jointly to discuss and to formulate goals for your students. Once these goals have been stated, ask the Board, the faculty, and the constituents to adopt them as the school's official statement of purpose.
2. Before the opening of each school term, devote a meeting of the faculty to a discussion of these objectives and make provision for improved formulation.
3. Before any curricular changes are approved, insist that the objectives to be met by those changes are sufficiently articulated and documented. Change for the sake of change, or change for the sake of conformity is not adequate justification.
4. Encourage teachers, students, and parents to reflect seriously on the relationship between purposes and curricular experiences.

112

5. When students raise such questions as, "Why must we study this material? ," try to give them answers that they can comprehend and that will give meaning to their study. If the teacher cannot give meaningful answers to such questions, it is presumptuous to think that the students will find meaning in the experience.

6. Avoid excessive involvement with questions of methodology. Protracted involvement in methodology detracts from the more significant and prior questions of purpose. Contemporary educational practice is losing its sense of purpose just because of such distracting emphasis on method.

Chapter IX

DEFINITIONS OF EDUCATION CONSIDERED

The word "education" is one of the more popular words in the vocabulary of the Western world, but also one that is often left undefined. Since parents are expected to pay for the education of their children, it is reasonable to expect that they be told what education is. The same could be said for teachers. Since their task is to teach, that is, become active participants in that endeavor called education, one would expect them to know the meaning of at least two words, namely, "education" and "teach."

It is rather distressing to note, however, that many educators and teachers have never bothered to define the very words which they insist on appending to themselves. In fact, the vast majority of books on education that the author has examined do not define these central terms. In spite of the above observations, definitions of these central terms occasionally do slip off-handedly, but not overtly or intentionally, from the many volumes that boldly purport to be textbooks on education and teaching. A few of these definitional clichés should be scrutinized for the sake of determining their validity and value. If one should be found that withstands careful Scriptural examination, that one should be ardently propounded, while the others may be summarily discarded.

One of the more common definitional slips is stated as follows: "Education is preparation for life." In analyzing such a definition we would be found acceptable in presumably all quarters if we stated that preparation means "to get ready for." Life is something that all human beings have at least from the moment of their birth and quite probably from the moment of their conception. According to this definition, education is the getting ready for that which man received no later than the moment of birth. It becomes definitely ludicrous to prepare for something which already is.

The same line of argument could be used against those people who define education as "preparation for citizenship." Again, citizenship in a state or country is accorded to most children at the moment of birth as an accompanying right of birth. For all naturalized citizens such a definition becomes gross redundancy. Now, if the proponents of these definitions wish to argue that the child does not have either life or citizenship by virtue of his birth, those proponents will have to conclude that the child who comes to their so-called educational institutions is characterized by non-citizenship and non-life, that is, alien status and death. The Christian may readily agree to such designation and may be warmed by the promise of further discussion on the matter, but the non-Christian is apt to find such designation repugnant and preposterous.

Now, admittedly, the original formulators of these superficial "definitions" intended to include more than the current catch-phrases contain. For example, the definition "Education is preparation for life" presumably referred to *life* in other than the physical sense. If some other meaning of *life* was intended, it is compulsory that the proponents of such a definition state their intended meaning. They are compelled, if they desire credibility, to say what it means *to live*. What is the essence of living? Is it existing? Is it loving? Is it acquiring? Is it serving? On the other hand, if such definition is now incomplete because the phrase "preparation for life" was originally intended to mean "preparation for *adult* life," the formulators are confronted with an equally difficult problem: How does *adult* life differ from *pre-adult* life? Is there essential difference, or is life continuous? Assuming that there are essential differences which could be claimed, the ambiguity of the word *life* remains. Thus, the definition remains ambiguous at very best.

Similar ambiguity and superficiality characterizes the definition which states that "education is preparation for citizenship." Presumably the formulators of that definition intended to mean "preparation for *responsible* citizenship." But additional questions rise to plague such advocates. For instance, what constitutes "responsible citizenship? Paying taxes? Voting in every election? Staying out of jail? Obeying laws? If such is meant, the Christian finds no disagreement. Nevertheless, the definition remains unsatisfactory for two reasons: (1) the definition offers no fixed reference point by which to measure responsibility, and (2) the definition concerns itself with nothing more than terrestrial existence. Some better, more precise and yet all-inclusive definition must be found.

Another common definition of education is this: "Education is the transmitting of ideas, values, and knowledge from the older generation to a younger generation." Implied in this definition are two significant admissions. First, it must be admitted that only those things can be transmitted which are already held in possession. One cannot transmit those things or that knowledge which he does not have. Secondly, in all transmitting there is a loss of power, a seepage, a resistance to that which is being transmitted. Human experience tells us that the student imbibes only a small portion of that which the teachers, individually or collectively, attempt to transmit to him. The net result of all this attempted transmitting of ideas, values and knowledge means, then, that each generation receives less knowledge than the preceding one. Even when one considers such inanimate devices as books and objects as aids to the transmission process, one realizes that a stream cannot rise higher than its source. If education is *merely* the transmission from generation to succeeding generation, the trend must inevitably be downward. If, however, there is some transcendent, omniscient, super-human "teacher" that compels men to rise above the collective human source, then such definition becomes credible. But this definition makes no such reference.

Given the definition as stated, the generation that is currently receiving the transmitted information would be far less knowledgeable than the generations of the Civil War or of Colonial eras. The most knowledgeable persons, by this definition, would be the first generation, the first set of parents that inhabited the earth. Taking into account the fact that Adam lived to be 930 years old, whereas current generations consider 65 to 70 years as an average length of life, one might be inclined to accept this definition as having some validity. Adherence to it, however, would lead to progressive despondency, for all succeeding generations would inherit diminishing shares of that which is being transmitted.

Yet another definition of education, one which can be found in many dictionaries, says "education is a process." Admitting that there is some kind of process involved, we would nevertheless be considered somewhat mystic and evasive if we said that students go through life and school to receive a process. Instead of saying, "He has an education," we could just as meaningfully say, "He has a process." Also, if education is to continue as long as life, as current educators and this author insist, a person would spend his whole life, right until the time of death, acquiring a process. But as the justification for any process is the acquisition or formation of a product, it would be speciously partial to define education only as a process. Obviously, education must also be considered as product. Persons undergo *the process* of education in order that they may acquire an education, that is, *a product.* Such distinction between process and product is necessary, but is also insufficient. No active mind would be content with a definition which merely stated that education is a process which results in a product. With such general terminology, the manufacture of automobiles could be labelled rightly as education, for both process and product are inherent in such manufacture.

In order to differentiate the educational process and the educational product from other processes, some educators have specified that education is what takes place in schools. Such a definition may serve to delineate, but it leaves two basic questions unanswered. On the one hand, the definition implies that education is confined to the schools. But does not education also take place in the home, in the church, or at the place of employment? If education takes place in the schools, then homework is not educational. On the other hand, this definition implies that whatever takes place in the schools is education. Knowing that cheating, fighting, sleeping, and love-making all take place in schools, we would have to conclude that these are integral to education. Being part of education by very definition, the school would have to encourage and organize such activities, for the school has been assigned the function of promoting and organizing education.

Such a definition, however, is plainly deficient and nonsensical, for it offers no normative standard for judging either the quality of the process or the quality of the product. By such definition all activities and all endeavors would be equally justifiable, provided that they were carried out within the confines of the school.

One final, non-Christian definition needs to be examined before a Christian definition is proposed. That is the definition made famous by John Dewey and the Progressive Education Movement. Quite simply, it states: "Education is life." Looking at this definition from a positive viewpoint, it is very beneficial in that it does not attempt to make any radical distinctions between what should be going on in the school and what should be going on outside the school. It constructs no untenable dualisms or dichotomies. It treats life as an organic entity, not to be artificially divided. So much in its favor. On the negative side, however, this definition merely solves one problem by substituting for it a problem of equal if not greater magnitude. By stating simply that education is life, attention is no longer focused on the word education. For those not dulled into insensitivity by such subtlety, the problem created by such facile definition is that of defining life. If education is life, what is life?

As often happens, a phrase or term becomes acceptable or unacceptable according to the meanings read into that phrase or term. In the Progressive definition offered above, "Education is life" could become a very satisfying phrase to the Christian if only the word Life might be packed with Scriptural signification. For Christ said not only that He was the Way and the Truth, but He also said that He was Life (John 14:6). Incorporating such Scriptural meaning, education could be defined as the process whereby persons become united in their totality with the Christ, who is the only avenue by which to know God, and in Whom the whole universe has its meaning. If such definition were allowed to stand, education would be synonymous with the Spiritual sanctification that must follow regeneration — the new life in Christ. Such an equation may seem strange at first, but, if the very concept of education is to arise out of Christianity as we have previously insisted, then education and sanctification must not be separate and distinct. Education, in order to be God-glorifying, must be a sanctifying experience with spiritual blessings for those who undergo it.

Such synthetic definition must be rejected, however. It not only creates potential confusion, but deliberately alters the meaning originally put into it. Because Dewey's conception of life is naturalistic positivism and evolutionary pragmatism, it is both dishonest and perilous for the Christian to engage in such definitional shifting. Moreover, the definition *remains* ambiguous and fails adequately to account for all the facets of an admittedly complex process. In order to formulate an adequate Christian definition, some of these complexities will first have to be recognized.

In the first place, any restoration of true beliefs or knowledge must involve the work of the sovereign God. Since knowledge has previously been characterized as a gift from God, and since the sovereignty of God is a central doctrine of Scripture, any partial or complete restoration to that position enjoyed by Adam and Eve before the Fall must include the recreative work of the Triune God. Second, this recreative work of God does not take place apart from the work of man. Human responsibility is also a central doctrine of the Bible: man is called to aid in that restoration. This religious function of man, in keeping with current terminology about the developmental nature of children, can simply be labeled a redeveloping function. Third, our definition must also involve the understandings and relationships which existed between Adam and God, between Adam and Eve, and between Adam and the physical universe. Seeking a restoration of those understandings and those relationships, the Christian recognizes that there is no other way to such restoration than through the last Adam, the Christ. Desiring true understandings and true relationships between himself and the world of nature, the Christian accepts Christ's claim that He is the Truth. All those understandings and all those relationships, finally, must be focused on Him if they are to be true. Constantly striving for such restoration in and through the Christ, education for the Christian will most certainly be sanctification. Such education will not operate apart from or alongside of faith, but will be a growing in faith.

By conjoining these elements, a satisfactory (Christian) definition of education can be formulated. Education is the recreation and development of the True understandings and relationships between God and man, man and fellowman, and man and the physical universe. In alternate wording, education is the divinely instigated and humanly cooperating process whereby persons grow and develop in Life, that is, in Godly knowledge, faith, hope, and love through Christ. So stated, the prefacing adjective Christian is superfluous to the word education. Any process, any growth, and any development which takes place apart from the Truth is false. Any education which is not Christian is not education. It is pseudo- or mis-education. As Henry Zylstra once said, "We hold that education being a human enterprise is inevitably religious, that except it be religious it is not education, . . . and that the alleged neutrality of the public schools must — if their education is to be real education — turn out to be a mere allegation" (*Testament of Vision,* p. 101). All education, then, is religious; but not all religion is Christianity. And any form of education in which Christ is not acknowledged as King is ultimately Satanic, *anti*-Christianity.

What then is schooling? Using a contemporary distinction, we could say that schooling is formal education. We could thus distinguish it from informal education, preserving the basic assertion that education is not confined to the school. Helpful though this distinction may be, it does little to characterize the differences between what goes on inside the school and what goes on outside the school. Obviously there is a difference, for if there were not, schools would lose all justification for existence.

Using the concept of formal education already mentioned, we can use the word formal to mean structured or methodical, or systematic. Through this structuring and systematizing, more of God's revelation and more of human experience can be brought within the purview of the individuals being educated than would be possible if the situation were informal or unstructured. Contrary to the thinking of the eighteenth and nineteenth century educational realists, the distinction is not one of life outside of school being real, with life in school being unreal. Both should be very real, for life is one. Rather, the distinction should only be as we have just noted: formal education is structured and compressed revelation and experience, whereas informal education is unstructured and not compressed. Essentially there is no difference between what goes on within or without the school. Although the home and the church are not within the school, they are also concerned with the understandings and relations of children considered to be Christian; there should be no *foundational* differences between what the school and the home and the church are trying to accomplish. All, rightfully functioning, are trying to educate the child in the fear of the Lord, which is the essence of wisdom.

Chapter X

THE RESPONSIBLE INSTITUTION

In the history of education three separate institutions have contested for the right and duty of establishing schools. These three institutions have been the state, the church, and the home. In ancient Sparta the government established and regulated formal education, thus producing a public or state form of school. In medieval Europe the Roman Catholic Church assumed this prerogative, making education in its organizational dimension parochial. The third distinct type of education is called private. Historical examples of this type can be seen in both the colonial South and in the Middle Colonies, especially Pennsylvania. In these areas the home was designated the institution responsible for the establishment of schools; for it was parents, acting individually and collectively, who organized, financed, and controlled the instructional program.

In any comprehensive discussion about education, this placing of responsibility and assignment of duty must be determined. If the state is to be responsible, public schools are a necessity. If the church has the high calling, parochial schools are the proper form. But, if parents are given the assignment, private schools should be everywhere in evidence.

The arguments involving these three societal institutions have been in contention throughout history. If any theoretically sound and final answer to this question is to be found, such finality will not come from a study of history. History abounds with examples of each type of school, and, besides, historical precedent is always judged acceptable or unacceptable by the use of other, higher criteria. In fact, historical examination will only complicate the question, for various additional solutions have been attempted. In late medieval Europe, for example, the emerging universities proclaimed institutional autonomy, deliberately trying to divorce themselves from state, home, and church. If such tradition were allowed to extend itself to the elementary and secondary level, schools would need to be considered as separate institutions and thus be neither public, parochial, nor private. Even the most cursory examination of such an independent institution makes it unthinkable and unworkable.

Another solution that has been found unsatisfying was tried in Massachusetts during the seventeenth century. In the Massachusetts laws of 1642 and 1647, the state and the church jointly assumed the responsibility of education. Such cooperation was possible as long as church and state were synonymous in membership. Such a solution might even be considered desirable by some in twentieth-century America, for every person wishes the state to guarantee and protect his own religious commitment.

A third solution is the one currently being practiced in the United States. It is the pluralistic answer. All three forms of educational institutions are given legal protection and right of existence. Public schools, parochial schools, and private schools are all allowed to participate in the educating process. Such an arrangement may seem to be the only workable one in a society that is pluralistic in its religious, cultural, and ethnic make-up. However, pragmatic considerations can not be satisfying to anyone who is concerned with truth. Anyone who desires to know which institution is rightfully responsible could not possibly conclude that all three are correct in their roles. If the home is the God-directed agent for education, then the church and the state should not usurp that function. Any usurpation on their part would be impermissible and would thus make the resulting educational units illegitimate and erroneous. Furthermore, if parents are responsible, but are derelict in their task, such dereliction does not justify the taking-over of responsibility by other societal agencies.

For the egocentric person, the easiest answer is the pluralistic one. Because the pluralistic arrangement guarantees the existence of all forms of schools, and because the selfish person is not concerned about the rightness or wrongness of other people's choices, he smiles tolerantly upon relativity. The ultimate rightness or wrongness of other persons' choices is of no concern to him. Permitting others the right to be wrong seems to be his highest creed. A Christ-centered and Biblically loving concern for the rightness of fellow Americans' decisions seems an exotic irrelevancy.

Whoever persists in thinking of education as a secular and neutral activity will not be disturbed by our pluralistic system. Alarm over the inadequacy of the pluralistic answer can only come when the believer accepts the religious nature of all education. Correctly understanding education as allegiance or disobedience to the Sovereign God, the sincere Christian cannot ignore the Christ-rejecting iniquity of those who persist in denying God's relevance to the schooling process. When education is understood as a means of sanctification and the process of inculcating religious beliefs, the state's role as educator becomes not only very tenuous but also extremely dangerous. With the state in its educational program indoctrinating students in the concepts of neutrality and secularism, and with the church preaching the sovereignty of God in every sphere, the child is coerced to believe opposing philosophies. Over against the church, then, the state is not really neutral. To the extent that the religious philosophy of secular public education is accepted, the Christ-obedient witness of the orthodox Reformational church is weakened.

This obviously raises the crucial question: Does the state, the church, or the home have the God-ordained responsibility for education? Clearly, this responsibility should not belong to the state. Even though the Tenth Amendment to the Constitution has long been considered as justification for the states' role as educator, it should be observed that those functions not specifically assigned to the federal government are the duties of the states *or* the people; by not specifying which, the framers of the Constitution made it easy for state governments to assume educational duties not willingly accepted by the people. If not by design, then at least by default, the government has gained a stranglehold on most American education. As a result, the purpose in education has shifted from the glorifying of God to the preservation of American society. Education for national defense and for material security, rather than education for the Kingdom of Christ is the predominant motif.

Scripture is very clear in its placement of·educational responsibility. After his descent from Mt. Sinai, Moses exhorted the Israelites with the words that God had spoken to him. God said, "Gather me the people together, and I will make them hear my words, that they may learn to fear me all the days that they shall live upon the earth, and *that they may teach their children*" (Deut. 4:10). Just prior to this, Moses had instructed the people to keep God's laws and statutes, and to "teach them [to] thy sons, and thy son's sons" (Deut. 4:9). With equally explicit commands Moses told the parents, "And thou shalt teach them diligently unto thy children, . . . and thou shalt bind them for a sign upon thy hand, . . . and thou shalt write them upon the posts of thy house" (Deut. 6:7-9).

But the dubious reader may question the applicability of such Scriptural injunction to contemporary education. Gerhard Kittel, renowned German Bible scholar, explains the original meaning of the word *teach* in such a way that its intent and current appropriateness are inescapable. He states,

> In the Septuagint it is no more possible to restrict the Greek word to teach than the Hebrew word to teach to the religious sphere. In both cases the term can be used for instruction in the use of weapons or practicing a song (Deut. 31:19-22). The particular object of *to teach*, however, is the will of God in its declarations and demands. Thus in Psalm 94:10 it is said of God that he teaches men knowledge, and in Job 12:20 God is called the teacher of understanding and·intelligence. It makes no difference whether the one who gives the instruc-

tion is God Himself (Deut. 4:10), the head of the family (Deut. 11:19), or the righteous (Psalm 37:30). The term is always marked by the fact that it has a volitional as well as an intellectual reference. The Greek word to teach of the Septuagint always lays claim to the whole man and not merely to certain parts of him . . . The Total claim associated with *to teach* made it peculiarly fitted to become the word for God's presenting of His will to His people in order to subject the people to this will and to fashion it accordingly (Kittel, *Theological Dictionary of the New Testament*, Vo. II., pp. 136-137).

God's injunction to parents may not then be confined to moral or religious teaching (wrongly limited in present usage), but must extend to all instruction. Simply because the mind of modernity seeks to divorce the Scriptural intent from contemporary, "secular" schooling is no justification for the Christian's accepting such altered meaning. In Jesus' day, too, the meaning of *teach* had been perverted. However, in opposition to the Semitic usage of the word, "Jesus resumes the true line of the Hebrew word to teach in the Greek word to teach attributed to Him. For He is again advancing the claim of God to the whole man in a way which does not allow either contradiction or theoretical reflection. This is a total claim which is not bound to any intermediary authority and which is completely independent of the perception of the one who is claimed. This claim, which has as its goal the education and reformation of man according to the will of God (Matt. 5:48) becomes a reality in the teaching of Jesus" (*ibid.*, p. 140). Clearly such mandates are not directed to the state. It is not the state that has been enjoined by God to educate and reform the total man to the will of God.

In the beautiful words of Psalm 78, Asaph poetically reaffirms the promises which the Hebrew people had made to God. In response to God's demand that His people give ear to His law, Asaph replies for all true believers with these words:

> We will not hide them from their children, shewing to the generation to come the praises of the Lord, and his strength, and his wonderful works that he hath done. For he established a testimony in Jacob, and appointed a law in Israel, which he commanded our fathers, that they should make them known to their children: that the generation to come might know them, even the children which should be born; who should arise and declare them to their children: that they might set their hope in God, and not forget the works of God, but keep his commandments (Psalm 78:4-7).

This incontrovertible placement of educational responsibility on the shoulders of parents is also expressed in the Proverbs of Solomon. In the abundance of Proverbial references to learning, understanding, wisdom, and knowledge, the language is always that of parent to child.

The father-son relationship is repeated over and over (for God often addresses His people in this way), each time intimately fusing this relationship with the quest for education. Following are some of the examples:

> My son, hear the instruction of thy father (1:8).

> My son, if you receive my words, and treasure up my commandments with you, making your ear attentive to wisdom and inclining your heart to understanding; yes, if you cry out for insight and raise your voice for understanding; if you seek it like silver and search for it as for hidden treasures; then you will understand the fear of the Lord and find the knowledge of [that belongeth to] God (2:1-5).

> Hear, ye children, the instruction of a father, and attend to know understanding (4:1).

> My son, attend unto my wisdom, and bow thine ear to my understanding . . . that thy lips may keep knowledge (5:1).

In the comparatively uncomplicated life of the Old Testament Hebrews, most, if not all, of the instruction could be accomplished by the parents in the home. In the New Testament dispensation, however, life had become more complex. Paul then speaks of children who were "under tutors and governors until the time appointed of the father" (Gal. 4:2). Unable to deal domestically with all the educational requirements of a complex society, delegation of this parental function had apparently taken place. The responsibility, nevertheless, remained with the parents, for Paul continues to exhort fathers to bring up their children "in the nurture and admonition of the Lord" (Eph. 6:4).

Further support for the placing of educational responsibility with the parents comes from a simple, but often overlooked fact: children enter the temporal life only through parents. Children are not born to the state, nor even to the instituted church. Children are given to parents by God. Children are first, foremost, and always God's children, to be nurtured for God and to be presented back to Him. Hannah, the mother of Samuel, most beautifully expresses this conviction in her prayer to God: "Remember me . . . but give unto thine handmaid a man child; then I will give him unto the Lord all the days of his life" (I Sam. 1:11). Gordon H. Clark negatively illustrates the same concept when he asserts, "Under any government the Christian principle is plain: Render unto Caesar the things which are Caesar's, and unto God the things that are God's. Children do not belong to Caesar" (Clark, *A Christian Philosophy of Education*, p. 195 f.). In a covenantal relationship, children of believing parents are united to God through their parents. Christian parents acknowledge and confirm the blessedly significant relationship in the sacrament of baptism. By so doing, parents confess before God and His church that these infants are really God's and that it is their responsibility to train and educate them for Christian service. Scripture's pointed and repeated admonitions to parents are given, therefore, to ensure that the covenantal relationship between children and God is not violated.

Reflection on this doctrine of the covenant, however, complicates the question of educational responsibility. The question would be simple enough if we could finalize our answer with the Scriptural directives to parents. Children are born *to* parents, but, by virtue of the covenant, are also born *into* the church of Christ. Thus the church, as the body of Christ and also in its instituted form, is, or ought to be obediently interested in children and their education. For the church to claim an interest in its children members while ignoring the education they receive would be to fragment life and deny its essential wholeness. The church, properly using the means at its disposal, thus stands as a very necessary aid to parents in presenting their children back to God. In the preaching of the Word, the administering of the sacraments, and the application of discipline, the church also seeks to redevelop those true-to-Christ relationships existing between God and man, between man and fellow-man, and between man and the physical universe.

Further awareness of the Church's involvement in the educational process can be gained from a study of Christ's mandate to His disciples and from Paul's charge to Timothy. In what has come to be called the missionary mandate, Christ instructed the eleven disciples, "Go ye therefore, and teach all nations, baptizing them in the name of the Father, and of the Son, and of the Holy Ghost: Teaching them to observe all things whatsoever I have commanded you" (Matt. 28:19-20). Christ's use of the word "teach" strongly implies that the work of the church is not totally different from the work of parents and schools. Also, in Paul's epistles to Timothy it is twice stated that bishops must be "apt to teach" (I Tim. 3:2 and II Tim. 2:24). Given this instruction, any attempt to divorce the work of the church from the work of teaching would be unscriptural. The question, then, is not whether the church should be engaged in a teaching function. Rather, the question should be: whom and what is the church required to teach?

In reflecting on the Scriptural mandates that were addressed specifically to parents, it should be remembered that the language used always stipulated a parent-child relationship. Parents were called to educate their children. In the missionary mandate the subject is seemingly much broader. The disciples were not therein instructed to teach only their children, or even just the children of the established church. Rather, the disciples, as leaders in the church, were directed, to "teach all na-

125

tions, baptizing them." The clear implication is, then, that the message of the church of Christ is a call to teach the Truth of God to the unregenerate. The church must go into those areas and those communities where baptized Christ-believers are not yet present, calling those people to repentance and admonishing the parents to train up their children in the fear of the Lord. In such missionary outposts the church is called to assume a primary role in the educational enterprise, not for the sake of displacing parental responsibility, but for the sake of awakening parental awareness to responsibility. Paul, in his first letter to Timothy, further clarifies this teaching function of the church when he says, "I am ordained a preacher and an apostle, . . . a teacher of the Gentiles in faith and verity" (I Tim. 2:7).

Paul's charges to Timothy are of a basically similar nature. The injunctions to Timothy to "command and teach" (I Tim. 4:11) and to "teach and exhort" (I Tim. 6:2) come not as admonitions to a parent. They are instructions to a missionary who is engaged in the establishing of new congregations of converts. The teaching that was required was not primarily directed to children, but was part of the preparation of men for the offices of elder, deacon, and evangelist. Paul summarizes this in the second epistle when he writes, "And the things that thou hast heard of me among many witnesses, the same commit thou to faithful men, who shall be able to teach others also" (II Tim. 2:2).

It should be clearly understood, in the light of the above discussion, that the church is not called to assume the educational responsibility of the believing parent. Over against the believing parent, the church has not a conflicting teaching function, but a complementary and expanding one. Furthermore, it should be stressed that the nature and the practice of the parental educational endeavor may not be markedly different from that of the church, for believing parents are always members of the church, and the church is always a collection of believing parents and their children. To permit dichotomies and conflicts between the work of the home and the church would be to encourage warfare with oneself. The home cannot condone adherence to the pseudo secular and neutral philosophy of twentieth-century public education while the church advocates total commitment to Biblical belief. Being one in membership, mutual toleration of such an antithesis will destroy both home and church.

An additional complicating factor is the person's relationship to the state. Not only is the Christ-believing child born *to* parents and *into* the church, but he is also born *into* the state. By birth the child becomes a citizen of a temporal, geographical, political state. True, a person can repudiate such governmental right and responsibility in the same severing way that a covenant child can renounce his membership in the

126

church. Until such alienating renunciation, however, every child is a member of the state into which he has been born. As citizen he is responsible to it and subject to its laws. As citizen he must conform to the state's compulsory school-attendance laws. Growing into responsible adulthood, that citizen must honor additional educational statutes, such as those regulating teacher certification, length of school day, building codes, and financial regulations. The person must do this, however, not primarily because of his citizenship, but because the Word of God demands it as follows: "Let every soul be subject to the higher powers," said Paul by the inspiration of the Holy Spirit. "For there is no power but of God . . . rulers are not a terror to good works, but to the evil . . . for he [the ruler] is the minister of God to thee for good" (Rom. 13:1-4). The Christian citizen does not scorn and violate his citizenship in the temporal state; he accepts it as a necessary and legitimate dimension of his life. He accepts the God-ordained government as being instituted for his welfare. He accepts the responsibilities that are concomitant with citizenship, and he accepts them *in addition to* those responsibilities which he has inherited as a member of a home and of a church. Those various responsibilities in no way cancel each other. Rightly functioniong, the home, the church, and the state are all institutional agents of God. Simultaneously holding membership in all three institutions, the covenant-honoring individual is aided by them in the re-establishing of those true relationships in Christ which were previously discussed.

Because of inadequacy of preparation or lack of time, parents usually cannot fully carry out the development of the child and the further refining of the person that Scripture has stipulated. Recognizing, however, that the responsibility is, and remains theirs, the parents join with other parents to form a school, an association through which they employ other, qualified individuals to carry on the work for them. The school, then, is a humanly originated institution, an institution growing out of and standing in the place of the home. It is this concept of "in loco parentis" that is essential to our understanding of the school as a God-worshipping and God-approved institution. Not existing independently, it is an extension of the home which seeks to carry on the functions and duties that the home has delegated to it. The school, as institution, derives its authority from the home. The teachers, however, individually and collectively standing *in loco parentis,* are also persons with individual relationships to God, and as such, are individually responsible to Him. Their acceptance of delegated duties from the home in no way diminishes or negates their functioning all the while as prophet, priest, and king. If the home, the state, or the church violates the revealed will of God, liability for such offense remains with the disobedient institutions. The school and its member teachers can foolishly concur with such violation, or they can honor their individual commitments to God and address the offending institution through their office as prophet.

The following illustration will help to clarify the complex, but complementary set of institutions into which the child is born. Each, if faithfully fulfilling its Scripturally-assigned functions, will aid in returning to God the children who come as a gift from God.

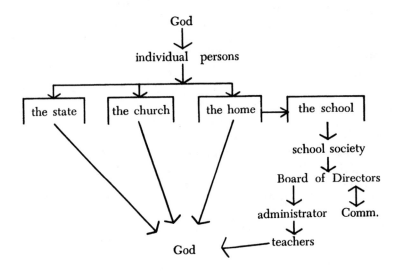

Fig. 14. The Structural Pattern for Education

The above scheme is not only foreign to Western educational thought, but is anathema to it. Having grown accustomed to the concept of the complete separation of church and state, the Western world has not been content merely to separate the peculiar functions of the state from those of denominational churches, but has also attempted to separate the state from all religion. In practice, no one wants such separation. Everyone wants the state to encourage and ardently support his particular religion. Actually, no such separation is possible. *All* men are religious, and all men are religious in *all* of their human activity. The state, composed of men and ordained by God, is also religious in all of its human governmental functions. The men who comprise the government and who enact its legislation, whether recognizing it or not, are also subject to the commands of God and are under His control.

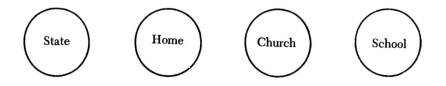

Fig. 15. *A Misconception of Sphere (institutional) Sovereignty*

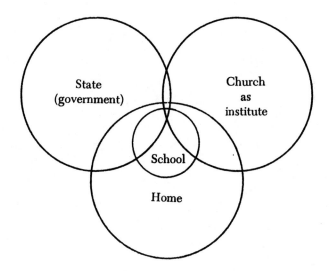

Fig. 16. *A Misconception of Sphere (institutional) Sovereignty*

The question is not one of being able to separate the state from religion, but one of whether those men who comprise the state are in conformity with the true, Christocentric religion or whether they are acting in conformity with a pseudo religion, with some anthropocentric idolatry. The question is not whether men can separate themselves, albeit temporarily, from the directives of the sovereign God, but whether they are obedient or disobedient to those commands.

Pluralism is, then, only an historical, humanly-conceived, and God-allowed expedient. Having refused to confess that government exists primarily of God, and for God, men, and Christians included, have humanistically proclaimed that government exists of the people, by the people, and for the people. However, in the best traditions of the Roman Catholic church, Calvinist Geneva, Lutheran Germany, and Puritan Massachusetts, the church and the state were not totally separate. Whole men, divinely attuned, were members of these two institutions simultaneously. In every function and in every thought, those men sought to obey the voice and will of God. For them, God was still the cause, the means, and the end of every human endeavor.

CHAPTER XI

IMPLEMENTATION OF GOALS AND OBJECTIVES

In February of 1967, Dr. Frank Cassell of North Dakota State University delivered a series of lectures at Dordt College. His stated purpose was to encourage the improvement of instruction in the natural sciences. However, he also addressed a gathering of faculty and students on the topic: "Quality Teaching." One would expect a speaker who had chosen such a subject to do at least two things: (1) define teaching and (2) state his criterion for determining quality. Although the speaker did give an off-handed and seemingly uncalculated definition, he did not posit any criterion or yardstick by which to judge quality. Dr. Cassell did, however, list four common characteristics of good teachers:

1. Know your subject.
2. Be interested in your subject.
3. Know your students.
4. Be interested in your students.

That these are necessary to good teaching one would not deny. But, to accept the superficial secular explanations of these four points as given by contemporary educators would make one guilty of theoretical naivete, as well as of man-centered apostasy.

To know one's subjects and to know one's pupils implies that we ought to know them for what they Truly and, therefore, really are. To know a subject (an artificial human division of knowledge) for what it Truly is, we need to go to our source of all knowledge, our All-Knowing God, our Originator of knowledge, and learn from His revelation. To know a student for what he truly is, we need to go to the Creator of man, the Giver of all children, and ask of Him.

To know our subjects and to know our students, we need to turn to God's revelation of Himself. Scripture becomes the repository of all true knowledge and thus becomes our only criterion source for determining quality. If a teacher *knows* a student as God wants him to know that student (according to His Word), and if a teacher *knows* his subjects as God wants him to know them (according to His Word), then that teacher has met two qualifications for quality work. If a teacher is *interested in* a student as God wants him to be interested, and if he is *interested in* his subjects in the way that God wants him to be interested, then he has met the remaining characteristics stated by Dr. Cassell. For the Christian is rightly confident that the Holy Spirit, through God's infallible Word, will illumine him, will sanctify him, and will lead him into *all* truth in Christ (John 16:13; 17:19).

The End of Teaching

The seemingly uncalculated definition of teaching that Dr. Cassell offered was, "Teaching is communication of that which one wishes to communicate." This is a contemporary secular definition, mechanistic enough to be acceptable to most academicians and educationists. The purpose of citing it here is not to cast aspersions on the lecturer who uttered it, but to elucidate a very erroneous concept that is darkening American education. The definition is not only theoretically unsound, but also very dangerous if believed by teachers.

The theoretical insufficiency and the perilous aspects of this definition come to focus when the question of "What do you teach: subjects or kids?" is considered with it. Although this question is often considered a rhetorical one, it must be seriously considered if we are to gain an adequate understanding of the concept "teaching."

When examined grammatically, we notice that the verb teach requires an object. One cannot teach without teaching someone or something. If we say that a person teaches a subject, for example, history or music, that subject becomes the object or end of the verb "teach." We could then posit the situation where one person is in a room by himself. Assuming that he knows his subject, that person could then engage in teaching. The teacher is there, the teacher is capable of activating the verb, and the object is there. Accepting this choice of solution to the previously raised question, we would have to conclude that, theoretically, teaching could be taking place.

Hopefully nobody is going to agree, because it is almost universally accepted that teaching cannot take place without learning (an associated human experience) going on. Presumably this would require the presence of a second person in the situation, since we can assume that the teacher, who knows the material to be presented, would not also be the learner.

If the reader is willing to accept the foregoing assertion, what relative position must the learner occupy in the pedagogical situation? Does the learner become the medium? The tool by which? A parallel object? Dr. Cassell, when confronted with this question, naively asserted that the student and the subject are parallel objects. He said, "We have to teach both the kids and the subjects." Grammatically again, we could say that the use of *and* as a coordinate conjunction leaves the originally proposed situation unchanged except with the addition of another object. Addition of one to one in no way removes the theoretical inadequacy suggested above. What position, then, should the student play in this grammatical structure?

To make the student anything less than the object of the verb would be to relegate the student to a lower value station than that of the subject. Regrettably, many educators are only too willing to regard the subject as sacrosanct and the student as expendable. In their minds, what happens to *persons* is not nearly as important as what happens to the *subject*. If their subject or course is presented fully and the students go home as neurotics, egocentrics, agnostics, or rationalists, they still maintain that good teaching has taken place. Although it will soon be evident that course content and the student are both essential if any teaching is to take place, the relationship of these two elements to the verb "teach" must be correctly understood. Consistent with the entire philosophy proposed in this book, the end must determine the means and not vice versa. If the child is the correct and only legitimate object of the verb "teach," then the subject must be something other than the end — presumably the means. If that is true, the subject must be considered flexible so as to attain the desired objectives in the lives of the students.

The entire problem should also be approached from the position of the contemporary, secular definition of teaching. Abbreviating Dr. Cassell's definition to its essentials namely, "teaching is communicating," we can further see the inadequacy of the definiition. Also, the fallaciousness of setting up both subjects and students as joint objects for the verb "teach" will become more apparent. By substituting the word "communicate" for "teach," notice what happens:

a. I teach history.   b. I teach students.
   I communicate history.   I communicate students.

Obviously, *a* is grammatically satisfactory, whereas *b* is unsatisfactory. Since Dr. Cassell offered his communication definition first and then strongly asserted that we teach both subjects and students, it is safe to say that he failed to see either his own dilemma or the inadequacy of this secular definition.

Looking at the definitional problem from still another angle, we can see that this answer is also educationally dangerous. Since many persons have accepted "education as communication," they have become guilty of grossly perverting the whole teaching concept, and this with good logic on their side. They have argued along the following lines:

I have been employed to teach history, that is, to communicate history.

When I am communicating history, I am teaching and am fulfilling my contractual obligations.

When I am not communicating history, I am not teaching.

When I am disciplining a child for misconduct, I am not communicating history. Therefore I am not teaching.

When I am supervising the hallway or patrolling the playground or keeping the "lid" on a study hall, I am not teaching.

I agreed only to a teaching contract and am obligated only to fulfill my job as teacher; therefore, the school cannot force me to do these "babysitting" jobs.

Many schools have been pressured by this type of logical reasoning to employ squads of underlings and non-professionals to take over the "non-teaching" functions in the school. In the "teacher's" minds, all these so-called "non-teaching" activities, including discipline, are relegated to lower status. Discipline (establishing obedience to law and authority) becomes of secondary importance, and, where still practiced, is merely a means to an end, a necessary evil so that knowledge may be accumulated. Concerning the relationship of discipline to teaching, many new teachers have been given faulty advice. Because these recruits are usually very concerned about discipline, and because discipline is still considered important in many schools, principals are inclined to advise, "Get your discipline under control first. Don't worry about teaching anything those first few days. Once you have discipline, you can start teaching."

Although the intentions and sentiments behind such advice may be praiseworthy, the advice itself is poor. That such counsel is misleading should be readily apparent. From a practical viewpoint, any experienced teacher would know that to attempt to control a class without giving the students positive work and study in which to engage would be to invite problems. The only sensible procedure is to work toward control and discipline *as* the students begin their encounter with the curricular content. But such advice is also unwise from a theoretical viewpoint. The implication in such advice is that discipline is basic to good teaching but separate from teaching itself. The implication is there because teaching is again considered solely as the communicating of knowledge. In the purview of Scriptural objectives, no such distinction can be made. Obedience, knowledge, love, and freedom are all Christian complementary objectives. There are no contradictions or disjunctions among them. Moreover, such thinking has led many persons away from the teaching profession. Looking at discipline as an accompanying evil rather than as a vital objective of education, they have excused themselves with, "I wouldn't mind teaching if it weren't for those naughty kids."

134

To the modern mind, knowledge is power, and knowledge is salvation. In this intellectual idolatry, the *quality* of education is determined by the *quantity* of knowledge accumulated. The more knowledge, the better the teaching and the better the education. In extending this erroneous concept, our state Departments of Public Instruction and our college Departments of Education have blandly specified precise quantities of schooling as the only real prerequisite for obtaining teaching certificates. Within this extension, too, quantity is the implied determinant of quality.

In God's Holy Word we find quite a different emphasis. As noted in the chapter on objectives and aims, obedience remains the primal demand of God. If the reader scans Scripture, he will find one theme constantly reiterated: "Obey my voice and I will be your God" (Jeremiah 7:23), "To obey is better than sacrifice" (I Sam. 15:22), and "Salvation to all that obey" (Heb. 5:9) is the command that unifies the Old and New Testaments. Cassell's theoretically and Scripturally unsound construct relegates obedience to an inferior status, as it does such other primary objectives as love and freedom. Although teaching certainly involves the communication of course content, it would be inadequate, and therefore deceptive, to say that communicating is the meaning of the word "teach."

This brings us back to the question: What should be the relative position of the words "teacher," "subject," and "student" (learner) in our definitive grammatical construct? Keeping in mind that our definition should be both grammatically correct and theoretically sound, let us examine other possibilities. Another common and widely held definition is as follows: "Teaching is the communication of a subject to a student." This might be acceptable to many persons, but a restatement of the essential thought in this definition into two alternative grammatical forms will again leave the original problem unsolved.

Form A: He teaches history to the student.

Form B: He is teaching the student history.

Notice here that the learner takes the grammatical position of object of the preposition in Form A and that of indirect object in Form B. In either arrangement the meaning is essentially the same. Moreover, the word history remains the direct object of the verb "teach," thus leaving us with the philosophic inadequacy already cited.

Again positing a situation in which only a teacher, subject material, and a learner (student) are present, let us reconstruct the situation so that the learner becomes the object (end) of the verb "teach." Let us, furthermore, leave the subject (history or whatever) entirely out of the construct, but consider it as an abstracted and structured catalyst which will activate the teaching-learning process. Now, by constructing our answer to read: "He teaches students (learners)," we will find that we can no longer define teaching as communicating. We then have to formulate a new definition for teaching. A definition which is philosophically and practically satisfying involves a two-step process. It simply states: "teaching is educating." This, of course, rules out history or music or chemistry as the object of "teach." One can educate students, but would find it rather difficult to educate history, math, English, or chemistry. If teaching, then, is educating, we must say that we teach pupils and not subjects. This will put the Christian on the same side of the argument as the Progressives in this definitive problem. The Christian, however, need take no alarm about this temporary theoretical alignment, for the previously completed step of defining "educate" leaves the two groups poles apart.[1]

By defining teaching as educating, we not only reject the concept of teaching as communicating, but now we can accept the concept offered by Cornelius Jaarsma, who describes teaching as a "dynamic interplay of personalities" (*Human Development, Learning and Teaching*, p. 254). In this dynamic interplay, in which the teacher attempts to direct and mold the learner, the communication of beliefs and information is essential. But other, less prominent facets are also involved.

The Multi-faceted Nature of Teaching

Those teachers who have either consciously or unconsciously assumed that the dispensing of knowledge is the only real function of the teacher are likely to make a number of professional mistakes. In the first place, persons of this opinion tend to feel that they must be a walking encyclopedia, capable of providing answers to all questions and feeling incompetent when not able to do so. Secondly, they often feel compelled to *talk* all the while that students are within their range of supervision. And third, these persons are apt to feel guilty when the class discussion deviates from that prescribed body of information which they feel compelled to disseminate. These are the teachers who become addicted to a textbook and have as their primary goal the completion of a table of contents. What happens to the students, or what does not happen, is not their first concern. Finishing the book is their main objective; the stragglers can flunk.

An even more important role than that of knowledge communicator,

---

[1]The definition of education, as given in Chapter IX is as follows: Education is the recreation and redevelopment of the True understandings and relationships between God and man, man and fellowman, and man and the physical universe.

however, is that of substitute parent. Although many teachers have openly rejected this role because of its babysitting connotations, this function is of long standing and extreme Biblical importance. When the parent sends a child to the school, that parent is asking the teacher to stand in his place, to act *in loco parentis*. Long upheld by the courts of the United States, this legal and Scriptural principle has many implications. Standing in the place of the parent, the teacher is thus required to love and discipline the child in the way that the parent ought to love and discipline. Since the parent may not be concerned only with the child's acquisition of knowledge, neither may those who have been employed to take the parent's place be content merely with the pupil's ingestion of data. The substitute parent, like the natural parent, must be deeply concerned with development of Godly character and manners and values. The teacher, like the parent, is a designer and builder of the child's value structures. He unavoidably, if not deliberately, tells the child what to value and what not to value. Whether the teacher is more successful than the parent in these matters is not our immediate concern. What is important, however, is the fact that this function of the teacher is constantly being executed. The teacher may exercise this function overtly by advisedly telling the child what to value, or he may exercise it subtly by the selection and interpretation of curricular ingredients and experiences.

A closely aligned role of the teacher is that of security symbol. Having previously described the child as a voracious security-seeker, it should not now be surprising that the respected teacher stands as a symbol of security for the child. Much of the teacher's success or failure will depend on whether the child feels secure or insecure in the teacher's presence. Significantly, it is the demands of this role which unconsciously sends fear into the hearts of most beginning teachers, for students are quick to test the mettle of any new teacher. Finding a teacher to be firm, fair, and concerned about their welfare, students extend their trust, confidence and friendship to that person. Having found a personified symbol of security, they become increasingly receptive to the beliefs which that instructor is trying to transmit.

Another unavoidable role that the teacher always plays is that of master craftsman. Because technique is involved in much, if not all, of learning, it is also important that the teacher see himself as technician or craftsman. In teaching a child to read, for example, it is assumed that the teacher be skilled in the techniques of reading. The same may be said for the skills of typing, spelling, map-reading, singing, and experimenting. Although it is conceivable that a teacher could be successful without having a mastery of the skill superior to that of the student, such apparent lack of mastery would be sufficient excuse for most students to withhold their confidence from that unskilled teacher. In short, the teacher's security and credibility ratings would drop to a distracting low. The role of master craftsman is not identical to that of knowledge communicator and security symbol, but it is intimately related to them.

Regrettably, the role of craftsman is the one which has been given inordinate attention in Departments of Education since the advent of scientistic humanism. Again acting like the six blind men of Indostan, educationists have proclaimed that technique is the essence of teaching. A preponderance of methods courses in teacher-training curricula is the present inevitable result. Methods of teaching reading, methods of teaching arithmetic, methods of teaching language, methods of teaching science, ad infinitum, are proliferating redundantly. Not only does such curricular construction distort any true conception of teaching, it also helps to pervert the (Christian) reality of unified knowledge. It secularizes both teaching and knowledge, for it seeks to establish that teaching and knowledge can rightly be understood apart from God. In insidious and subtle form such curricular arrangement negates belief in the Sovereign God as the Meaning-Giver and Origin of all knowledge in its integrity.

One final facet of teaching is so common as to be often neglected. Not only is the teacher a communicator of beliefs, a substitute parent, a designer of values, a security symbol, a disciplinarian, and a master craftsman; the teacher is always and foremost a person. Persons teach, not machines or books. Machines, gadgets, books, and workbooks are tools used by persons. The teacher can rely overmuch on the tools of the profession; but he can never avoid the finality that it is he who teaches. As organic person, he enters the teaching situation with all his values, all his beliefs, all his mannerisms, all his sins, and all his faith-commitment(s) to his God or gods. True, the skillful person may temporarily prevent exposure of certain unpleasant personality traits, but such a person is eventually detected as a sham. He is not what he pretends to be. Instead of entering the teaching situation as a person, he enters as a pseudo-person. Dishonest with himself, he is not worthy of belief nor worthy of trust.

Teaching, then, is not only a very complex task; it is also a very responsible one. James warns the Christian Jews: "Let not many of you become teachers, my brethren, for you know that we who teach shall be judged with greater strictness. For we all make mistakes, and if anyone makes no mistakes in what he says he is· a perfect man, able to bridle the whole body also" (James 3:1-2, RSV). Commenting on this passage, Cornelius Jaarsma observes that "In a day of teacher shortage and when ever greater demands are being made upon the classroom teacher, these words are not too encouraging. One would hesitate to undertake so great a responsibility if it were not that the Lord himself calls to service and promises to qualify when he calls. Let a teacher be assured of a call to service" (Jaarsma, *Human Development, Learning and Teaching*, p. 253).

Science, Art, or Commitment?

Amongst educators and educational theorists, teaching has traditionally been considered an art. By this designation it was understood that persons were born with an aptitude for teaching. "She was a born teacher," was, and still is, a common phrase. Since a person was presumably born with a high aptitude for the teaching function, it was even thought that this aptitude would evince itself naturally and without training or preparation. Once a certain age level and maturation level were reached, the "born teacher" would be ready to enter the teaching fraternity, almost irrespective of the type of academic program he had followed.

Regrettably, however, the conception of teaching as an art is appearing frequently in intellectual wastebaskets. Although this theoretical and traditional explanation is far from sufficient by itself, it has enough validity to warrant its retention in our thoughts. Scripture itself approves this idea when it states that some have been called to be teachers. When Christ "ascended up on high, he led a host of captives, and he gave gifts to men. . . . And his gifts were that some should be apostles, some prophets, some evangelists, some pastors and teachers" (Eph. 4: 8, 11 RSV). One direct meaning of this passage is that some, but not all persons, have been divinely endowed by the Savior-King with the abilities demanded of teachers. For, to say that some have been called to be teachers is also to confess that some have not been called. When viewed as a Godly calling, accompanied by divinely bestowed abilities, teaching can legitimately be called an art.

To identify teaching as an art should not lead one to conclude that formal preparation is not required. The aptitudes that lead to success in the classroom will not spring to full fruition of their own accord. Neither will the talents of painter or poet. Only after repeated exposure to the demands of the art and systematic development of the latent but recognizable qualifying abilities will that person be ready to engage in the art to which he has been called. Jesus Himself, called Teacher by His disciples, spent thirty years in preparation for His brief earthly ministry. When considered in His divine nature, Jesus lacked nothing from the moment of His humble birth. But, considered in His human nature, Jesus needed to increase in wisdom and stature, and in favor with God and man (Luke 2:52). Simply because some intellectuals have abused and misinterpreted the concept of teaching as an art is no justification for dispensing with the concept.

A more recent trend in educational circles is to think of teaching as a science. In the minds of devout empiricists, teacher preparation programs must be *scientifically* engineered and executed. The information and the theories that issue from educational research must be *scientifically* based and tested before they deserve inclusion in the education curriculum. Teaching method, curriculum structure, and learning theory are considered of no value unless previously tested and proved in a laboratory situation. In the philosophy of "scientific educationism" the hope or salvation of education rests with the total adherence of teachers to this concept. Recognizing that current educational practice is woefully unproductive of desirable outcomes, it is thought that success, yes, even professional salvation, lies with the improvement of method and technique. In discussing the academic deficiencies of the American secondary school, Bent and Kronenberg give unquestioned allegiance to this scientific approach. They say, "The remedy does not lie in pupil selection or in reverting to a more academic type of curriculum for all. The solution is to be found in methods of teaching or in organization" (Bent and Kronenberg, *Principles of Secondary Education*, 4th ed., p. 106).

John Dewey, recommending scientific analysis as the educational panacea, has argued that pedagogy was failing because the field lacked the "existence of systematic methods of inquiry, which when they are brought to bear on a range of facts, enable us to understand them better and to control them intelligently, less haphazardly and with less routine" (John Dewey, "The Relation of Theory to Practice in Education," *National Society for the Scientific Study of Education*, Third Yearbook, 1904. Reprinted by the Association for Student Teaching, Bulletin 17, 1962. Cedar Falls, Iowa: State College of Iowa, p. 8). Expanding on this, Dewey asserted that education needs to rely less on the intuition (that is, the creative, artistic expression) of practitioners and more upon the methods of science.

For those who have blandly accepted this dogma of Dewey, research in education is the only sure savior and preserver of the teaching profession. The U.S. Office of Education, created to give leadership in education, but unswervingly dedicated to the doctrine of scientific humanism, has established regional research centers for the pursuit of this secular ideal.[2] It should be obvious, by now, that the field of educa-

---

[2]For review of governmental involvement in educational research, see (a) *Phi Delta Kappan*, Vol. XLVIII, No. 1, Sept. 1966, and (b) *Phi Delta Kappan*, Vol. XLVIII, No. 5, Jan. 1967.

tion is not now lacking in the volume of research. Unreadable amounts of statistically organized research findings are disgorged from colleges and universities, as well as from private and government research centers. Each masters and each doctoral candidate in education — as well as in various other fields — is expected to contribute to this flood of computerized data. Rather than saving the prospective educator, this massive production of research evidence has had the effect (if any) of either stultifying or maddening the teacher who tries to worship the variable and self-negating data-deity.

Furthermore, research and the scientific attitude in education have been noticeably ineffectual in directing teacher habits. Educationists sadly concur that teaching practice is not consistent with the educational theory that is disseminated in pre-service and in-service training programs. If it were, education might not only be more effective, but the entire profession would be viewed with greater esteem. The respect would not necessarily be deserved — for the results would be positivistic grotesques like the science-regulated half-humans of Huxley's *Brave New World* — but the credibility gap between the training institutions and its products would be narrowed. Recognizing the gulf between theory and practice, Dewey once said,

> The student [soon to be teacher] adjusts his actual methods of teaching, not to the principles which he is acquiring, but to what he sees succeed and fail in an empirical way from moment to moment. . . . In this way the controlling habits of the teacher finally get fixed with comparatively little reference to principles in the psychology, logic, and history of education. In theory these latter are dominant; in practice the moving forces are the devices and methods which are picked up through blind experimentation; through examples which are not rationalized; through precepts which are more or less arbitrary and mechanical" (Dewey, *ibid.*, p. 7).

What Dewey is here arguing for is a more scientific approach to the actual classroom situation, but in this demand he is, ironically, giving support to the traditional concept of teaching as an art. By condemning teachers for their failure to act in accordance with the educational theory that they have received, Dewey is admitting what every good teacher intuitionally accepts: that teaching is an address to continually varying situations and continually varying persons. No two situations and no persons are identical; therefore, teachers must continually be adjusting and adapting both their methodology and course content — since objectives are the fixed points of reference and remain constant. To make such adjustment and adaptation is to be creative. To be creative is to be artistic.

That Dewey did not recognize this is surprising, for he, along with the noted pragmatists William James and Charles Peirce, believed in the concept of eternal change. In this important doctrine of pragmatism, the only absolute is change. Once this doctrine is accepted, teaching as science is of negligible value. Scientific endeavor, by its very nature, depends on constancy. Educational situations, as part of this eternal flux, could then never be amenable to the scientific method. No sooner has one situation been scientifically analyzed than that very situation has changed. Given this pragmatic assertion, no situation could ever be duplicated, and no scientific experiment could ever be repeated. The pragmatically oriented scientist is thus forever doomed to basing his conclusions and laws on a random sampling of one. If he tries to increase the sampling, he is being inconsistent with his philosophic bias, or he is engaging in the scientific method with all variables and no constants.

Nevertheless, teaching must still be considered as science, if the term science is rightly understood. Using the definition of *science* offered in chapter one; namely that science is confined to taxonomy (systematic arrangement) and to methodology, it must be acknowledged that teaching is a science. That the term teaching implies a systematic arrangement of knowledge about itself should be obvious. If there were no systematic collection of knowledge about teaching, the only alternative would be an unsystematic or disorganized collection. Since our library shelves and this discussion testify that there *is* knowledge about teaching, the accompanying hope is that this knowledge be organized rather than disorganized. That same systematic arrangement is characteristic of good education, of true education (and that means education in Christ the Truth), we trust that the reader will accept.

The second criterion is equally easy to meet. Laying claim to the fact that educating and teaching are also process, it must be deduced that teaching always involves methodology. The activity of any person who is engaged in a process is method. The method may be inconsistent or it may be consistent. It may be good or it may be bad, but there is always some method involved. Simply because current connotation suggests that the word refers only to those approaches that are systematic and successful does not negate the fact that *every* approach to a process is rightly called a method.

With science so understood, teaching is legitimately defined as both art and science. Jaarsma recognized this dual nature of teaching when he wrote, "Teaching is an art based on a growing science" (*Human Development, Learning and Teaching*, p. 253). To confine ourselves to an understanding of teaching as nothing more than science would be naively wrong. But to confine ourselves to the dual characteristics that Jaarsma recognized would also be an error. For teaching must be considered in still another way. Teaching is more than art and science. It is also commitment.

In order to understand teaching as commitment, let us return to the situation described by Dewey. When he discussed the gap between theory and practice, he was not implying that the students and teachers were ignorant of educational theories and principles. Presumably those persons knew the theories and principles well enough to receive passing grades and teachers' certificates. Presumably, also, they believed the information that was received from instructors and textbooks. Why then did they fail to act accordingly? Lack of commitment! Simply stated, they did not hold to this knowledge with sufficient psychological strength. The disseminated information failed to touch them at other than the cognitive level; it was mere verbalization and therefore not strongly enough held to alter their behavior patterns. Looking at the theory-practice schism from another vantage point, the offered information also lacked significance for their lives. So what if Skinner observed the pecking of a stimulated chicken in 1950? What significance do the eating habits of caged chickens have for the future disciplining of a love-starved, spiritually — and overtly — rebellious boy?

This is not to intimate that *all* research information is useless. Rather, the intent is to stress the fact that some knowledge which is arrived at methodically and presented in systematic fashion is not worthy of commitment. Much of the knowledge currently being promulgated in the name of education deserves no more than peripheral rating. Since the body of knowledge about teaching is large, some of this knowledge will be more significant and more deserving of commitment than will other. If a teacher refuses to address himself and his class to the basic, significant issues of life and persists in dealing with the trivial and peripheral, then his student's lack of commitment to his conjectures is understandable if not laudable.

A further insight into the concept of teaching as commitment was afforded the author during his tenure as school principal. In the process of choosing a method for the teaching of phonics, the faculty was indoctrinated by the sales promotion of one phonics textbook publisher. Thoroughly convinced that this method was the right one, the faculty pitched into their fall assignment with exceptional fervor. They were committed to a method. The results were highly satisfying: the children learned to read with gratifying speed and proficiency. The true method had been found and all doubt vanished for a time. But eventually a teacher from a neighboring school stopped by to report the equally satisfying results that their students had produced with a basically different method. Subsequent checking of periodical contents and sales promotion pieces revealed that still other, widely varying methods had also produced "sensational" results. Obviously, the key to success lay not in methodology. Seemingly incongruous methods had all been successful. With the methods themselves becoming variables, therefore, the commitment of the teachers became the only recognizable constant.

Such denigrating of methodology is not the mark of one "conformed to the present worldly scheme" (Rom. 12:2, Berkley Version). Teacher training centers and research-oriented institutes expend vast allotments of money, time, and effort in blind pursuit of improved method and advanced technology, those glorious elixirs that will solve current educational ailments.

With this attention on methodology permeating the classroom, J. M. Stephens offers a refreshing reminder. In *The Process of Schooling* he turns the methods researchers on themselves with the following summary:

> It is part of the folklore that, in educational investigations, one method turns out to be as good as another and that promising innovations produce about as much growth as the procedures they supplant, but no more. Nachman and Oopchinsky (1958), to take one example, feel safe in stating, as a matter of common knowledge, that "Reviews of teaching procedures produce little or no difference in the amount of knowledge gained by the students." In truth this has been a refrain ever since Rice (1897) discovered the surprising constancy of spelling attainment in the face of marked variations in the time devoted to study and since Merriam (1915) reported regular growth in school subjects in the absence of formal instruction in those subjects.
>
> These classical conclusions are echoed when we turn to the most recent studies of television and programmed instruction. . . .
>
> Bracketed between the ancient and the most recent investigations are scores of studies to show that pupils learn about as much in large classes as in small classes (De Cecco, 1964; Fleming, 1959); in homogeneous groups as in heterogeneous groups (Ekstrom, 1961); in core curricula as in traditional curricula (Michelson, 1957); in lecture classes as in discussion classes (Churchill and John, 1958; McKeachie, 1963); in teacher-centered approaches as in group-centered approaches (Stern, 1963); in small schools with indifferent facilities as in large schools with lavish facilities (Lathrop, 1960, p. 10).

But, what is commitment? In the first place, it is not empirically evident and thus not analyzable by the scientific method. Commitment is somewhat analogous to emotional expression. An emotion itself cannot be seen or analyzed, although emotional expression can. So, too, with commitment. A commitment is internal, but the expression of that commitment demonstrates itself in the actions, the overt emotional responses, and the speech of a person. Because of man's organic unity, any attempt to further define a commitment must be in the abstract. We can make this abstraction, however, because we have previously seen that man believes in psychological strengths. Having defined core beliefs in chapter one, we can now assert that a person's commitment is an outward expression of his core beliefs. Since core beliefs rather than peripheral beliefs are the determiners of action or behavioral direction, it is these beliefs which form the root of commitment.

Every person, and thus every teacher, has a commitment. Every person has a set of core beliefs which give direction to his life. Core beliefs and behavioral direction vary widely from individual to individual. Many persons are committed to material or financial gain for themselves. Strongly holding to the popular idolatry that the dollar solves all problems and saves all people, such persons bend every effort and devote every opportunity to the acquisition of temporal wealth, the "almighty buck." That may not be the commitment of the Christian, for Scripture warns, "The love of money is the root of all evil" (I Tim. 6:10). For others, intellection or prestige may be the end of their aspirations. For still others, power or peace or happiness.

By referring to money, fame, and power as commitments, the word commitment has taken on added meaning. No longer does the word mean only that internal motivation which propels a person towards a goal. The goal itself has come to be called a commitment. For example, when a person strongly believes that an increased salary will solve his problems, this belief results in action that he believes will most likely produce the increase. Unable to separate the propelling action from that goal towards which the person is moving, the word commitment is amplified to encompass the entire range of belief, action, and objective.

In the same sense, then, that wealth is a commitment, so, too, is teaching. In order to use the word in such a way, however, one thing must be remembered. When we say that teaching is a commitment, we mean that teaching is an end in itself. Not an ultimate end, certainly, but an end nevertheless. It is not merely a stepping stone to another goal. A person who is committed to teaching does not use his professional membership as a means of acquiring wealth, fame, or power. Such professional abuse will lead only to bitter disappointment and a hasty departure from the ranks.

That such faulty purpose, however, is characteristic of the American teaching fraternity can be illustrated as follows: In a ten-year study at the University of Illinois, 40% of the graduates who were qualified to teach never entered the profession. Of those who did enter, half had dropped out within two years. Of a thousand teachers, fewer than one hundred continued to teach more than ten years. In some states teachers are leaving the profession at the rate of 20% per year (Havighurst and Neugarten, *Society and Education,* p. 534). Discounting a small fraction for illness and accident, it would be safe to say that the bulk of the dropouts are not committed to teaching. Teaching, for them, was a means of reaching another, more profoundly determinative commitment.

Within the teaching fraternity, the current outcry for collective salary negotiations is a not very subtle betrayal of a commitment to financial and material gain. Other, presumably more dedicated teachers, are committed to a body of secularized knowledge. Not dedicated to the welfare and needs of the students, their only guiding concerns are the preservation of English, history, mathematics, or foreign languages and of their personal involvement in them. These are the persons who adamantly teach subjects and not students. These are the teachers who will associate themselves with schools whose faith-commitment contradicts their own *outward* profession, so as to preserve their *inward* idolatry toward their favorite subject.

But for the sincere Christian, the only legitimate and obedient commitment is to serve Christ. To make that Christ-serving concrete, the Christian serves the students in the name of Christ. Teaching for the Christian is not an ultimate end; it is the way by which he can fulfill his calling and serve the Lord of his life. It is not an attempt to gain reward, but, if it is done in the name of Christ, it will certainly bring rich blessings. "For whosoever shall give . . . a cup of water to drink in my name, because ye belong to Christ, verily I say unto you, he shall not lose his reward" (Mark 9:41). And whoever will lose his life for Christ's sake — and that means also in the teaching profession — will certainly find it (Matt. 10:39). Solomon expressed the same truth when the Holy Spirit directed him to write, "For whoso findeth me [Godly wisdom] findeth life, and shall obtain favor of the Lord" (Prov. 8:35).

In conclusion, teaching as commitment should not be confused with teaching as calling. Calling is not of human origin; it is God's choosing and equipping of His servants for their particular functions. Commitment in Christ is the called person's affirmative response to selection. Commitment, then, is the self-consecrating, unswerving response to God's call.

The Means to the End

In the theoretical construct (He teaches students.) previously discussed, course content was briefly mentioned as being the catalyst in the teaching-learning process (see p. 178). Not intended to diminish the importance of God-given knowledge, the purpose of that construct was to show the correct relationship of knowledge to the teacher and the student. The structured bodies of knowledge that we have come to call subjects must always be kept in that relationship: they must always be considered as means and not as ends in the education process. Yet, they are essential. Without subjects, without the transmission of knowledge, the educational process could never be started. This is why we have chosen to call the various courses catalysts. As in certain chemical experimentations no action or reaction can take place until the catalyst is added. Just as with most analogies, this description of the curriculum as analagous to a chemical catalyst is intended to have significance at only one point. The function of a catalyst is to accelerate the chemical process. The function of a systematically structured curriculum is to speed the educational process. The curriculum must accelerate the student in the development of his true relationships and understandings. On that central point of acceleration the analogy holds. However, it does not retain its validity when the unchangeableness of the chemical catalyst is considered. The teacher must be willing to change and adapt course content as his insights deepen or as the needs of students vary.

The apostle Paul clearly explained the necessity of transmission of knowledge between persons. Addressing himself to the Roman Christians, he wrote, "But how are men to call upon him in whom they have not believed? And how are they to believe in him of whom they have never heard? And how are they to hear without a preacher [or a teacher]?" (Rom. 10:14 RSV). In the personal interaction that is called the teaching-learning process, the student will not be recreated and redeveloped in his true understandings and relationships until knowledge has been employed as the medium of interaction. Teaching and learning cannot take place within a vacuum. Jaarsma illustrated this concept with these words: "In addition to a learner and a goal, learning involves a medium, a something through which a learner reaches a goal. For our purpose this medium is the organized program of the school as we know it today" (*Human Development, Learning and Teaching*, p. 173). Henry Zylstra also clearly recognized this and graphically stated it thus:

> It is so easy in the name of Christianity to turn one's back to art, to science, to politics, to social problems, to historical tensions and pressures, in one word, to culture, if you will. But once the conviction seizes on you that these all, precisely because they are cultural realities, exhibit a religious allegiance and an ultimate loyalty, that none of them is neutral but rather that all of them are faith-founded, all laid on an altar, all dedicated to a god, then you realize that they are at the very least important. Then you realize, too, that the true discernment of the God behind the culture, the assumption underlying the thought, the dogma beneath the action, the soul in the body of the thing, are precisely what it is the business of our schools as schools to disclose and judge. In that lies the strengthening of the moral sinews of our young Christians. It is so that their choice for Christ and God can

147

become a meaningful human choice. Christianity versus culture: no, it is the fundamentalist heresy. Culture alone: indeed not; it is the liberal heresy. Christianity through culture: the religious in man governing, shaping, determining the scientific, artistic, social in him, precisely; it is the Reformed truth (*Testament of Vision*, p. 99).

Developing Christians through the medium of, or by means of, culture is the task of teachers. Subjects are windows through which God's revelation may shine so that faith is expanded and strengthened. To divorce faith from culture is not possible, for whoever denies God as the source of all culture and the Christ as He in whom all culture coheres, must choose an apostate faith in something or someone else.

The use of culture as the medium for learning will either strengthen or weaken faith in God. If Christ's relevance to history or arithmetic or English is denied, either by word or by lack of reference, the student's faith in God will be threatened, and the teacher will have incurred the anger of the Christ. For our Lord Himself warned, "So every one who acknowledges me before men, I also will acknowledge before my Father who is in heaven; but whoever denies me before men, I also will deny before my Father who is in heaven" (Matt. 10:32-33).

But which subjects shall we use? Within recent centuries, and especially during the past few decades, there has been almost uncontrolled proliferation of courses in the schools. The limited trivium and quadrivium curriculum of the medieval schools has mushroomed to monstrous proportions. In a report issued by the U.S. Office of Education in 1962, 800 "separate" subjects were being taught between grades 9 and 12 in the nonpublic schools of the United States. By comparison, only 150 "separate" subjects were reported by the non-public high schools in 1933 (Gertler, Diane, *Subject Offerings and Enrollments, Grades 9-12, Nonpublic Secondary Schools*, U.S. Government Printing Office, frontspiece). This represents a 533% increase over a thirty-year period, and that only among the nonpublic schools.

All these humanly organized bodies of knowledge are legitimate tools when it is acknowledged that all knowledge is still unified, still emanates from the Giver of all knowledge, and still is revelational of the omnipotent, sovereign God. Jan Waterink, noted Dutch psychologist, testifies to their legitimacy when he says, "All culture-products are the creation of God. Every product of culture comes from God and it must also serve God. Since this is true, no product of culture can be sinful in itself. This does not imply, of course, that people are not able to use some specific culture-product in a sinful manner" (Waterink, *Basic Concepts in Christian Pedagogy*, p. 103). He goes on to say that some of these culture-products may have been so perverted through their continuous use for non-Christian purposes that they are no longer fit tools for the Christian to handle.

All knowledge is God-given, yet most of the recent knowledge-divisions are the result of secularizing influences. Most of them are products of man's innate destructive urge to fragment and disintegrate. They are sinful attempts, piously executed, to abolish the name of God. Holding to a form of Godliness by the retention of courses in theology, secular minds have denied the power thereof by attempting to divorce God from everything else. By continued fragmentation, deicide has been committed not merely in the structuring of advanced linear geometry, radio-TV repair, advanced placement English, mechanical drawing, and economic problems. Each little subject comes neatly pre-packaged, complete with specified objectives. Schools no longer choose their tools on the basis of the goals to be reached, but choose their goals on the basis of the tools being dangled tantalyzingly before them.

Every school faces important and recurrent decisions regarding curriculum. Which subjects and which activities should be included in the school program? With such a proliferating array from which to choose, some guiding principles must be formulated. Without such principles, curricular growth becomes haphazard, subject to whim, and contributory to educational chaos. In order to prevent such wild, cancerous development, the following general principles are offered:

1. Subjects and activities must be judged and evaluated in the light of objectives, and must be discarded or rejected if they fail to aid substantially in reaching those objectives.

2. Subject matter and curricular experiences must be chosen according to a priority system:
   (a) Those which can best meet the primary objectives must be given primary importance.
   (b) Those which can best meet the secondary objectives must be given secondary importance.
   (c) Those which can be considered incidental may be included only if time permits.
   (d) Those which are structured for the sake of meeting false objectives must be rejected.

3. The curricular program must be capable of being related to all the students in the school if it is intended to implement either the primary or secondary objectives; for it is these objectives that are aimed at, and considered important to, all students. (For example, if the essay is considered an essential means by which to show man's search for Truth, that is, the Christ, then study in the essay

149

should be required of all students. Also, if a course in civics or government is considered an essential means by which to show the proper relationships between man, God, and the state, then this course should be required of all students.)

4. Before a curricular experience or course may be introduced into the students' program, the specific content of that course should be evaluated and structured so that immediate, attainable objectives can be articulated in complete agreement with the ultimate, primary, and secondary objectives.

5. Subjects and activities are not ordinarily to be considered wrong in themselves. The important considerations are the way in which those subjects or activities are used, the motives for using them, and the results that they tend to produce in the educand. For example, "auto mechanics" is not wrong inherently, but it becomes wrong if it is used for the sake of making "hot-rods" or if it contributes to making the car an idol in the mind of the student.

6. The curricular program must be capable of relation to the student in a way that is consistent with his physical and psychological characteristics, always aiding the child in his developing spiritual-moral relationships. Age or size may not be our principal criteria; rather, the child's over-all ability to cope with and profit from any given experience should be our guide.

7. Subject matter and experiences may not be included if they are contrary to the principles of the state or church of which the student is a member. For example, ballet may be an excellent means of developing muscular control, but must not be required of the student whose church has taken a prohibitive stand on dancing.

8. The program of subjects and activities must be so regulated as to allow the home and church adequate time to meet their unique objectives. The school officials must remember that the home has prior claim to the child under God because He has established His covenant with the *parents* and their children, and not with the officials of the school — even though the latter are delegated *in loco parentis* powers by those parents.

Having formulated these guiding principles for making curricular decisions, we can now address ourselves to the actual choices to be made. By which courses can we best develop a child's true understanding of God and the proper relationship to Him? Through which subjects can we best reach the goals of love, knowledge, obedience, and freedom? Quite obviously, the best and most direct method is through study of the Bible. The Bible ought to have the prominent place in the school

150

as well as in the home and church. But, because of the inherent unity of knowledge, the Scriptural teachings and their implications can be instructively objectified and illustrated through the immediate aims of all the subjects in the curriculum. History, for example, can be used as the medium for conveying and concretely demonstrating significant spiritual lessons. Wars can be illustrative of man's spiritual-moral degradation or of his resistance to obedience. Each society's historical emphasis on religion can be used to show man's innate religious urge. The common traits of divergent societies can also be used to show the common Adamic origin of man and the highly similar characteristics of all men. Furthermore, the vast accumulation of interpreted facts that characterizes the subject called history can promote a Christian attitude of insignificance and piety in the contemplation of God's all-controlling providence, rather than a foolish pride in man's accomplishments. A man approaches wisdom when he begins to realize how ignorant he is, when, through the enlightenment of the Holy Spirit, he begins to fear the Sovereign God and keep His commandments in *every* aspect of his life.

Literature can also be used as a medium for developing spiritual understandings and relationships. Tragedy, for example, shows man's tendency toward willful self-destruction. Comedy further displays human depravity by exposing the foibles of men. In comedy's lower, more farcical forms — which are inferior materials for school use — only a spurious and momentary escape from sinful reality is offered. In more thoughtful comedy, however, the need of solutions is admitted although, grievously, the Christian solution is very seldom preferred. Fiction, because of its more elaborate plot structure presents a concept of destiny and an interpretation of life that may be romantic delusion, bleak fatalism, optimistic humanism, Christian realism — but finally it is either instructively, persuasively, dedicated (by the author) to Christ the Truth or to the darkness and despair of the Satanic lie: "Ye shall not surely die" (Gen. 3:4).

Sociology, which could just as aptly be called group behavior, collective belief patterns, or mass psychology, could effectively be used to illustrate various conditions under which human attitudes and beliefs are strengthened or altered. By studying the actions which accompany changes in belief, the student may come not only to understand himself better in his relationship to God, but he may also become more aware of the universal human need for reconciliation with the Savior and for citizenship in the Kingdom of Christ on earth as well as in heaven.

The natural sciences, too, if included in the curriculum, must be used to strengthen the student's faith in God. The necessity of all scientific endeavor's being based on *a priori* assumptions must be used to show man's ultimate dependence on God-given know' dge and belief rather than on method, observation, or reason. The scientific dependence on generalization can illustrate the order, consistency, and planning in the universe, thus becoming another apology for the being and faithfulness of the One True God. Also, the fact that matter cannot be destroyed, but only changed into different forms, illustrates the completeness and perfection of God's creative act.

This same completeness and beauty can also be suggested — though imperfectly — through the study of music and art. Man, re-creatively functioning, is confined to making good or evil use of the materials and opportunities afforded him. Offered the whole universe as material, man can shape, re-arrange, and form for prasise to God, or he can shape, re-arrange, and form in denial of God, but he can never originate. Also, in music and art history, the predominance of cultic, religious themes vividly portrays man's inescapable religious desire to praise, pacify, or provoke God.

The child's true understanding of his relationship to other men can also be developed through the studies discussed above. Again, the only source of true information is the Bible. Not only the real is therein described, but also the ideal. Man's inhumanity to man is clearly presented in Scripture, but so, too, are all the principles and precepts for correct, Christ-centered relationships. History can also awaken the child through a vast storehouse of covenant-keeping, that is, God-oriented, and covenant-breaking, that is, God-rejecting, examples. Sociology, correctly studied, not only creates an awareness of human misery, but establishes an outlet for the young Christian's developing love for fellow humans. Geography not only illustrates the interdependence of all men, but also affords countless manifestations of Providential care and man's total dependence on God.

In addition to the subjects discussed above, many activities can be structured for the sake of developing Christian interpersonal relationships. Games can be played and contests can be organized, not for the sake of avoiding obedience and mutual concern, but for the Biblical purpose of teaching obedience to rules and of showing the necessity of love through concrete, child-level activities. Recesses and noon-hours are not to be considered as a respite from the demands of Christianity, but as practical, refreshing opportunities in which to live Christianity. For Christianity is not tedious, unbending sobriety. In Christ our Liberator, it offers happiness, fun, and freedom that no other way of life can promise.

Our purpose here is not to construct a curriculum. Curricula will always be changing because they are always abstractions from a unified whole and because not many teachers correctly understand their purpose. Furthermore, because man moves through time toward the

Judgment, curricular contents will have to change if teachers are to use them effectively in addressing the student to the peculiar challenge of his day. The core and essence of the curriculum must not change, however, for the Bible is its focal point and guiding light. Our purpose, rather, is to accent the importance of directing the entire school program to the honor and praise of God. Whatever activity or subject is admitted to the school's curriculum must be included, not because it is traditional or because it is popular in the public schools, but because it contributes significantly to the development of the Christian.

The goals and objectives of public schools are necessarily different from those of Christian schools. Consequently, their curricular contents are selected for different reasons and are used in different ways. Herein lies one of the major differences: both God-honoring and God-rejecting schools may include history, geography, arithmetic, and music in their curricula. Both schools may even use identical textual tools for these courses. At this point, however, similarities should cease. The interpretations, the emphases, the internal structuring, and the daily objectives should all differ. For this reason the Christian teacher may not proceed through the study of a subject only in logical, systematic fashion.

Bent and Kronenberg, correctly aware of the fragmenting and disintegrating effect of rigid, systematic curricula, express a concern that should evoke a felicitous response from the Christian educator. In their jointly authored *Principles of Secondary Education* they explain,

> When subject matter is logically arranged and presented, pupils are likely to leave school with an accumulation or collection of isolated facts and skills, but with no ability to organize them. This is comparable to teaching the parts of a clock but never teaching how they are assembled so that the clock may function (p. 235).

They further argue that "units should be organized around some nucleus which becomes the point of view, central theme, or center of interest" (p. 235).

The Christian may readily accept such explanation and may give Christ the nuclear position, but such arrangements have been tried before and are, reservedly, principally, inadequate. Although such clustering of bits and pieces around a nucleus represents an improvement over any atomized arrangement, this approach to curriculum construction fails to expose knowledge in its essential character. The curriculum, by such arrangement, coheres only because human ingenuity has succeeded in synthesizing a satisfying configuration of elements, theoretically judged to be secularistic if considered in isolation.[3] When the student

---

[3]It is this type of curricular organization that is portrayed in Figure 4 on p. 47.

is confronted with such an array, the most enlightened concept that could be deduced is that somehow, in some mysterious way, all of the events and ideas in time must be focused on the Christ. Certainly the universe and human history, cosmically envisioned, do cohere in Christ who is one with the Father. But the sovereignty of God must not only become evident on such a grand, impersonal scale. He must become more than a distant revolving point for men and history. His omniscient power and directing providence must be seen in the personal and minute affairs of individual living. In order to make both the comprehensiveness and narrowness of Christianity real to the student, all phenomena, eras, and ideas deemed worthy of protracted study must be displayed and examined in their significant dimensions and modes. If, for example, the record of ancient Greece were chosen for extended examination (and well it might), the political, military, economic, technological, and artistic dimensions should be considered. But, to confine oneself to these would be to ignore the most crucial and the only all-encompassing dimension: the spiritual-moral relationship of these people to the God who created them and allowed them existence. Examined spiritually-morally, the Spartan confidence in stately princes and the Athenian idolatrous emulation of man's law-making rather than law-abiding function become the prime topic of interest. The internecine warfare of the Greek city-states then constitutes collective human tragedy potent with admonition for the spiritual-moral guidance of the questing student.

But, due to long exposure to a necessarily and arbitrarily divided curriculum, other, more direct organizational techniques may periodically be required. The teacher, mindful of the seamless unity of knowledge, should choose some single significant element and repeat its use in differently-labelled courses. A Psalm of David, for example, could be used to equal advantage whether in music, literature, grammar, history, psychology, or Bible classes. And not only such positive spiritual responses need be selected. Negative responses to the God of the universe, abundant in every traditional course folio, can and should be used to the same end. Not only is the Christian called to think on those things that are true, honest, pure, lovely, and of good report (Phil. 4:8); he is also instructed by God's Holy Word to "try the spirits whether they are of God: because many false prophets are gone out into the world" (I John 4:1). By this edict, evolution, segregation, scientism, communism, democracy, and secularism, among others, become legitimate and necessary studies for the school.

Having a vision of God's universal sovereignty, the Christian teacher must attempt to transmit that vision by repeatedly illustrating the unity of knowledge and by demonstrating the coherence of all knowledge in

154

Christ. Moreover, the Christian teacher, in his deployment of the curriculum, must address himself to the entire child and not just to his mental dimension. Love, obedience, and freedom do not develop apart from knowledge, but simultaneously with it. All these Christian gifts are facets of the organic, human response that the teacher seeks to elicit from God's covenant youth. To shape, to mold, to develop the whole child according to the will and revelation of God is his all-consuming task.

CHAPTER XII

CONSIDERATIONS OF LEARNING

In contrast to the words *educate* and *teach,* the word *learning* has been the object of much discussion. Many textbooks have been devoted to attempting, but seldom completing, its definition. The typical result of such attempts has been the formulation of a number of propositions *about* learning, all of which avoid its essential character. Furthermore, hundreds of theorists have devoted their lives to a contemplation of the learning process. One of the reasons for this twentieth-century surge of epistemological activity is the attempt on the part of educational psychologists (already discussed in Chapter I) to transform their specialized area of study into a laboratory science. It is as though some magic elixir lies undetected, either in the wastes of research diggings or unobtrusively within the human psyche. Once this elixir is found, the scientific humanist believes, teaching can become fully successful.

The implication of all this "scientific" research into learning is that earlier generations of teachers did not know what they were really doing. It is implied that teachers of thirty, twenty, and even ten years ago did not have the knowledge that teachers of today have. Unless the survivors of those by-gone myth-ridden eras "keep abreast" by in-service training, they must be hastily pensioned off, or even dismissed if possible. Not having as much scientific knowledge about learning as the teachers of today, they obviously knew less about good teaching, for, as Pestalozzi once said, "As the child learns, so must one teach."

This statement of Pestalozzi, accompanied by the contemporary, frantic searching for an understanding of learning, presents an interesting enigma. If Pestalozzi's remark is adjudged true, and I believe that we must so consider it and if there has yet been discovered or understood no definitive theory of learning, a number of deductions can be made. First, if we do not know how the child learns, it is implied that we do not know how to teach him. Second, any learning which has taken place in the past — and surely no one would deny that much learning has occurred — would then have come about by accident and apart from correct learning theory. Third, any successful teaching either by our contemporaries or by our forebears will have to be completely discounted as mere happenstance. This, of course, puts the learning theorists themselves in a deserved predicament, for they also are the products of the old-fashioned schools and unscientific teachers who presumably knew nothing about learning. Thus, even the learning theorists would have to discount all their own learning, in that way disqualifying themselves for their prophetic employment.

Despite the currently excitable emphasis on learning theory, learning has always taken place. The difficulty lies not in the establishing of learning, but in describing the nature of it. Again, it is believed that once the correct nature of learning is understood and articulated, teachers will be able to work more effectively and efficiently because teaching activities will be able to be correlated with learning characteristics.

This whole attempt at explanation, however, is almost without exception a blasphemous one, for the proponents of all the popular learning theories have attempted their explanations on the temporal, God-denying level. To study learning theory in typical secular fashion is to re-enact the foolish searching of the six blind men of Indostan. Operating apart from God's Scriptural Revelation, men like Pavlov, Thorndike, Watson, Guthrie, Skinner, and Wertheimer have groped for understanding that always remains partial and elusive. With a blindness that is characteristic of all those who refuse to take the Scriptural light on their theoretical journeys, they have grasped segments of the learning phenomenon, grossly misconstrued their character, and absolutized their findings as depicting the whole.

Although a detailed analysis of the extant learning theories would be redundant, some of the blind spots in these theories must be discussed.[1] Jaarsma classifies the secular learning theories under four main headings, namely: the conditioning theory, the trial and error theory, the field (or gestalt) theory, and the reasoning and creative expression theory. This arrangement may or may not be considered acceptable; but Dr. Jaarsma served the Christian community well by attempting to formulate an additional Christian theory, or view, as he called it. Winfred Hill, however, places all secular learning theories in two main categories — the connectionist and the cognitive. A third category that he tentatively suggests is designed for those theories that attempt to combine the ideas of the cognitive and connectionist approaches. These two main classifications are most convenient because they attempt to divide the theories between those that deal with visible, external phenomena and those that emphasize hypothetical assertions about the invisible,

---

[1]For those who are interested, but not familiar with these theories, the following resources are recommended: Jaarsma, Cornelius, *Human Development, Learning and Teaching*, Chapters 12-17, and Hill, Winfred F., *Learning: A Survey of Psychological Interpretations*. Chandler Publishing Company, San Francisco. 227 pp.

internal character of learning. The former theories are classified as connectionist because they represent attempts to connect stimuli (input) with responses (output). The latter are classified as cognitive because they attempt theoretically to describe the activity that takes place within the mind at the moment of learning.

Within the connectionist tradition are found the classical conditioning theory of Pavlov, the behaviorist theory of Watson, the contiguity theory of Guthrie, and the reinforcement theories of both Thorndike and Skinner. In the most radical of the connectionist theories, attention was focused almost exclusively on the physiological aspect of learning. The mind was considered identical with the brain, and was analagous to a telephone switchboard. Learning was explained on this physiological level, in much the same way that an electrical engineer would describe the electrical activity of the telephone system. B. R. Bugelski, a physiologically oriented psychologist, defined learning in this way:

> Learning is the process of the formation of relatively permanent neural circuits through the simultaneous activity of the elements of the circuits-to-be; such activity is of the nature of change in cell structures through growth in such a manner as to facilitate the arousal of the entire circuit when a component element is aroused or activated (Bugelski, *The Psychology of Learning*, p. 5).

Unable to explain learning adequately on such a limitedly physiological level, educational psychologists in the connectionist tradition have swung to virtually opposite positions. Lowell Schoer of the University of Iowa typifies this theoretical change when he confines his learning explanations to the externally observable stimuli and responses, while labeling the learner as a complete mystery, as the "little black box." For him, man remains an unknowable entity. The only possible hope for success lies in the finding of a certain pattern of stimuli which will be productive of certain desired patterns of response. The manner by which such patterns will be discovered remains unexplained, but one thing is certain: religious and spiritual considerations must be excluded. Out of the desperate dichotomy that such an anti-Christian anthropology makes of life, Dr. Schoer once told the author, "I am a member of a conservative, orthodox church, but I'll have you know that my religion has nothing to say about the nature of the child."

It should also be noted that most connectionist learning theorists are proponents of the Darwinian evolutionary tradition. Still bound by ethical considerations and thus prevented from extensive human experimentation, these theorists have given religious assent to the idea that man is merely a rational animal. The animal part is comprehensible to them, but the rational mystifies them. Proceeding from rat mazes to monkey cages to dove cotes, they have sought the key to unlock the rational mind by observing the actions of beasts and birds.

Although some positive insights can be gained through a study of the connectionist theories, for God's common grace is also operative in the thought of the evolutionist and the agnostic, some of their heinous errors should be enumerated. The connectionist theories:

1. View learning as strictly a horizontal, human activity and ignore the vertical (God's involvement in the life of man).

2. Fail to consider man as an organic unity. By abstracting from the total man and absolutizing the physiological, the rational, or the sociological, they cannot understand learning as the activity of an organic person.

3. Are based on the pseudo-scientific assumption that there is an unbroken, evolutionary progression from animal to man. Simply because animals and humans both respond to stimuli is no justification for arguing that, therefore, they learn in the same way.

4. Are based on the empiricist belief that whatever cannot be observed by the human senses does not exist. Many proponents of these theories have argued that all learning can be reduced to observable, measurable responses. Whatever is not measurable, for them, is either non-existent or not worth measuring. (By such reasoning, the mind is either non-existent or not worth measuring.)

5. Fail to explain why the learner responds to some stimuli and not to others, or why the learner responds to certain stimuli at one time and not at another time. Although the child is constantly surrounded by a multitudinous variety of stimuli, the theories are based on unrealistic experiments in which one stimulus is isolated and accented. Furthermore, they are based on the assumption that there is a causal relationship between the stimuli and responses. Simply because a response occurs when a stimulus is present does not mean that the stimulus *causes* the response. Often when stimuli are present, no related response can be detected. Such thinking is fallacious, also, because the single most significant factor, namely the learner himself, is left out of the theoretical consideration.

If the connectionist approach to learning were the true approach, and if the internal, non-observable dimensions of the learner were as insignificant as these men would have us believe, the teaching process would be quite simple. Teachers could again resort to the rote memorization and drill that typified American education practice during recent decades. Rote and drill were the practical applications of connectionist learning theory, because permanent neural circuits, permanent S-R bonds had to be established. In God's providence, however, the materialist connectionist tradition has fallen into disrepute even among secularists. One of the reasons for this decline of reputation has been the presence of competing, cognitive theories.

Within the cognitive tradition, the Gestalt theory, as advocated by the German psychologists Wertheimer, Koehler, and Koffka, is not only the most popular, but is also the outstanding revolt against the connectionist position. This Germanic movement was not only a revolt against the externalism of the connectionists, but was also an attempt to deal with whole learning phenomena rather than minute, analytical segments. It was an attempt to hypothesize about the internal activity and structure of the mind. Also included in this tradition are Kurt Lewin's theory of life space and Edward Tolman's theory of purposive behavior.

The cognitive theorist, who also works extensively with animal behavior, is not a laboratory researcher in the same sense that the connectionist is. His purpose is not to systematically use the "scientific" method, for he recognizes that the human mind, which is the object of all his effort, is not amenable to such observation. Rather, his purpose in observing animal behavior is to play hunches. He does not systematically apply laws to the behavior being observed, but looks into his own cultural background for hunches or hypotheses that may credibly explain a change in behavior which has previously been labelled as learning. In contrast to the connectionist, the cognitive theorist is far more realistic, but less scientific. For every bit of nearness-to-the-real that is gained through their approach, a corresponding amount of control is lost. In the research-oriented approach of the connectionist, the opposite is true. For every measure of control that is gained through the laboratory, a corresponding intimacy with reality is lost. Even though both types are capable of recognizing an occurrence of learning, each is peculiarly frustrated in his attempt at explanation by the disadvantages of his partial and Truth-denying system.

The cognitive theorists, like the connectionists, are prone to continued embarrassment because they also are beset by serious, self-imposed weaknesses. Some of these weaknesses, or theortical errors, are the same as those attributed to their connectionist rivals. The cognitive theorists also:

1. View learning as strictly a horizontal activity and ignore God's involvement in the life of man.
2. Fail to consider man as an organic unity. Unlike the connectionists, however, they do not concentrate their analysis on the physio-

logical or the observable. Hypothesizing from the observable, they focus their analysis on the unobservable rational dimension of man. By abstracting the mind and considering it as a separate entity within man, they also violate man's oneness or wholeness. In moving away from the atomistic approach of the connectionists they have moved in the right direction, but not far enough.

3. Base their work on the pseudo-scientific assumption that there is an unbroken, evolutionary progression from animal to man. Again, they differ in the use of this presumed animal-human linkage. As was stated, the cognitive theorists do not use animals in the conventional "scientific" way. They assume, nevertheless, that the learning of animals is analagous to that of humans.

In addition to these common errors, the cognitive theorists are deficient on other, distinct accounts. Their theories also:

4. Fail to explain the reason for, or cause of, insight. In describing the learning of a person or animal, these theorists frequently append the terms *insight* or *understanding* to that situation or activity which in its largest sense is labelled learning. The German term *gestalt*, meaning shape, pattern, or form, is a forerunner of the American term *configuration* or *insight*. What is meant by these terms is that a person can be said to have learned when his perceptual field has been restructured and his behavior has been desirably altered. It is presumed that the alteration in behavior has occurred as a consequence of the restructuring of the perceptual field.

   All of this is mere hypothesis, however, and essentially differs little from the connectionists' approach. The cognitive theorists, although they presume to be preoccupied with the internal working of the mind, are also confined to external, observable phenomena. The cognitive theorist, instead of repetitiously presenting the same stimuli in the same pattern, juggles and re-arranges the stimuli in constantly shifting patterns. It is basically a trial-and-error method. The cause of success is not explained. The activity is merely labelled as a correct gestalt or arrangement of the perceptual field whenever the previously designated outcome is achieved.

5. Do not explain the failure or refusal of all persons to act similarly even after those persons have seen all the integral relationships within a perceptual field.

Any experienced teacher has been perplexed by children who had a high degree of insight into a particular issue or problem, yet failed or refused to think and act in the desired way. If learning were to be defined as the formation of insight, such a person must be judged as having learned, yet neither the cognitive theorists nor the author are willing to agree. For even in secular educational thought, learning cannot be said to have taken place until the desired objectives have been reached, until the sought-after response has become evident. Two examples from personal experience will illustrate.

During my student days, a professor of literature showed interest in my espousal of Calvinistic Christianity. Thinking that I understood the Calvinistic world-and-life-view quite well, I proceeded to elaborate for the sake of my mentor. To my chagrin, he corrected me on certain interpretations and added considerably to the explanation. Yet we might question whether he had ever *learned* Calvinistic Christianity, for he prided himself on being an agnostic. Closing our discussion, he said, "If I ever decide to accept Christianity, I am going to be a Calvinist." He saw the integral relationships far more clearly than I did, yet the desired response was evident in my life, and not in his. In this instance it would be permissable to say that the professor had developed a cognitive awareness of Christianity, but could one also say that he had *learned* Christianity? He did not act in accordance with my Christian beliefs, but he certainly did act in accordance with his beliefs. In his cognitive awareness, he did not believe Calvinistic Christianity to be a true explanation of life. He believed it to be false, for he persisted in his agnosticism. Technically, then, he had learned. But whether he had learned what his teachers had intended is another question.

In any dynamic interplay of personalities, the one who professes to know asks his hearers to do either of two things. The professor of knowledge asks his students either to accept the disseminated information as true, or he asks the hearer to accept as true the assertion that the disseminated information is false. For example, when a Christian teacher asks a class to learn Darwinian evolution, he is not asking the student to learn *about* evolution. Such use of the word *about* implies a response of neutrality, with which neither the teacher nor the student can be content. What the teacher really desires is that the student accept his explanation and interpretation as a true explanation of Darwinian evoluion. But more is involved. If the teacher has asserted that the evolutionary interpretation of life is a false one, that teacher hopes the students are directed to accept as true that the evolutionary interpretation is false. If the students should, despite the teacher's best efforts, conclude that Darwin was true and that the teacher was false, the teacher must admit that learning has taken place. But the teacher cannot avoid the correlary conclusion that it is wrong, unchristian learning rather than right, Christian learning.

The second example involves a typical boy, my own son. Our goal as parents was to teach him to hang up his clothes. We explained to him the importance of keeping a neat closet and showed him how to carry out our wishes. After such procedure failed to bring the desired results, discipline was administered. Questioning followed further failures. Did he understand? Did he have insight? Yes, the level of understanding was more than sufficient, but we found ourselves using the common phrase, "When will you ever learn?"

The same phrase has often been used by exasperated teachers. After watching junior and senior high students persistently make simple spelling and computation errors, teachers are likely to ask, "Will you people ever learn?" The point is this: learning must involve a desired response. Correct insights are not enough; behavior must correspond to them. The commonly accepted proposition among both cognitive and connectionist theorists is that learning must produce a change in behavior. With this proposition I agree.

But learning must also involve the stimuli and the non-observable activity within the learner. It is inadequate to say that the stimulus or insight constitutes learning, but it is also inadequate to say that the response or change of behavior constitutes learning. Jaarsma came dangerously close to that mistake when he wrote, "We come a little closer to the true nature of learning when we see it defined as a change of behavior resulting from experience. If one's response to a given situation is different this week from last week, one is said to have learned" (*Human Development, Learning and Teaching*, p. 169).

Although the word *change* in this instance may have been used to indicate the total process which produced the new behavior pattern, the phrase normally refers to the new behavior pattern as compared with the old. When used in this traditional sense, the definition "learning is a change of behavior" is incomplete and incorrect. Defining it in that way would be analagous to saying that a motor is horsepower. Although the two cannot be separated, the horsepower is a product of the motor and not synonymous with it. So, too, with learning. Learning is an internal something with outward manifestations. The change of behavior that results from learning can be measured and observed, but learning itself can not. Since the change of behavior is indicative of internal activity, it thus becomes theoretically and practically safe to say that we can usually tell when learning has taken place.

Another, somewhat different approach to learning also deserves attention. Although first stated by Aristotle, the idea has gained recent attention because of its popularization by the Progressives. It is best summed up by the phrase, "We learn by doing." In Aristotle's *Nico-machean Ethics, Book II*, this concept is expressed in the following words:

> Virtues . . . we acquire by first having actually practiced them, just as we do the arts. We learn an art or craft by doing the things that we shall have to do when we have learned it: for instance, men become builders by building houses, harpers by playing on the harp. Similarly we become just by doing just acts, temperate by doing temperate acts, brave by doing brave acts. (Quoted from *Three Thousand Years of Educational Wisdom*, Robert Ulich, ed., p. 78.)

Extending this concept, we could say that a person learns to read by reading. He learns to write by writing. He learns to obey by obeying. He learns to swim by swimming.

Such an answer to our basic questions about learning may seem highly satisfying at first glance. No troublesome definitions to bother us. Just an easy solution to the whole problem of learning. Easy, that is, until one tries to practice it.

For the sake of analyzing this concept, let us take the example of a child who wants to learn to read. After being approached with the request that we teach him, we could simply respond: "We learn to read by reading. Therefore, start reading." The child obviously would be hopelessly frustrated unless we charitably and sensibly changed our method of instruction. A second example will also illustrate the danger of such a theory. It is cited here, not to be facetious, but because it is rumored to have been tried with recruits in the United States Navy. In attempting to teach sailors how to swim, the "instructors" reportedly dumped the non-swimmers into a pool. After all, we learn to swim by swimming, and no one learns to swim on a dry deck. (It is also reported that several survived and are now swimming nicely.)

These examples should illustrate two important ideas. The first is obvious: doing is impossible unless preceded by explanation of some sort. This explanation may be visible example or oral instruction, or both. The swimming teacher will have to explain the kinds of body movement required and may have to give additional actual or filmed demonstration. And the reading teacher, of course, will have to make extensive explanations about letters, syllables, and sounds.

The second lesson one should draw from these examples is that there is, after all, a definition of learning implied in Aristotle's discussion. The implied definition, which was formally articulated by William James, is "learning is habit formation." If such a definition were accepted as a correct and true definition, then the concept of learning by doing must also be accepted.

164

But the definition "learning is habit formation" is far from acceptable, for it is more deficient than any of the other theories already discussed. This Jamesian definition pretends to explain only that part of the total learning process which follows the first desired response. It neglects to explain the appearance of the first desired response, and also ignores the internal activity of the learner and the stimuli that impinge upon the learner.

At the same time, this concept of learning as habit formation does have something significant to add to our total perspective: the term learning is not correctly applied to a single, unrepeated response. Learning must involve a notably extended change of behavior. For example, if a child were instructed to obey a certain rule, and then promptly complied, we might be inclined to judge that he had learned. If, on subsequent days, however, the child did not obey that rule, we would be right in reversing judgment and saying that the child had not learned.

In order to formulate an adequate definition of learning, several concepts must be included. Some of these concepts, stated here as propositions about learning, will conform to truths already disclosed by the partial, incomplete explanations of the connectionist and cognitive theoreticians. These propositions are as follows:

1. All learning involves the connection of stimuli and responses.
2. All learning involves an internal activity of the learner.
3. Because learning involves the connection of stimuli with responses, as well as with internal activity, the learner must internalize these stimuli through one of the five senses.
4. All learning presupposes a cognitive encounter with the object or idea to be learned, but also presupposes encounter in the physiological, emotional, and social dimensions of man: in *all* the functions of man's whole-being integrity as God's image-bearer.
5. Any comprehensive definition of learning must be expressive of man's organic unity and of his spiritual-moral relationship to God.
6. Any correct understanding of learning must include the direct involvement of God as well as the horizontal relationships between man and his environment.
7. All learning must express itself in some outward manifestation. This overt demonstration will be a changed way of thinking, feeling, acting, or communicating.

Remembering man's organic unity, and mindful of all the above propositions, we offer the following definition: Learning is the process of accepting for oneself that which one comes to believe is true. By

165

formulating our definition in this way, the truths expressed by the connectionist, cognitive, and pragmatic theorists are not denied, while their basic weaknesses are avoided. Also, belief again becomes the basis for conduct or behavior. Furthermore, the relationship between learning and the psychological needs of the learner can be understood. Jaarsma illustrated this relationship when he wrote,

> When one has come to accept truth for self-discipline, one has truly learned. There may be momentary slips into deviations, but they represent what one has learned to do under certain conditions. The evidence of heart acceptance is not in the isolated doing, but in the consistency of integrated action.
> It should become increasingly evident how understanding and a feeling of security are related to learning. These constitute the keys to acceptance. As religious beings we are relentless security seekers, and we find security only through understanding. We commit ourselves only to that which we understand or [to that which] discloses meaning to us (*Human Development, Learning and Teaching*, p. 170).
> The Scriptures tell us, and we see it evidenced in human life, that the religious being, made in the image of God, finds his final and deepest security in what he feels to be true. . . . As he forms concepts, truth is disclosed to him which he relates to himself. Truth understood in relation to felt needs cultivates a feeling-tone of identity, of being one with. Truth felt is accepted as that to which one surrenders for control. It is in this surrender that one's personality is formed (*ibid.*, p. 22).

When learning is understood as the process of accepting that which one comes to believe is true, the contemporary discussion in political editorials and council chambers about "credibility gaps" takes on special significance for teachers. Teachers, as well as politicians, government officials, and preachers can all be frustrated by credibility gaps, for all attempt to convince others of the truth of matters within their respective domains. If their credibility rating is low, truth will not be established in the minds of their constituents.

Since the establishing of truth is the heart of teaching, and the acceptance of truth at the center of learning, the statement of Pestalozzi becomes completely credible: As the child learns, so must one teach.

Practical Suggestions for Teachers

1. Be consistent in your own thought, in your administration of discipline, and in your demands on the students. Inconsistencies are more easily detected by those who observe than by those who practice them.
2. Make your life conform to your teaching. Teachers must practice what they preach. Remember that examples speak louder than words, and that teachers are always examples.

166

3. Be committed to those truths which you are attempting to teach. No one should expect others to come to firm belief in a truth if the conveyor of that truth does not firmly believe it himself.

4. Try to represent a common faith with other teachers and parents. Conflict of belief between the parent and the ones who stand *in loco parentis* is the surest way to make students rebel against the truth.

5. Avoid, especially, the "open-minded" presentation of conflicting ideas with the intention of letting the students decide. Unless the response has been predetermined by previous learning — in which case the whole procedure would be pointless — the emotional insecurity that results from making undirected decisions is damaging to further learning. Such practice makes doubt, rather than belief, the basis of action. Children want to know; they want to believe.

6. Try to be a symbol of security for the child. Children are quick to notice signs of insecurity in a teacher, and will consequently withhold allegiance to the truth of what is taught. Insecurity is a sign of doubt rather than of commitment.

The Necessity of Frustration and Success

The proposition that learning must involve permanent changes in behavior is an important one. It leads us to reflect on the whole matter of goals and objectives, as discussed in chapter eight. Schools exist and education is carried on for the purpose of bringing about changes in students. These changes are always from existing characteristics or existing modes of thought and behavior to desired characteristics or desired modes of thought and behavior. In our formulation of educational objectives, the ultimate, primary, and secondary objectives represent the desired characteristics. The existing characteristics or modes of thought and behavior are not always stated, but are always implied. For example, the ultimate objective of honoring and enjoying God forever implies that the child who has not yet experienced the restoration and sanctifying power of Christ-centered education is characterized as dishonoring God. For, as the *Heidelberg Catechism* states, "I am prone by nature to hate God and my neighbor" (Lord's Day II, Question 5). Similarly, the objective of love implies that hate (sometimes evinced by apathy) is the existing characteristic. The objective of knowledge implies that ignorance is the existing characteristic. The objective of communication skills implies that lack of such skill is the existent condition. The objective of obedience implies that disobedience is the present characteristic.

When students come to school, they come with individualized, highly differing characteristics. Some students, because of divine endowment and prior parental teaching, possess more of the desired characteristics than do others. Their behavior is already such that not many changes must be made. Some children may already be characterized by high degrees of academic diligence, obedience, knowledge, and love. Others come to school with these desired behavior traits noticeably lacking. Recognizing these differences, one will conclude that more changes will be required and expected (by God's grace) in the lives of those students who are deficient in the desired characteristics than will be required in the lives of those students who already possess the desired characteristics.

Those students who are already in possession of many of the desired characteristics the school has traditionally labelled as good. This labeling takes the forms of social approval, letter grades, honors, and report cards. By giving good reports and good grades the school is telling the student, in effect, that it does not wish to change him drastically, that he is already in possession of those characteristics that are deemed desirable. There is always need of further developing and strengthening of those characteristics — growth and maturation are also forms of change — but at least the desired responses have been developmentally evident.

No one desires change in his personal life, that is, in his existing modes of thought and behavior. Everyone — considered apart from external forces — resists change. The anti-intellectual wants to remain anti-intellectual. The liberal wants to remain a liberal. The conservative wants to remain a conservative. The Christian wants to remain a Christian. Jacques Barzun recognized this truth when he wrote,

> Even under the best conditions of fair play and deliberate spontaneity, the pupil, while needing and wanting knowledge, will hate and resist it. This resistance often makes one feel that the human mind is made of some wonderfully tough rubber, which you can stretch a little by pulling hard, but which snaps back into shape the moment you let go.
> It is exasperating, but consider how the student feels, subjected to daily and hourly stretching. "Here am I," he thinks, "with my brains nicely organized — with everything, if not in its place, at least in a place where I can find it — and you come along with a new and strange item that you want to force into my previous arrangement. Naturally I resist" (*Teacher in America*, p. 22).

Jaarsma, too, recognized the innate resistance of the learner. Correctly relating this innate resistance to the doctrine of total depravity, he said that the child resists "accepting truth and surrendering himself to it in humble obedience. Man, dead in trespasses and sins, resists the discipline of truth because he lacks righteousness" (*Human Development, Learning and Teaching*, p. 260).

C. S. Lewis, with his typical comprehensive and yet succinct expressions, gives further insight into the significance of pain. In his sanctifying little book, *The Problem of Pain*, he writes as follows:

> Now the proper good of a creature is to surrender itself to its Creator — to enact intellectually, volitionally, and emotionally, that relationship which is given in the mere fact of its being a creature. When it does so, it is good and happy. Lest we should think this a hardship, this kind of good begins on a level far above the creatures, for God Himself, as Son, from all eternity renders back to God as Father by filial obedience the being which the Father by paternal love eternally generates in the Son. This is the pattern which man was made to imitate — which Paradisal man did imitate — and wherever the will conferred by the Creator is thus perfectly offered back in delighted and delighting obedience by the creature, there, most undoubtedly, is Heaven, and there the Holy Ghost proceeds. In the world as we now know it, the problem is how to recover this self-surrender. We are not merely imperfect creatures who must be improved: we are, as Newman said, rebels who must lay down our arms. The first answer, then, to the question why our cure should be painful, is that to render back the will which we have so long claimed for our own, is in itself, wherever and however it is done, a grievous pain . . . But to surrender a self-will inflamed and swollen with years of usurpation is a kind of death. We all remember this self-will as it was in childhood: the bitter, prolonged rage at every thwarting, the burst of passionate tears, the black, Satanic wish to kill or die rather than to give in. Hence the older type of [teacher] or parent was quite right in thinking that the first step in education is "to break the child's will." Their methods were often wrong: but not to see the necessity is, I think, to cut oneself off from all understanding of spiritual laws. And if now that we are grown up, we do not howl and stamp quite so much, that is partly because our elders began the process of breaking or killing our self-will in the nursery, and partly because the same passions now take more subtle forms and have grown clever at avoiding death by various "compensations." Hence the necessity to die daily . . .
>
> The human spirit will not even begin to try to surrender self-will as long as all seems to be well with it. Now error and sin both have this property, that the deeper they are the less the victim suspects their existence; they are masked evil. Pain is unmasked, unmistakable evil; every man knows that something is wrong when he is being hurt . . . And pain is not only immediately recognizable evil, but evil impossible to ignore. We can rest contentedly in our sins and in our stupidities . . . but pain insists upon being attended to. God whispers to us in our pleasures, speaks in our conscience, but shouts in our pains: it is His megaphone to rouse a deaf world (pp. 78-81).

Wanting to introduce the study of learning in a personal way, and hoping to gain additional evidence for this concept of resistance to learning, I once surprised my classes in educational philosophy with a brief, subjective-objective questionnaire. Since the subject of learning had not previously been discussed with these students, they had no advance warning as to how the questions were to be answered. Included in the questionnaire were the following questions:

Question 1   What are two of the most significant things (or concepts) you have learned in life that have been influential in changing your life?

Answer: The respondents gave purely subjective answers without coaching as to type of answer or wording. Their responses were then placed in one of the following categories, which were later drawn up by the questioner.

Categories	Responses
spiritual	58
philosophic	27
social (friends)	17
social (family)	9
moral	5
artistic	5
vocational	2
literary	1
scientific	1

Question 3   Which of the following adjectives would best characterize your learnings referred to in No. 1?

Answers:

Categories	Responses
exhilarating	23
pleasant	26
devoid of emotion	7
frustrating	44
painful	18

One of the more interesting and admittedly gratifying results of the questionnaire came from the answers to question 3. Of the sixty-three students responding, most of them felt it necessary to use two polar adjectives to describe their learnings. On the one hand, they found their learning to be accompanied with exhilaration or pleasantness, but they also vividly recalled the frustration and pain that attended it. In discussing the results of this questionnaire with the class, the students concurred in the opinion that the feeling of frustration or pain always preceded the feeling of pleasantness or exhilaration. They were also convinced that the intensity of both the pain and the joy diminished with the lessening significance of the material.

In reviewing the secular learning theories, we noticed that little attention was focused on this aspect of learning. In the research studies of Thorndike, Spence, Guthrie, and other connectionist theorists it is significant that well-fed, contented animals were never used for experimentation. The animals always were given meager diets before the experiments. They had to be hungry. They had to be compelled by hunger pangs, by annoyance, by frustration. Yet it was only Thorndike who gave significant place to this annoyance in his theories. Interestingly, however, he too dropped this concept when he revised his theories in 1932. Skinner followed this trend of ignoring the painful aspect of learning by placing all his emphasis on reinforcement through rewards. As a result of his current popularity, the notion is becoming ever more prevalent that learning can be accomplished without pain or frustration. To this theoretical innovation the mind of modern, pleasure-seeking Americans is very receptive.

Kurt Lewin's theory of life space also gives indication of his having approached the problem, but he, too, is of little real assistance. He recognized that there is always a positive-negative counter-action in learning, as shown by his key terms "negative valence" and "positive valence." But, he, like all the other secularists, refused to allow spiritual considerations to influence his thinking. So, too, with Clark L. Hull and his formal connectionist theory. He also recognized that deprivation of food and water, plus painful stimulation were necessary factors in all animal learning situations. But he too refused to raise his theories above the animal and physiological levels: he refrained from consideration of the significant spiritual-moral learnings that give basic direction to life.

Why are pain and frustration essential to learning? Why is it that discontent with the present state of affairs must precede learning? Why is it that beginning students must feel frustrated with their inability to read before they can be taught to read? Why is it that students must feel a deep sense of guilt for their disobedience before they can learn obedience? Why is it that resistance to change is part of man's very character? Why is it that Eric Hoffer could truthfully write, "For men to plunge headlong into an undertaking of vast change, they must be intensely discontented?" (Hoffer, *The True Believer*, p. 20). Why is it that the gospel call to belief is always preceded by a call to repentance?

In one word, the answer to all these questions is the antithesis. Man is a battleground. God and His arch-enemy Satan are both operative in the life of God's creatures, and both work through human agents. God, the author of all truth, and Satan, the father of lies, are contesting for the minds and hearts of men. The child is not exempt from the battle, and the school is not a demilitarized zone. True, not all learnings that are attempted in school are equally significant, just as all battles in a war are not equally decisive. Consequently, the amount of resistance will vary from learning to learning. Learning that George Washington spent a winter at Valley Forge, for example, will be comparatively painless, for by itself such knowledge is insignificant. But learning that one's own people have been grossly inhuman and loveless to fellow humans — as has been true of the whites' treatment of the Negro — is far more significant and far more painful. Even more ultimately essential, and thus still more painful, is the learning of personal obedience to the will of God.

But the reader may object. After all, is not the best teacher the one who can teach the most while incurring the least resistance? Is it not generally recognized as sign of failure if one's students resist what is being taught? Not necessarily. Look at the Christ, called Teacher even by the Pharisees and scribes. In His work there were times when He was very popular with the people. Thousands gathered to hear His seaside and mountain-side teachings. As long as there was hope that Christ would give satisfaction to their desires for bread and for release from hated Roman oppression, the people stayed to listen. When asked to accept as true and individually relevant the truths that Christ used to induce the internal changes that would lead to eternal life, however, the crowds forsook Him. Those eternally significant changes in thought and behavior that Christ sought to effect in the lives of His hearers met with demonically violent resistance. Yet Christ remains the greatest of all teachers, the example for all Christians.

Such resistance to the truth-teaching of Christ is readily understood by the Bible reader. In the book of Isaiah, God already told His people, "Behold, I have refined you, but not like silver; I have tried you in the furnace of affliction" (Is. 48:10, RSV). With learning understood as the refining or changing of a person from less desirable to more desirable relationship to Christ the Truth, the relationship of pain and frustration to learning becomes clearer. The same symbolism of fire, purging, and pain is used in Zechariah. God Himself, there speaking through the prophet, says, "I will bring the third part through the fire, and will refine them as silver is refined, and will try them as gold is tried" (Zech. 13:9).

Again the reader may object. Such purgational symbolism has nothing to do with the learning that goes on in school. Taken literally, perhaps not; but taken metaphorically, indubitably yes. God, as the teacher of righteousness, has spoken to the Christian teacher through this language: the learnings, the changes that lead to sanctification and righteousness are not arrived at painlessly. If there were a less painful way, God, as loving Father, would use it; but, He, like the human father

172

referred to it in Hebrews 12 (who obeys God's example), disciplines because of love.

Malachi, prophecying the earthly appearance of Christ, and foretelling the Jews' reaction, continues the cleansing emphasis. "But who may abide the day of his coming?" he wrote, "And who shall stand when he appeareth? for he is like a refiner's fire, and like fuller's soap: and he shall sit as a refiner and purifier of silver: and he shall purify the sons of Levi, and purge them as gold and silver, that they may offer unto the Lord an offering in righteousness" (Mal. 3:2-3). Yet Jesus, when He came, could sit peacefully in a boat and teach the crowds on the hillsides. He never subjected people to the stocks, or the pillories, or the stake, but His words cut like a two-edged sword and His parables remove all self-righteous facade. His questioning probed the heart, and His precepts came with authority. With them He refined and purged and pained. In this Christly tradition Saint Augustine could later write, "When a being is compelled to something better, the pain is useful, when to something worse, it is useless" (Oates, *Basic Writings of Saint Augustine*, p. 438).

In mystical but God-ignoring wonderment, Van Cleve Morris expresses the same general concept. Writing the introduction to Bernard Johnston's *Issues in Education*, he states,

> Somehow the mind of man carries on the enterprise of thought most effectively when, like an ax, it is grinding against an object somewhat but not entirely like itself, i.e., another mind. If sparks fly, as they sometimes do, their flickering light is at least a symptom that we may be getting near the cutting edge of things (p.v.).

If one is willing to accept this frictional characteristic of effective teaching, another secularized, jargon-heavy phrase will take on new meaning. That very common phrase denotes the teacher as a "creator of felt needs." The full import of this phrase frequently eludes the teacher-training students with whom the author has worked, but the description should be recognized as a polite, couched way of stating that teachers must provoke slight, controlled frustrations in the students they intend to affect. If the student has no unfilled need, if he appears smug, content, and blatantly self-sufficient, the teacher's natural and necessary response must be, not to gloat on the self-sufficiency, but to present new challenges, new problems of greater difficulty and greater complexity. In short, the wise teacher must initiate restricted frustrations, never for frustration's sake, but always toward fuller reformational development, that the student's "joy may be full" (John 16:24).

Why, then, do some teachers maintain that they never meet resistance? Why, then, do some teachers boast that they never have disci-

173

pline problems? A number of explanations might be offered, but the following ought to be principally considered. Probably those teachers have never really taught. They may have disseminated some information, but the information may have been offered on a "take it or leave it" basis. Such teachers do not easily become frustrated, but neither do they experience the joy and reward of having brought children into a true relationship to their God in Christ, to their fellowmen, and to their God's creation. A second explanation is that they probably "never bothered with" significant truths. Some teachers have an amazing instinct for the peripheral and trivial. In such situations, students do not resist. They merely exist.

Teachers must have the courage to act as God's vicegerents. They must be deeply committed to Him if they are to act as human agents responsible for bringing about Godward changes of behavior that will unavoidably and knowingly be painful. If, however, a real concern for the temporal and eternal welfare of his students is the teacher's primary motivation (for God's glory) then such instruction in the truth will certainly occur.

But this question remains. If all men resist change, why do men still seek it? What is it, for example, that the Psalmist David, after his sin with Bathsheba, could still say, "Behold, thou desirest truth within the inward parts, and in the hidden part thou shalt make me to know wisdom. Purge me with hyssop" (Ps. 51:6, 7)?

The answer lies not in man, but in the working of God. The human teacher by himself can accomplish nothing, but God works in and through each of us, giving knowledge, giving obedience, giving love, and giving freedom. God's divine revelation reminds us of this truth in the words of Proverbs 2: "Yes, if you cry out for insight and raise your voice for understanding, if you seek it like silver and search for it as for hidden treasures; then you will understand the fear of the Lord and find the knowledge of God. For the Lord gives wisdom; from his mouth come knowledge and understanding; he stores up sound wisdom for the upright" (Prov. 2:3-7, RSV). The same thought is expressed by God through the words of Jeremiah. In chapter 31, God speaks by his servant thus: "I will put my law within them, and I will write it upon their hearts" (Jer. 31:33, RSV).

With such Biblical statements, however, the empirical educational psychologist will undoubtedly disagree. This is not surprising, however, for many "realists" in the history of educational philosophy have also disagreed. Men such as Francis Bacon, René Descartes, John Locke, Rousseau, Herbart, and numerous lesser figures long ago discarded any Christian concept of epistemology. Unwilling to accept the authority of Scripture, these men wanted to know how men "really" came into possession of knowledge. Like doubting Thomas, they had to see with their eyes before they would believe. As with Thomas, Jesus answers them with the words, "Blessed are they that have not seen and yet have believed" (John 20:29). For these presumptive realists, however, the answer lay not in the working of God, but in the gap between mind and matter, as these two entities comprised their dualistic constructs. Somewhere between the mind, defined as the residue of knowledge, and matter, which encompassed all observable phenomena outside the mind, lay the key to epistemological understanding. For them, the only possible answer lay in an understanding of the senses, for the senses were the only apparent bridge between mind and matter.

In their approach to the problem of the origin of knowledge, the sensory realists of eighteenth- and nineteenth-century Europe differed little from the empirical educational psychologists of twentieth-century America. The question to which these schools have addressed themselves is essentially the same, but the language used to describe the issue differs markedly. The following figure will illustrate.

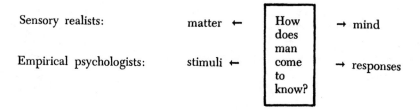

Fig. 17. The Problem

As already stated, the sensory realists attempted to solve this question by focusing their attention on the senses. But for the pseudo-scientific educational psychologists of twentieth-century America, no answer has yet been found. They continue to search frantically, beset by the devilish notion that truth can be found apart from God and His Word.

For the faithful Christian, however, intellectual calm is assured, for the answers that have been given in God's Word will be accepted as true. Although all answers have not yet been fully understood, there is also the promise that if we seek earnestly, we shall find, and if we knock, the door to Godly understanding will be opened. Then, though mysteries will remain, God will reveal to us by His Holy Spirit (who leads us into *all* truth) all that we need to know. And we also have the assurance that someday we will see God, the Teacher of righteousness and truth, face to face. "For now we see through a glass, darkly; but then face to

175

face: now I know in part, but then shall I know even as also I am known" (I Cor. 13:12).

Pressing on to those fuller answers that we have been promised, we ask how the sensory realist is to be answered. What is the role of sensory perception in the learning process? Is learning in this life confined to what we can apprehend or perceive through the senses, as the realists affirm? Somewhat surprisingly, the answer is yes. The book of Romans gives us insight into this human state of affairs, as Paul, expressing concern for the salvation of the unregenerate, says, "How then shall they call on him in whom they have not believed? and how shall they believe in him of whom they have not heard? and how shall they hear without a preacher? So then faith cometh by hearing, and hearing by the word of God" (Rom. 10:14, 17). The sense of hearing is thus stipulated as a *medium* for faith, but so are the other senses of sight and touch and taste and smell. Exhorting His disciples to renewed belief after His resurrection, Jesus instructed them to use their senses of touch and sight. He said, "Behold my hands and my feet, that it is I myself; handle me, and see" (Luke 24:39).

In our understanding of sensory perception as the God-ordained *media* for faith, all five senses must be included. Attention must not be narrowed to one or two senses as empiricists would have us do. These positivists have argued that man comes to know only as the mind comes into contact with *observable phenomena* through the senses, thus subtly suggesting that we reduce the significant senses to those of sight and, possibly, touch. According to them, that which is to be known is *material* (matter). These philosophers, in the tradition of Galileo, were rebelling against excessive dependence on the hearing sense (which was the tradition of the Roman Catholic Church) and were refusing to accept information or ideas on the basis of *authority*. They were saying, in effect. "Show me or I won't accept it," but they couched their unbelief in the persuasive postulate "Seeing is believing."

Scripture offers a different emphasis, however. The senses are not equated with believing, for the Psalmist wrote concerning the unregenerate, "They have mouths, but they speak not: eyes have they, but they see not: They have ears, but they hear not: noses have they, but they smell not: They have hands, but they handle not" (Ps. 115:5-7). The importance of the senses as a media for faith is nevertheless accepted, for God instructed His messenger to His rebellious people, "Make the heart of this people fat, and make their ears heavy, and shut their eyes; lest they see with their eyes, and hear with their ears, and understand with their heart, and convert, and be healed" (Isaiah 6:10). The same power of God over the effectiveness of the human senses is illustrated in Isaiah 44:18. In that passage it is written, "They have not

176

known nor understood; for he hath shut their eyes, that they cannot see; and their hearts, that they cannot understand."

The Christian, then, does not try to emphasize the value of one sense as compared with another sense. He makes meaningful use of them all. He uses sight, not in rebellion against his Lord, but in reading the Word which his God has given and in viewing the creation which the Almighty has fashioned. Sensory perception, for the Christian, is not the *essence* or *basis* of real knowing. It remains the *media*. The essence of knowing is *belief* or *faith*. This is what is significant. This is what makes all the difference.

But what is faith, and what is belief? It is "the substance of things hoped for, the evidence of things not seen" (Heb. 11:1). But it is also the *gift of God* which in itself is not received through the senses, but which is *applied only to* that which has come through the senses. It is the power which enables us to accept as true or reject as false those ideas and observations which we have become aware of through the senses.

Such a definition makes teaching and preaching a fundamentally necessary task. It demands of us that we cooperate to bring the young child into a cognitive awareness of God, salvation, truth, beauty, natural phenomena — of all that is eternally important. And it demands that we do this through the senses of the child in order that faith may become operative.

Sensory realists:	matter← the senses →		mind
Empirical psychologists:	stimuli ← unknown, but → searching		responses
Christian:	all that ← faith (the → is outside implanting, the self by God, of sensory perceptions in the heart of man)		the self

Fig. 18. The Answers

To define *faith* as the implanting, by God, of sensory perceptions in the heart of man is not to disagree with other Reformationally Christian meanings of the word. Faith, defined in this way, rightly attributes all human knowledge to the power of God. It is the power of God which makes possible our believing the Scriptures to be true, but it is also the power of God, working in us, which makes possible our believing a mathematical formula or a poem or a piece of music. It attributes the power of the intellect not to man, but to God.

The Christian, like the disciples in ancient Palestine, must stand "amazed at the mighty power of God" (Luke 9:43) and with new meaning pray: "Lead us not into temptation, but deliver us from evil: for thine is the kingdom, *and the power,* and the glory, for ever. Amen" (Matt. 6:13).

"For by grace are ye saved through faith; and that not of yourselves: it is the gift of God: not of works, lest any man should boast. For we are his workmanship, created in Christ Jesus unto good works, which God hath before ordained that we should walk in them" (Eph. 2:8-10).

CHAPTER XIII

EVALUATION OF EDUCATION

"I am Alpha and Omega, the beginning and the ending, saith the Lord."
(Rev. 1:8)

One of the significant aspects of any educational system is measurement or evaluation. School systems of one state are judged in comparison with school systems of other states. Schools within states are constantly being compared with other schools in the same state. Teachers are judged by parents, administrators, and supervisory boards. Students are constantly being measured by their teachers, but also by their peers. From national and international levels of judgment down to the individual student level, evaluation is an ever-present process.

But by what standard is judgment made? Is there one yardstick for measuring all that is measurable in education? Or are there many yardsticks, one for each situation? Are national systems of education judged with a different standard of judgment from that used in state systems? Are the schools of one philosophic-religious orientation judged with a different set of principles from that employed in the schools of another philosophic-religious orientation? (For example, are private Christian schools judged by the same set of standards as those by which secular public schools are judged?) And what about individual teachers: Are they all judged by the same standards? And also the pupils: Are white pupils judged by the same standards as black children? Are Christian students judged by the same standards as non-Christian students?

All of these are answer-begging questions. All of them need resolution; but the answers can be given only if we discover the standard(s), the absolute(s), by which we can make our many evaluations integral to the whole human adventure of education.

Certainly questions on evaluation are fair and fundamental questions. They need to be asked by everyone who gives leadership in education. Whoever dares not answer them is intellectually dishonest. There are always the evaders, who would like to sidetrack the question by replying that there are no valid yardsticks for making educational comparisons and judgments. These are the persons who say that comparisons and judgments really cannot be made because no two situations or schools or teachers or students are the same. They argue, moreover, that it is impossible to compare different things. Such negation would be more hon-

179

orable if the persons protesting were to stop their own comparing and evaluating. If they themselves desisted from making judgments and comparisons, their position might be tenable. But such restraint from judgment has not characterized education in the past; nor is it possible that it will be in the future. Judgment, evaluation, and comparison are a part of everyone's integrity of human-being as an image-bearer of the One True God.

As soon as the original questions about evaluation are approached, the ogre of "double standards" and "multiple standards" presents itself. The questions themselves imply that double and multiple standards are possible. To the American, reared in the tradition of justice and equality for all, such implication sounds treasonable. Of course, there may be no double standards! Of course there may be no multiple standards! If such should exist, no self-respecting American may take pride in it or condone it. Neither may any Christian.

That would be a typical American reaction. It should be no different. Neither Christian nor non-Christian should want it any other way, for inequality and injustice must inevitably result from multiple standards. Within both the American and Christian tradition justice and equality are essential blessings. By God's goodness, they have been granted, up to the present age, both to covenant-keepers and to covenant-breakers.

But such commonality does not solve the problem: By what criterion do we evaluate so as to determine whether true, quality education is being carried on? By what standard is judgment made?

Contemporary Criteria

In contemporary educational endeavor, there is an astonishing, almost inordinate amount of judging and evaluation. Recently there has been an international evaluation of mathematics instruction. Regional and state accreditation agencies make annual and bi-annual evaluations of schools from the primary to the university level. State departments of education make annual judgments of schools in their states. Civil rights advocates repeatedly compare the schools attended by white students with those attended by Negro students. All such evaluation and judgment implies that there is some standard or some set of standards by which judgment is made. Hopefully there will appear only one standard or only one cohesive set.

In this generation of hyper-specialists, few persons have sufficient vision to see beyond their little niche and cranny. Few have the all-encompassing vision which allows them to see their relationship to the whole. Primary teachers, for example, can become so engrossed in the validity and reliability co-efficients of a grade-two spelling test that they fail to see beyond the child of age eight. High school coaches can become so engrossed in their hedonistic pursuit of athletics that they come to believe that the quality of their school is determined by the size of their salaries, gyms, banquets, and trophy cases. University publicity personnel become so enamored of their files of philanthropic commitment that they find themselves judging a school's quality by the size and frequency of its collections.

But other criteria are also very common. Among the followers of James Bryant Conant, who is far more popular than he deserves to be, and among the ardent advocates of consolidation, size has become the determiner of quality. Within Conant's narrow utilitarian philosophy, a school can only be considered good if it has a specified, minimum number of students. If a school is big, it is therefore good — so goes the assumption. Among those embroiled in matters of teacher certification, the number of academic degrees and certificates held by a faculty is the prime determinant of quality. In such thinking, the school with the highest percentage of degreed and certified faculty members must be the best school, and the school with the smallest number of degreed and certified faculty members is incontrovertibly worst.

With administrators and boards, the splendor, novelty, and cost of school buildings are conjointly used as the standard of judgment. For example, the following illogical assertion may sometimes be heard, "That school really has beautiful buildings. That sure is a good school." If what were meant by such a phrase were that the school has beautiful buildings *and* is a good school, the logic could not be impugned. The phrase, however, is intended to imply that the goodness of the school is somehow consequent from the elegance of the buildings. But in schools, as in persons, the quality is not determined by external appearances. What goes on inside is crucial. Many clean-cut, well-dressed persons turn out to be criminal; and many dishonest and vicious persons live in lavish, immaculate homes.

Within the field of comparative education an important principle of evaluation has been enunciated. Among those who devote their energies to a comparison of national educational systems, there has been a growing awareness that some single principle (or measuring standard) must be employed. In its most succinct form, this principle states that quality must be determined by the measure of success. Unable to find any other yardstick, the comparative educationists have concluded that national school systems should be judged by the degree to which those systems meet the objectives that they have set up for themselves. For example, when making comparative evaluations it would be unfair to criticize the schools of Canada for not having taught vocational skills well if it had not been their intent to teach vocational skills. Simply be-

181

cause one national system does not show the same results as another national system is no justification for rating the first system as inferior or the second system as superior.

The same principle of evaluation can be applied to schools within a country or state. School X in suburbia can not be rated superior for having taught foreign languages while school Y in rural Podunk is rated inferior for not having taught foreign languages. At the same time, if it could be clearly demonstrated that school Y should have taught foreign languages, but failed or refused to do so, that school could be rated as poor for not having done what was required. The same principles apply to teachers and to students, for it would be gross unfairness to judge a school, teacher, or student for not having done well that which he was not even intended to do.

In order to use this principle comprehensively, it becomes apparent that the objectives of a teacher or school or nation must first be clearly articulated. Then, with objectives vividly in mind, one can determine quality by measuring the degree to which the objectives have been met. If school X meets its objectives 60% of the time, and if school Y meets its objectives 90% of the time, regardless of what those objectives are, it now becomes evident that school Y is better, by the success standard, than school X. If teacher A has set as her objective the teaching of allegiance to racial segregationist principles and is 80% successful, and if teacher B has set as her objective the teaching of Christian principles of integration and is 70% successful, teacher A must be rated as being better, despite the fact that her objective is sinful — as well as humanitarianly disagreeable. Since schools are concerned with quality, and since teacher A is the better of the two, it would seem reasonable that teacher A should be employed and teacher B by-passed.

But there is obviously a corrupting fly in the dialectical ointment: quality and success simply cannot be equated. If they were synonymous, the schools of Nazi Germany would have to be judged as being qualitatively superior to the schools of the United States. Yet no humane person would want his children educated in one of the Hitler-dominated schools. Still, they were amazingly successful, as Zeimer testifies in *Education for Death: the Making of a Nazi*. In the field of formal, sectarian religion, Mormonism would have to be judged one of the best religions, not because it most closely approximates the truth, but because of its amazing missionary success.

American citizens are certain of disclaiming the superior status of the Nazi schools, and Reformed Protestant Christians are certain of disclaiming the superior status of the Mormon church. In fact, success is desirable only if right goals are being pursued.

Despite the inadequacy and falsity of success as a standard for judgment, the determining of effectiveness must go on. Schools and teachers must try to determine whether their objectives are being met. In doing this, however, certain difficulties and limitations must be recognized; but those limitations should not force a change in direction. The first of these difficulties is that the success of schools in meeting their various objectives is not easily measurable. In the philosophy that we have developed as the Biblical-Christian truth, the ultimate aim is the increased honor and praise of God through the lives of the students (as well as the teachers) being educated. That is, we have said that the only validating aim is the producing of responsible, effective citizens of the Kingdom of Christ as it is already evident here on earth. The extent to which Christian schools meet this ultimate objective is not easily determined. Christ-believing teachers, although constantly attempting such discernment, cannot adequately measure the heart-commitments of their students and graduates. For such measurement there are no neat mathematical scales and objective instruments of testing. The scribes and Pharisees of Jesus' day, for example, boasted that they were glorifying God, but Jesus saw through their piosity and called them hypocrites. "By their works ye shall know them" seems, often, to be counterbalanced by "judge not that ye be not judged."

The objectives of love, freedom, and obedience are especially difficult to measure in their degrees of attainment. Again, pretense, peer pressure, and local mores serve to cast shadows and distort appearances so that it becomes almost impossible to determine whether students have grown in these virtues. Even in knowledge, reliable measurement is extremely difficult. It is only, in fact, when one deals with secondary and tertiary objectives that measurement seems to become easier. Moreover, the fact that success in reaching ultimate and primary goals is difficult to measure, further detracts from the use of success as a standard for judging quality.

Earlier in our discussion, attention was focused on the distinction between education as *product* and education as *process*. In our observations on success as a possible yardstick for determining quality, our attention was directed to education as product. Because it is almost impossible to determine whether our students have acquired the product that we call education, we devise all kinds of peripheral and incidental goals, falsely considering them products to be attained. The number of volumes on library shelves, the number of films in the audio-visual supply, the number of technological gadgets at teachers' disposal, and the brilliance of band uniforms — these become our goals, our ends toward which we move. In short, our insistence on equating quality with quantity has become an obsession. Any financial retrenchment is met with loud outcries that quality is being eroded.

Upon attaining these unessential pseudo-products, we activate the publicity committee and oil the propaganda machine — all with the hope that the rest of the world will heed and move our quality rating one notch higher. But even such shenanigans are not productive of contentment and inner peace. Those wildly pursued goals, along with all those of our predecessors, are mere mirages. Quality is not to be found in their pursuit, but new frustration and self-contempt are.

Because of such recurring disappointment, state and national leaders have subtly and devilishly substituted the process for the product. Unable to measure neatly the quality of education *as product*, we have been led to believe that *uniform process* will produce *uniform product*. It is reasoned, albeit wrongly, that similar processes will produce the similar products that the advocates of the statist educational concept ardently desire. Twisting and perverting the concept of equality — a Godly virtue, if defined rightly, which is agreeable to Christian and non-Christian alike — state departments of instruction have insisted on uniform process. This insistence has been supported by legislatures and courts to such an extent that conformity to the process employed by the majority has become the yardstick of quality. To be approved and accredited as a good school, that is, as a school of acceptable quality, a school must conform in its process to those specifications laid down by the federal and state power structure. If a school does not conform, it is labelled deficient and removed from accreditation and approved lists.

Such a standard of judgment is insidious in its influence and crushing in its power. It makes might the determiner of right and causes the definition of quality to shift with every political current. The process becomes all-important, whereas the product should be. The process should always have its justification as a means to the end, but in such systems the means has become both the beginning and the end.

Nevertheless, fixing our attention on uniform process as a pseudo-yardstick of quality also has its benefits. Such focus reminds us that there ought truly to be considerable uniformity in process. There ought also to be far greater agreement on the choice of objectives. All schools would improve by working toward the objectives of God-honoring love, obedience, freedom, and knowledge. Also, there ought to be far greater agreement on the choice of a firm and durable foundation. If there should not be multiple standards for judging quality, neither should there be multiple bases for education: and neither should there be conflicting sets of objectives.

The Normative Standard

But what is the only sure measure of quality? For Christian and non-Christian alike the only valid approach lies with the truth or falsity of what is taught and what is learned. If a teacher, whether by word or example, by precept or action, communicates that which is false, that teacher is of inferior quality. By the same token, if a teacher communicates that which is true, that teacher is of superior quality.

The same principle holds true for the objectives that a teacher or school or national system has set for itself. Even though a specific teacher or school or system has had success, the determination of quality must always be decided by the truth or falsity of the goals that have been established and the progress made toward them. If a teacher, in violation of the authorities' expressed demands, communicated the skill of theft by pointed switchblade, the authorities would find ready justification for dismissal on the basis of improper teaching, success or failure not withstanding.

But such relationship of objectives to quality leaves our basic question still unanswered. For by what standard is the truth or falsity of objectives determined? Obviously, to determine their truth or falsity, their authenticity and validity, one must go back to the basis from which they are derived. If even that is false, unwisely chosen, then there can be no hope for good, quality, true education.

The Christian, however, has a sure knowledge and a hearty confidence that his foundation is eternally true. Having this hearty confidence, a single standard of quality not only becomes possible for him, it becomes a necessary concomitant of his total faith-commitment.

The quality of education is determined by the proximity of that education to truth. Since God Incarnate (the Christ) is Truth, and since the Word is the divinely inspired revelation of the God of Truth, the quality of education is determined by its proximity to Christ and the Bible. Quality is not determined by material wealth, by high salaries, by the size of audio-visual collections, by academic degrees, by certificates, by buildings, or even by any secular standard of success. It is determined by the relationship of the total process and the total product to Christ, who is "The image of the invisible God, the first-born of all creation; for in him all things were created, in heaven and on earth, visible and invisible, whether thrones or dominions or principalities or authorities — all things were created through him and for him. He is before all things, and in him all things hold together. He is the head of the body, the church; he is the beginning, the first born from the dead, that in everything he might be pre-eminent. For in him all the fulness of God was pleased to dwell, and through him to reconcile to

185

himself all things, whether on earth or in heaven, making peace by the blood of his cross" (Col. 1:15-20).

"Christian education is education *in Christ,* and presupposes a certain relationship of the person who receives it to Christ. Eliminate that relationship and the education ceases at once to be Christian for him who receives it" (Allen, Roland, *The Spontaneous Expansion of the Church,* p. 122).

If any person desires to know the quality of a particular teacher, of a specific school, or of a certain system of schools, that person need only determine the proximity of that teacher, that school, or that system to the inscripturated Word of God and to the Christ, who is the Word of God Incarnate. If anyone wishes to know whether the schools of Russia are better schools than those of America, let him determine the relationship of those schools to the God of the Scriptures. If anyone desires to find out whether school X in suburbia is better than school Y in rural Podunk, let him examine the relationship of those schools to the Word of God and to Christ the Truth.

But such may seem too narrow for all except the fundamentalist palate. However, such need not be so. The Truth of God is all comprehensive. In it can be found the only true description of the student and the teacher. In it can be found the valid goals of love, obedience, knowledge, and freedom. In it can be found illuminating examples of the teaching-learning process. In it can be found the only sure measure of evaluation.

If a teacher does not conform to that model in his formulation of goals, in his insistence on discipline, or in his establishing of values and priorities, that teacher is not deserving of the appellation "quality." Though that teacher "have the gift of prophecy, and understand all mysteries, and all knowledge; and though [that teacher] have all faith, so that [he] could remove mountains, and have not love [for his students], [he] is nothing" (I Cor. 13:2).

The written revelation of God is the only yardstick of quality. It is the only criterion by which men may judge in education and elsewhere. For in it God speaks. And God speaks only truth.

186

QUESTIONS FOR DISCUSSION

1. Trends and emphases in evaluation are extremely influential in determining teachers' attitudes and ideals. Due to the necessity of articulating quantitative differences in mass schooling, attention is often shifted from the significant concern for *quality* to the less significant concern for *quantity.*

    (a) What is the relationship between quantity and quality? Can the two be totally divorced?

    (b) What dangers are attendant on teachers' day-to-day involvement with measurement of outcomes of immediate objectives?

    (c) Are qualitative concerns necessarily diminished as class and school sizes increase? If so, why?

2. Ortega y Gassett makes the following observations in his book *Meditations on Quixote:*

"The *minimum* is the measuring unit in the realm of quantity, but in the realm of values, the *highest* values are the measuring unit."

"The heart of man does not tolerate an absence of the excellent and supreme, and so the ranks are filled by objects and persons less and less fit for them."

    (a) On the basis of these comments, what would be the criterion for judging a diamond? a person? a teacher?

    (b) Whom would you consider to be a *perfect* teacher? What teaching tools or technological devices did He use? What were His primary characteristics as teacher?

    (c) Would it be impractical to attempt to imitate the highest example or pursue the highest ideal?

    (d) If we stop measuring values by their highest possibility, what inevitably happens to our standards?

3. James B. Conant has observed, "It is hardly necessary to emphasize that on the quality of the teachers the quality of the education must ultimately depend" (*The American High School Today*, pp. 38-9).

    (a) If the quality of education *ultimately* depends on the quality of teachers, no further questions may be asked and the issue must be considered as resolved. Does Conant resolve the issue? What obvious, additional question must be asked?

    (b) Are teachers first, foremost, and always persons? If so, what determines the quality of persons?

4. In their textbook, *Teaching in Elementary School*, Marie A. Mehl and her co-authors comment,

"The greatest asset of a teacher is to have an understanding of human nature. The humane qualities of teachers that are rated high are those which tend to regard the personalities of children and to give them a feeling of security. In recent years the need of American children for affection and for a sense of security has been greatly intensified by several social and economic changes" (p. 483).

(a) Does every teacher have an understanding of human nature?

(b) Are teachers' basic understandings of human nature ultimately true or ultimately false?

(c) What is the primary source of knowledge for an understanding of human nature?

(d) Does the quality of a school decline in direct relationship to its diminishing ability or desire to enforce discipline?

(e) Are the basic problems of inner city students lack of love, lack of firm and consistent discipline, and lack of security? If so, will an increase in technological devices or elaborate classrooms alleviate their problems? What will?

5. Consistency has been declared a jewel. Is it logical and essential that the philosophic basis also represent the normative standard for determining quality?

PART II

RELATED PROBLEMS

CHAPTER XIV

IS TEACHING A PROFESSION?

The essence of living is loving, and the essence of loving is giving.

Is teaching a profession or is it merely an employment — a vocation? This question is repeatedly asked by many, both within and without the ranks of those called teachers. It is asked by teachers, not out of idle curiosity, but out of desire for the prestige that is conferred by the word profession. If this term can validly be appropriated by those engaged in the teaching function, not only will teachers assume greater respectability, but the undesirable implications of the word "vocation" as occupation will be avoided. By those who would depreciate the work and worth of teachers, the question is asked with derogatory emphasis. Whether such disjunction of "vocation" and "profession" is defensible is not our immediate concern.

In order to determine whether teaching is, or is not, a profession, we must engage in what is by now an habitual necessity. We must attempt a definition of the word; for if we say that teaching is a profession, or is not a profession, it is implied that we know the meaning of "profession."

Webster's New Collegiate Dictionary defines the term as follows: A profession is "the occupation, if not commercial, mechanical, agricultural, or the like, to which one devotes onself; a calling; as, the profession of arms, of teaching; the learned professions of theology, law, and medicine." Teachers who trust in Webster may be warmed by such a definition, for teaching is included in those occupations that are lexicographically labelled "profession." The case is closed; the problem is affirmatively resolved.

But the question is not really answered. If *Webster's* is to be approved, if this answer is to be definitive, very few occupations will incontrovertibly claim the appellation "profession"; for only arms (the military), teaching, theology, medicine, and law are listed. By whim, tradition, or unexplained rationale, "commercial, mechanical, agricultural, or the like" occupations are denied the prestige of "professional" denomination. How is such definition to be considered? Is the list of "professions" complete with five, and if not, which occupations are to be added so as to make it complete? Is it justifiable automatically to exclude commercial, mechanical, and agricultural occupations? Is the banker to be arbitrarily excluded? And are the merchant, the highly trained diesel mechanic, the architect, the musician, and the farmer relegated to lower societal status because their work is merely vocational and not professional?

Obviously, *Webster's* definition is inadequate. Yet it is highly contemporary, for it attempts definition by empirical evidence, by a simply descriptive norm. In a society such as ours, one that is entranced by "science" and the empirical approach, such a definition may be unquestioningly accepted; but from such an arbitrary definition we will not be able to arrive at a true understanding of the term "profession."

Any attempt to define the word on a positivistic, empirical-evidence basis will prove invalid. If one attempts to list professions (for example: law, medicine, theology, teaching), the implication is very clear that the person making the list already has a definition of the word he is trying formally, self-consciously, to define. He has previously formulated a definition and now is citing examples of what he has unthinkingly (subrationally) defined. If it is already known what a profession is — and any listing is a practical assertion of such knowledge — then any further definition is superfluous and redundant. We must simply trust that those who have tacitly defined the term have done so adequately, and that they are willing to share their preconceived notions. But, as Arthur Bestor rightly asserts, "Educationists are morbidly self-conscious about the standing of their profession. They exhort one another to be 'professional-minded', and each one feels his pulse from time to time to make sure it has the right professional beat. Beneath it all, however, lies a frightened uncertainty concerning the exact nature of a profession."[1]

On the other hand, if we do not know what a profession is, and consider a definition necessary, then any listing is invalid because we do not know what it is that constitutes a profession. And not knowing what a profession is, any definition by example becomes farcical.

As we cannot progress with the method used by Webster, we must attempt a second and an even more common technique. With this method, definition is attempted by the delineation of characteristics. By listing the characteristics of professions we will, hopefully, come to a clearer understanding and, thus, to satisfactory definition. Some of the characteristics which are commonly ascribed to "professions" are listed below. A profession is an occupational group:

1. Which has the power to regulate its membership;
2. Which is autonomous in setting standards for practice;

---

[1] Bestor, "The Professional Standing of Classroom Teachers," *Issues in Education: An Anthology of Controversy,* Bernard Johnston, editor, Houghton Mifflin Co., Boston, 1964, p. 34.

3. Which has its own code of ethics;
4. Which requires specialized preparation, preferably resulting in a college degree, as a requisite for membership;
5. Which has the power to internally police its membership (through censure or expulsion);
6. Which has as its primary motivation that of service; and
7. Which engages in a unique function.

Abraham Flexner, highly touted advocate of teaching as profession, enumerates these six criteria of professions:

1. They involve essentially intellectual operations.
2. They derive their raw materials from science and learning.
3. They work up this material to a practical and definite end.
4. They possess an educationally communicable technique.
5. They tend toward self-organization.
6. They are becoming increasingly altruistic in nature.[2]

This list, which has been endorsed by the National Education Association, was drafted more than three decades ago. But because of the continuously changing concept of "professions," two additional criteria formulated by Myron Lieberman are considered necessary to bring this list up to date. By his judgment, professions also:

7. Enjoy a broad range of autonomy for both the individual practitioners and for the occupational group as a whole; and
8. Require an acceptance by the practitioners of broad personal responsibility for judgments made and acts performed within the scope of professional autonomy.[3]

Adding the two Lieberman criteria to Flexner's original six makes the two sets of characteristics essentially similar. This likeness exists, not by inexplicable coincidence, but for reasons which will become evident in the following paragraphs.

Any attempt, such as the above, to list the characteristics of a profession should precipitate a legitimate question: From what source are these characteristics derived, that is, are these characteristics arbitrarily chosen by the person composing the list? If they are, then we must

---

[2]Stinnett, T.M., "The Current Status of the Teaching Profession," *Crucial Issues in Education*, 3rd ed., Ehlers and Lee, editors, Holt, Rinehart and Winston, 1965, p. 307.
[3]*Ibid.*, p. 308.

accept all claims to professional standing and all definitions. Since all men are considered equal, all groups and all persons must have the right to submit their lists and their definitions. Obviously the result would be meaningless multiplicity of interpretation. "Professionals" would have no set of standards or criteria outside of themselves by which to be judged. A "profession" would then be anything a "professional group" says it is.

But we need not worry about such professional chaos, for the listed characteristics are not derived arbitrarily. They are drawn selectively from that roster of occupations which has previously been labelled "professions." What we have then is a dizzying example of circular reasoning. By selectively drawing characteristics from those occupations that whet the human appetite for God-denying autonomy, the proponents of "professionalism" seek to strengthen the claim of their occupational group to membership with the self-designated elite. And, by limiting the list of professional occupations, they seek more exclusive ownership of those ennobling traits that they wish to be associated with themselves. The following figure may help to illustrate their neatly monopolistic reasoning:

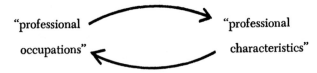

Fig. 19. The Circular Route to Professionalism

Why should those persons whose occupations are notably intellectual engage in such giddy reasoning? Are they not capable of recognizing their own fallacies? The answer lies not with the mental acuity of those who argue thus, but with the incredible irony that they have not been taught to examine fundamentally their own claims and motivations. But there is also Biblical reason to believe that this uncritical stance is deliberate, for this approach to professionalism is not an objective, neutral approach. It is an expression of an underlying philosophic bias: it is an expression, at bottom, of the classical humanist tradition which has its roots in the Platonic conception of man. This classical humanist emphasis, confronted by the scientific humanism of the twentieth century, has temporizingly capitulated to the positivist by attempting to assimilate (indigestible) empirical methodology.

The contemporary approach to professionalization is a manifestation of the humanistic philosophies which have previously been judged unacceptable by the Christian. Recognizing this, the Christian finds himself at a crucial juncture. Shall he dismiss all consideration of professional standing? Or shall he redeem the professional concept for Christ's glory by redefining the term? The latter course is obviously preferable, for the Apostle Paul encourages us, not only to cast down vain imaginations "and every high thing that exalteth itself against the knowledge of God," but also to bring "into captivity every thought to the obedience of Christ" (II Cor. 10:5).

Our assignment, then, is clear. We must attempt a Christian definition: We must consciously proceed from a Scriptural religious-philosophic position and seek to avoid the pitfalls of the empirical approach. Moreover, in doing so, we must strive for consistency with all the points of our previously articulated philosophy. We must recognize, for example, that all men have worth in God's sight, for all are His creatures. We may not denigrate the manual occupations nor may we exalt the intellectual, for Christ was as wonderfully willing to commission publicans and fishermen as He was to disciple and employ the scholar Paul and the physician Luke. We must also deal with individuals primarily and with groups secondarily, for the person's relationship to truth and to virtue is first and finally a decisively individual one. Also, we must recognize the fact that "professional" is a derivative of "profess." And "to profess" means "to vow," "to acknowledge," "to own," "to proclaim." Now, by correctly understanding man's prophetic function as that of outwardly owning, of proclaiming the truth of God, we can see the very close relationship between man as professional and man as prophet. Finally, we must consider that the term "professional" suggests commendation, that it implies an exceptional service.

With these criteria to guide us, we adduce the following re-definitions: (1) A professional is any person who *professes to know* (both the how and the why of) some phase of human culture more profoundly than does the rest of society; whose *primary motivation* is that of loving service to fellowman; and who has the *authority to act* on the knowledge given to him by God. (2) A profession is any occupation which is predominantly composed of persons who display the three characteristics enumerated in (1) above.

In this definition there is, clearly, ample room for teachers. The teacher who understands his theoretic and functional relationship to Christ-centered truth and who dedicates his life to proclaiming that truth to students rightly claims the nomination "professional." But, the teacher who blindly follows a tradition (whether Christian or anti-Christian) does not deserve the honorary designation.

If teachers collectively evince the attributes mentioned in our definition, then teaching deserves to be labelled a profession. If, however, the aggregate of teachers displays an attitude of self-seeking, or luxuriates in the relative ease of methodological discussion (the how) without ever examining religious-philosophic justification (the why), then teaching is merely another "vocation" in the most unbiblical and debased use of that beautifully significant and potentially Christ-praising word.

Chapter XV

GOVERNMENT SUBSIDY TO NONPUBLIC SCHOOLS

Should federal, state and local governmental funds be made available for private and parochial schools? This question is both current and controversial as evidenced by the space devoted to it in such books as *Crucial Issues in Education* and by the volume of articles and letters which have appeared in the nation's press. In addition, litigation on this matter has repeatedly been brought to state and federal courts during the last few decades.[1]

When the question of public funds, often erroneously dubbed "federal aid," for private and parochial schools is broached, one frequently finds it necessary and difficult to arrive at a specific definition of the point at issue. With current discussion on public aid involving many different forms of aid, it must first be determined whether the argument concerns income tax deductions for tuition, released time programs, shared time programs, free public transportation, federal and state scholarship offerings, or free distribution of textbooks to all school children. Even if this narrowing down were satisfactorily accomplished, it would be necessary to determine whether the principals in the discussion were members of CEF (Citizens for Educational Freedom) or POAU (Protestants and Other Americans United) or non-aligned. Still further, the question should be broached as to whether the discussion is principial in nature or aimed at the practicality and workability of existing and planned programs. If it is principial, are the arguments centering on the constitutionality of such aid? Are they concerned with justice and equality for all? Are they concerned with the nature and preservation of a pluralistic and democratic society? Are they arguing from an historical point of view and marshalling precedents?

Most of the publicized discussion seems to imply that "federal aid" or public funds is a bane or blessing which hopefully will or will not descend upon our society when the next legislative session convenes.

---

[1] Four of the most famous cases, as cited by Hamilton and Mort in *The Law and Public Education,* are those listed below:

    a. Cochran vs. Louisiana State Board of Education. (1930)

    b. Everson vs. Board of Education of Ewing Township. (1947).

    c. McCollum vs. Board of Education of School District no. 71, Champaign County, Illinois. (1948)

    d. Zorach vs. Clauson. (New York, 1952)

This implication that public funds for private and parochial schools is a thing of the future helps further to cloud the issue, because many instances of it are already in existence. In 1930 the United States Supreme Court decided that a Louisiana law making free textbooks available to all parochial and private schools was not unconstitutional. For more than a decade after World War II the enrollment in private and parochial colleges increased sharply due to the benefits of the G.I. Bill. At least three states, Michigan, New Jersey, and New York, now provide free public transportation to children in attendance at other than public schools. The federal milk and hot-lunch subsidy programs are also nondiscriminatory, as are National Science Foundation grants and National Defense Education Act funds. Because of action by Congress during 1965 we can now add to existing programs Public Law 89-10.

Nevertheless, the debate goes on while the recipients greedily accept the benefits. It almost seems as though everyone enjoys the 'moving impasse.' CEF members make bold preachments against "federal aid to education" while clamoring for equality of distribution when it comes. A notable exception to such a stance is that taken by the 1965 General Synod of the Missouri Lutheran Church when they voted by a two-to-one margin to refuse acceptance of public funds for their educational programs. Such action arouses many questions, but it also serves to further divide the issue between the points: "Shall public funds be offered?" and "Shall public funds be accepted when they are offered?"

Because of its many facets, as enumerated in part above, the issue almost defies concise definition. For the same reason, it seems difficult to find a common ground or battlefield for debate on which to clarify and resolve the question. If one chooses the ground of constitutionality, he finds himself bouncing between the "child benefit theory" and the First and Fourteenth Amendments to the Constitution. If one chooses to argue the questions of equality and justice, he finds himself in a heady type of discussion, in the likes of which even Plato and Socrates found it necessary to backtrack so as not to lose their way. If one chooses to argue the economic theories inherent in any such programs, he runs the risk of being labeled either "right-winger" or "pink," and then he either withdraws from embarrassment or loses his right reason in a fit of indignation. If one chooses to argue the necessity of maintaining a pluralistic society, he finds no agreement as to whether pluralism demands a one-school system where everybody acquiesces to everybody else's beliefs, or whether it demands diversified school systems where nobody acquiesces to anybody else's beliefs.

Any argument concerning the preservation of a pluralistic society will receive additional attack from those who rightly insist on grounding all of their argument in the foundation of Scripture. In a world marked and scarred by the antithesis, the committed Christian will Biblically argue, the preservation of pluralism is satisfactory to neither Christ nor Satan. The Christian may not rest content with claiming only segments of America for Christ; he must work actively, militantly, and daily, striving to bring all of America into subjection to the King of Kings. The Christian will further prick the pluralistic bubble by recognizing that the goal of pluralism, looming deceptively as a truce between antithetical factions, is actually a psychedelic mirage of Satan to delude the Christian.

The entire issue obviously will continue to produce more heat than light. All this emotion may serve to prick or salve consciences, but it does little to settle the issue. Even if we consider the question of the separation of church and state to be an age-old problem with which the formulators of the Constitution struggled, we must recognize that the problem remains and will not disappear because of our historical and philosophical naivete.

Assuming that the solution does not lie with any of the arguments set forth above, where then can we look? If we cannot agree on the surface issues, we will have to go beneath the surface and reclarify some of our underlying assumptions. To do this, a number of basic questions must be asked. Many of these questions have been asked previously in this volume, some in altered and some in identical form. They are repeated here, not for repetition's sake, but because this crucial issue, too, must be resolved by a re-examination of fundamental questions.

The first of these questions is this: On what authority or ultimate basis do we engage in education and make necessary decisions regarding that education? Is our authority certain human pronouncements such as our Constitution? our state laws? our federal laws? Do we use as our authority whatever practices and mores are current and socially acceptable? Do we operate from the pragmatic assumptions that whatever is workable and successful is therefore good and necessary? Or is our authority the sovereign, unchanging God who exists from eternity and has commanded His created beings to "Train up a child in the way he should go"? (Prov. 22:6) Other authorities could be suggested, but whichever one we choose, that choice is going to go a long way toward answering the question with which we are confronted.

Once we have determined that authority, what do we find the primary function or purpose of education, as defined by that authority, to be? If we choose a legal system as our authority, would the function of education then be that of exalting the character of man for his own sake? If we chose the "state" or government as our authority, would the primary purpose then be that of serving and preserving the "state" as our recent National Defense Education Act implies? If we chose the pragmatic, utilitarian, or existential philosophies as our basis, would the aim of education then be that of improving our social and civic relations so that life for man could be more successful and enjoyable? Or, if we chose the Sovereign Creator and His infallible Word as our authority, would the function of education then be that of bringing praise and service to that God?

A third basic question that we must ask is: What is the nature of our relationship to that authority? Is it a psychological relationship? Is it a physical one? Is it a legal one? Is it an economic relationship of provider to dependent? Is it a spiritual-moral relationship?

Since these questions have previously been discussed in greater detail, we need only to remind the reader of the answers already given. Most certainly, the foundation for all education ought to be the Sovereign God and His infallible Word. Most certainly, the purpose of all education ought to be the bringing of praise and glory to that Sovereign God. Also, the nature of our relationship to our God can most comprehensively be described as spiritual-moral, for the term is not a narrow one. Because of the organic unity which characterizes man, all the accompanying descriptions are analytic devices used to describe man more precisely in his organic, spiritual-moral relationship to God. By making such profession, the Christian concurrently recognizes that he stands in a legal, economic, physical, and psychological relationship to his Creator. Legally he stands guilty before God the Judge. Pardoned through Christ's redemptive blood, he is indebted to live a life of gratitude, willing to use his abilities, his wealth, and his time in Kingdom service. Psychologically and physically the Christian remains dependent on God as Providential Father. Obedient to God's demands, the Christian seeks no substitutionary source of aid. Recognizing that calamities and financial shortages are also within God's control, he professes with Jeremiah, "It is [because] of the Lord's mercies that we are not consumed, because his compassions fail not. They are new every morning: great is Thy faithfulness" (Lam. 3:23). Rejoicing with Paul, the Christian endures hardship because he knows "that all things work together for good to them that love God, to them who are the called according to his purpose" (Rom. 8:28).

Assuming for the sake of this discussion that the supporters of private (in this case defined as "church related") and parochial schools are willing to accept these answers because of their Biblical origin,[3] we

---

[3]Since the vast majority of the private and parochial schools in the United States are part of the Judaic-Christian tradition, and since the Bible is accepted by these groups as God's revelation of Himself, it seems reasonable to the author that these conclusions, or some slight modifications thereof, would be acceptable to them without further proof or evidence.

can now proceed to the solution that we are seeking. In order to do so, however, we must continue to ask fundamental questions so as to find our way.

If the supporting members of religiously oriented private and parochial schools decide that their relationship to their final authority — that is, God — is a spiritual one and also that they are dependent on Him as their Provider, how then can they best preserve this relationship while fulfilling the function of education that His authority demands of them? Can they best perform their task by demanding and accepting aid from the "state"? Or can they best perform their task by requesting their Provider for some other means of assistance, so as not to destroy that dependent relationship with their God, for whose glory they educate their children.

To arrive at an answer to this question and hence a solution to our whole problem, we must ask another, namely, what is the nature of the triangular relationship between our basis of authority (God), man, and the state? Is the state (federal, state, and local governments) a creation of man, as Rousseau's "social contract" theory or the Mayflower Compact suggests? Or is it a creation of God, as Romans 13:1-7 clearly suggests? Since we will again be so bold as to assert that private and parochial school supporters must, if they are to remain true to Scripture, choose the latter answer, for whose sake does this divinely ordained institution exist? Does it act for its own sake, or was it ordained to act for the welfare of man, as God's minister of justice for good? Is the state, in God's plan, to act as though it were an end in itself, or as a "power that is ordained of God" as a ruler that is a minister of God to man for good? (Rom. 13:1, 3, 4)

With the state, then, lies half of our solution. So long as the government legislates, allocates, and distributes aid for the sake of the people who comprise it, that aid can be considered good. But, so soon as the government legislates for its own sake, that is, when the government considers itself as an end rather than a means, then its action is wrong and evil. A few outstanding examples of such government would be Nazi Germany and Communist Russia. In so far as any government plans programs for the continuation of a particular party in office, rather than for the general welfare of "we, the people," that government is faithless and unjust. If any government dispenses financial aid to schools that embrace the secular-pragmatic religion while denying aid to those schools that actively promote the Christian religion, that government no longer seeks the eternal welfare of its constituent members, but coddles and encourages the God-denier in his vain and incriminating endeavor.

The other half of the solution to our problem lies with the persons who are the supporters of our private and parochial schools. If their relationship to their basis of authority and source of life undergoes change from what it originally was intended to be, that is, if man begins to regard the state as his ultimate authority and source of sustenance, rather than God, then they must reject the offerings of the state until such time as they can again regard the state as a means instituted by God for their good. In other words, the state may not be substituted for the Provider who ordained it.

In our earlier discussion (Chapter VII) we noted that man is first described in Scripture as created being. By virtue of his creation, man is dependent. He needs to rely on someone or something bigger than himself. This characteristic demands accomplishment. This need demands fulfillment. If a true relationship to God exists, that accomplishment or fulfillment can be found in God's generous grace. If a true relationshp to God does not exist, fulfillment will be sought from other sources. Because of this creative-Creator relationship, the Christian must seriously ask whether he should actively seek that government aid which is equitably his. And in addressing himself to this question he must again turn to the Word of God for his answers. Does Scripture encourage the sons of God to demand and claim that which may be justly and equitably theirs?

Although there may be Scriptural answers of which the author is unaware, the emphasis seems to be clear. Jesus' message repeatedly directs the Christian, not to acquire, but to give. When Jesus' disciples clamoured for Him to establish the earthly kingdom that they desired, Jesus answered, "If any man will come after me, let him deny himself, and take up his cross, and follow me. For whosoever will save his life shall lose it: and whosoever will lose his life for my sake shall find it. For what is a man profited, if he shall gain the whole world, and lose his own soul"? (Matt. 16:24-26). With similar response Jesus rebuked the rich man who sought to inherit eternal life: "One thing thou lackest: go thy way, sell whatsoever thou hast, and give to the poor, and thou shalt have treasure in heaven: and come, take up thy cross, and follow me" (Mark 10:21). Rich men are grieved by those words, but Christ's disciples were also astonished and disappointed. Nevertheless, in emphatic rebuttal Jesus continues, "How hard it is for them that trust in riches to enter into the kingdom of God! It is easier for a camel to go through the eye of a needle, than for a rich man to enter into the kingdom of God" (Mark 10:24-25).

Firmly entrenched in this Christian tradition, Rushdooney writes,

> The churches have not perished by being cut off from state funds in various countries. Rather, they have thrived and are gaining a new vitality and relevancy. In like manner, the "Dis-establishment" of the

schools will be productive of true scholarship and vital education (*Intellectual Schizophrenia*, p. 76).

In even stronger, but very defensible, language he also states,

> The Christian cannot rest content with extracting an indulgence for himself; he must attack the fundamental statist concept, separating all education, including parochial, private, and Christian schools, as well as "public" schools, from the state and from state financial aid in any form. Statist education is ultimately the annihalation of man as man . . . But the unavoidable issue remains: statist education is the bulwark of this statist concept of life, enabling it to mold the child to its faith and to obliterate every form of non-statist culture" (*op. cit.*).

In conclusion, then, public funds for private and parochial schools are not in themselves wrong or evil. The evil lies only in the intent and purpose of the government which makes those funds available and in the beliefs or attitudes of the recipients. If those who comprise the instituted government "seek first the Kingdom" (Luke 12:31), distribution of financial aid may be Biblically defensible. But, if in their hearts and minds, the recipients transfer their allegiance and feeling of dependence from God to a political party, a President, or a government, they will have violated the sacred pledge: "O my God, I trust in thee" (Ps. 25:2). Their usefulness to the Christian school movement will have been nullified.

CHAPTER XVI

RELIGION AND MORALITY IN PUBLIC SCHOOLS

Of all the critical problems facing American public education in the decade of the nineteen-sixties, the conflict between the churches and the schools has certainly claimed a great deal of national attention. Although Francis Keppel has argued that the 1965 Elementary and Secondary Education Act is evidence of new harmony,[1] the tug-of-war between religion and public education is again at the point of open warfare and can not be glossed over with polite terminology much longer. If we are concerned about the welfare of our educational institutions (and certainly we ought to be when our most powerful member, the public school, is caught in such a vicious struggle), we must address ourselves seriously to this problem.

In the first place, we ought to recognize that this problem has a long history. It not only dates back to the nineteenth-century establishment of the public high school, but even extends to the quasi-public schools of the Massachusetts towns in the early colonial period. Whenever education has been directly related to the state, this problem has succeeded in being immodest, and that simply because it is the offspring of the church-state controversy, which has an even longer record of immodesty. Although there is slight chance of satisfactorily solving the parent conflict, I believe that there is an achievable solution to the daughter problem.

Our aim must not be to cover up, but to solve. Patchwork solutions have been tried often enough, and their succession of futility should convince us that no more are needed. We need a final answer. However, to prevent our picking up an already outmoded and unworkable answer, we ought briefly to examine a few of the less-well-publicized answers that can be found on the ideological trashpile of history. The flaws which prompted their removal to the trashpile will be self-evident in some, but other solutions will have to be scrutinized so as not to raise false hopes regarding their value.

The solution tried by the citizens of colonial Massachusetts was most interesting. They controlled the beliefs that were taught in their schools simply by controlling the beliefs within the colony. They defined reli-

---

[1]Francis Keppel, "The National Commitment to Education," *Phi Delta Kappan*, Vol. XLVII, No. 4, December, 1965, p. 167.

gious freedom as the freedom to practice and think the Puritan religion. If the witch trials, heresy hunts, and outgoing invitations had been more successful, the solution might have worked.

A common and yet heavily veiled solution that was tried throughout the nineteenth century and well into the twentieth century may be called religious segregation. When groups of like religious persuasion banded together in a community, they could control the school district that encompassed that community. By legally controlling the school district, they could control the beliefs that were transmitted in the school. In Minnesota, for example, numerous communities were settled almost exclusively by Scandinavians who then set up Lutheranized public schools. In other areas we find similar patterns, with Baptized, Methodized, Reformed, and Catholicized public schools not uncommon. This kind of "solution" has worked well for many rural communities in the same way that *de facto* racial segregation has worked well for some cities. But, in either case, the workability does not make the practice morally or ethically sound. F. Ernest Johnson referred to the same kind of solution and lamented its potential hazards when he said,

> It was a painful experience to discover in the schools religious practices well established by custom and supported by strong community sanctions which did patent violence to the religious liberties of minority groups as any discriminating court might find them. Yet nothing was more apparent than the prospect of disrupted community life, with perhaps devastating consequences to the minority groups themselves, that would result from arbitrary interference with deep-seated community customs.[2]

It could be deduced from this kind of situation that the free public school is not a divisive influence in American life only as long as the various minority groups within the community do not assert their right to question the position of the school as dictated by the local power structure. Given one radical atheist with fortitude and finances, any school can quickly be transformed into the local powder keg. With a Supreme Court that increasingly seems to be directing its attention to individual rights, and with the willingness of many persons to test the authority of the established power structures, the public school can expect to experience increasing unpleasantries from the church-school conflict.

---

[2]F. Ernest Johnson, "Summary of Policies and Recommendations of the American Council on Education Committee on Religion and Education," *Educational Issues in a Changing Society*, Smith Kerber, ed., Wayne State University Press, Detroit, 1962, p. 91.

Other groups, some refined and others less so,[3] have argued that the root of the conflict lies with the private and parochial schools, and deduce that the solution lies in their amalgamation into the public-school system. For, they have argued, as America is so diverse in its religious, cultural, social, and ethnic make-up, what is needed is one cohesive agency that can resolve all our differences. Their line of argument continues that if we are to preserve our individual rights and choices, that is, truly preserve our pluralistic society, then we must find that one cohesive agency which can teach us how to live in that democratic, pluralistic, pattern. This agency, for these proponents, is the public school. The public school, they say, must become the microcosm of pluralistic America. If carefully evaluated, however, this solution — though outwardly tempting — is theoretically undesirable for, if our school system is to be a microcosm of a pluralistic society, then it, too, must be pluralistic. If, on the other hand, the pluralists advocate that each school be a microcosm of society, they will find their solution more than mildly unworkable, because *each* school must then contain Indians, Negroes, Jews, atheists, Catholics, Protestants, Moslems, and members of all races and faiths. Even if this were possible, it is precisely this kind of religious mixing that has caused most of our church-school conflict.

Because of the cubbyhole effect on religion and the irksome administrative mechanics imposed on the schools by the courts, the "released time" solution has also been generally rejected. But an interesting substitute, in many cases initiated by Catholics, has taken its place. This is a "shared time" solution built around the idea that the Catholics and other religious groups will maintain their present separate schools but will now transfer their students to the public schools for part of the day to take the supposedly "neutral" subjects such as typing, shop, and home economics. This move is so contradictory to the educational-religious position of most parochial and private school supporters that we could charge this solution with sacrificing principle for financial expediency.[4] If religion is of such significance that it must permeate the

---

[3]A few of the refined are Horace Mann and John Dewey. An example of the other class is the Ku Klux Klan of 1925 Oregon vintage.
[4]The following excerpt from Pope Pius XI's encyclical "Christian Education of Youth" would seem to principially contradict the shared-time solution: ". . . it is the inalienable right as well as the indispensable duty of the Church to watch over the entire education of her children, in all institutions, public or private, not merely in regard to the religious instruction there given, but in regard to every other branch of learning and every regulation in so far as religion and morality are concerned. . . ." from *The Papal Encyclicals*, Anne Fremantle, ed., New American Library, 1956, p. 226.

skills of writing, reading, and arithmetic, what kind of rationale would allow the vocational skills to be excluded? On what principial basis can we isolate religion from studies of one sort and not isolate it from studies of a similar sort?

This next proposed solution to the church-school controversy is the one that I wish to recommend because it is the only one that is theoretically sound. At the same time I hesitate to advocate it strongly because of the resulting chaos and also because the majority of Americans have legally expressed themselves as being opposed to this solution. In capsule form this proposal would eliminate the church-school controversy from the public school by simply eliminating the public school.

Although this may seem both radical and overly simple, it is based on a somewhat complicated argument and a rather widely held premise. The major premise of this solution is the idea that no one can be objective in teaching. Teachers are always selecting, presenting, and interpreting information on the basis of their religio-philosophical position.[5] Any educational position (not to be confused with individual bits of information) becomes, then, a religio-philosophical position. For example, whether a person teaches that man was created or was not created, each position is religious. If the teacher, either by word or example, teaches that there is or is not a God, he again is taking a religious position. If the teacher asserts that certain studies can be understood apart from God or can be understood only by reference to God, he is taking a religious position. If a teacher tries to rationalize his way out of every problem rather than self-consciously accepting certain solution on the basis of belief, he is again assuming a religious position. The manner in which the teacher makes known his position is not of importance in this discussion, but the fact that he is always taking a stance or position before the learner is important. Any educational position, then, is synonymous with or equivalent to a religious position; for man is by nature a religious, a faith-motivated, a believing, a worshipping being. God has so created him and he cannot repudiate his own nature.

If it is the business of schools, either in whole or in part, to transmit

---

[5]The following quotation from John Dewey should give credence to this assertion:

"A learned and self-conscious generation has fittingly discovered religion to be a universal tendency of human nature. Through its learning, anthropology, psychology, and comparative religion have given this testimony."
from John Dewey, "Religion and Our Schools," *Education Today*, G. P. Putnam's Sons, 1940, p. 74.

or inculcate an educational position, we can therefore assume that it is the purpose of schools, either in whole or in part, to transmit or inculcate a religious position. The state has said that it must educate all those children who are not in other acceptable schools, but it has also said, by its own dictum, that neither it nor its agents may establish or maintain (that is, inculcate or transmit) a religion or a religious position.[6] By conjoining these two, we find that the state has formulated for itself a contradiction of "thou shalt educate" and "thou shalt not educate." Therefore, by following either one of these contradictory dictums, the individual agent of the state (the teacher) has violated the other.

Out of this dilemma there are only two logical lines of escape. On the one hand, the state can decide that it shall not educate, thus choosing to invalidate the more recent of its dictums, but at the same time causing institutional chaos and reverting to the educational status of the 1820's. On the other hand, the state can decide that it has the right to establish or maintain a religion, thus putting this country back on the precipice of late feudal situations when institutionalized religion and government were openly vying for control of each other.

With neither of these avenues out of the dilemma very appealing at the present time, we might choose to ignore the situation; but such attempted indifference is also a decision for one alternative and against the other. If we truly wish to "solve" the church-school conflict as it confronts American public education, we must press for the removal of either of these contradictory dictums. Since America was founded in large part on the idea of religious freedom, I recommend that the former ("thou *shalt* educate") rather than the latter ("thou shalt *not* educate") be removed.[7] Any action on such a recommendation would cause sharp hostility, but no other honest course is evident.

If such action were attempted and proved successful, we would have removed the church-school problem from the public school, but we would not have eliminated the problem in itself. The public school's problem of conflict in belief between teacher's educational positions and church doctrines would appear with increasing frequency in the pri-

---

[6]Justice William O. Douglas reiterated this position in the Engel V. Vitale decision of 1962 when he said,

"The point for discussion is whether the government can constitutionally finance a religious exercise. Our system at the federal and state levels is presently honeycombed with such financing. Nevertheless, I think it is an unconstitutional undertaking whatever form it takes. . . ."

[7]The other avenue seems more tightly closed simply by the wording of the first and fourteenth amendments. No federal constitutional clause, however, protects the public school.

vate and parochial schools. The one redeeming factor in their situation, however, is that churches and private societal organizations that control and establish schools have the right to control or establish belief patterns. They have no basic restrictions which prevent them from establishing or maintaining a religious position. To do this, in fact, is their right and function. There has not been formulated for them a contradictory set of rules, the extraction from which can only be accomplished by self-extinction.

The fact that the public school may not regulate membership on the basis of belief makes public-school teaching and learning more difficult than private- or parochial-school teaching and learning. Having a relative homogeneity of religious and philosophical assumptions between the teacher and learner reduces the individual and internal interference or tension that so often retards learning. For example, a student could be expected to learn or accept an educational position more quickly if that position were in harmony with his religio-philosophical set than if it were in conflict. Since the public school, by the very fact of its being public, increases the probability of school-church conflicts, it also increases the learning retardation factor just mentioned. This ideological-religious schizophrenia has been one of the primary effects of the controversy on the student, and is further reason for my advocating the modest proposal that I do.

BIBLIOGRAPHY

Allen, Roland, *The Spontaneous Expansion of the Church*, William B. Eerdmans, Grand Rapids, 1962.

Barzun, Jacques, *Teacher in America*, Doubleday and Company, Inc., Garden City, New York, 1954.

Bent, R. K., and Kronenberg, H. H., *Principles of Secondary Education*, second edition, McGraw-Hill Book Company, New York, 1961.

Berkhof, Louis, *Manual of Christian Doctrine*, William B. Eerdmans, Grand Rapids, 1953.

Blamires, Harry, *The Christian Mind*, William Clowes and Sons, London, 1963.

Brameld, Theodore, *Education as Power*, Holt, Rinehart and Winston, Inc., New York, 1965.

Bugelski, B. R., *The Psychology of Learning*, Holt Publishing Company, New York, 1956.

Clark, Gordon H., *A Christian Philosophy of Education*, William B. Eerdmans, Grand Rapids, 1946.

Conant, James B., *The American High School Today*, McGraw-Hill Book Company, New York, 1959.

Dewey, John, *Education Today*, G. P. Putnam's Sons, New York, 1940.
————. "The Relation of Theory to Practice in Education," *National Society for the Scientific Study of Education*, Third Yearbook, 1904.

Ehlers, Henry, and Lee, Gordon C., *Crucial Issues in Education*, third edition, Holt, Rinehart and Winston, 1965.

Fremantle, Anne, ed., *The Papal Encyclicals*, New American Library, 1956.

Gaebelein, Frank E., *Christian Education in a Democracy*, Oxford University Press, New York, 1951.

Gertler, Diane, *Subject Offerings and Enrollments, Grades 9-12, Nonpublic Secondary Schools*, U. S. Government Printing Office, 1962.

Good, H. G., *A History of Western Education*, second edition, The Macmillan Company, 1960.

Havighurst, Robert and Neugarten, Bernice, *Society and Education*, second edition, Allyn and Bacon, Inc., Boston, 1962.

Henry, Matthew, *Commentary in One Volume, Genesis to Revelation*, Zondervan Publishing House, Grand Rapids, 1961.

Hill, Winfred F., *Learning: A Survey of Psychological Interpretations*, Chander Publishing Company, San Francisco, 1963.

Hillway, Tyrus, *Introduction to Research*, second edition, Houghton Mifflin Company, Boston, 1964.

Hoffer, Eric, *The True Believer*, Mentor edition, Harper and Row, Publishers, New York, 1958.

Jaarsma, Cornelius, *Human Development, Learning and Teaching*, William B. Eerdmans Publishing Company, Grand Rapids, Michigan, 1959.

Johnston, Bernard, editor, *Issues in Education: An Anthology of Controversy*, Houghton Mifflin Company, Boston, 1964.

Keppel, Francis, "The National Commitment to Education," *Phi Delta Kappan*, Vol. XLVII, No. 4, December, 1965.

Kerber, Smith, ed., *Educational Issues in a Changing Society*, Wayne State University Press, Detroit, 1962.

Kittel, Gerhard, *Theological Dictionary of the New Testament*, Vol. II, translated by Geoffrey W. Bromley, William B. Eerdmans, Publishers, Grand Rapids.

Lewis, C. S., *Mere Christianity*, The Macmillan Company, New York, 1960.

————., *The Problem of Pain*, The Macmillan Company, New York, 1961.

————., *The Screwtape Letters*, The Macmillan Company, New York, 1956.

Mehl, Marie A., et. al., *Teaching in Elementary School*, Third Edition, The Ronald Press Company, New York, 1965.

Mort, Paul R. and Hamilton, R. R., *The Law and Public Education*, second edition, The Foundation Press, Brooklyn, 1959.

Oates, W. J., *Basic Writings of Saint Augustine*, Vol. 1, Random House, New York, 1948.

Rushdoony, Rousas J., *Intellectual Schizophrenia*, Presbyterian and Reformed Publishing Company, Philadelphia, 1961.

————., *The Messianic Character of American Education*, Presbyterian and Reformed Publishing Co., Philadelphia, 1963.

Seaborg, Glenn T., "The Cybernetic Age: An Optimist's View," *Saturday Review*, July 15, 1967, pp. 21-23.

Stephens, J. M., *The Precess of Schooling*, Holt, Rinehart and Winston, Inc., Chicago, 1967.

Ulich, Robert, *Three Thousand Years of Educational Wisdom*, Harvard University Press, Cambridge, Massachusetts, 1963.

Van Der Laan, Harry, "Science and Faith — Dualistic Paralysis or Scriptural Vigor," Dordt College, Sioux Center, Iowa, 1967. 12 pp.

Van Til, Cornelius, *Common Grace*, The Presbyterian and Reformed Publishing Company, Philadelphia, 1947.

Waterink, Jan, *Basic Concepts in Christian Pedagogy*, William B. Eerdmans Publishing Company, Grand Rapids, Michigan, 1954.

Weiss, Daniel E., "Teacher Credibility in Christian Higher Education," *The Gordon Review*, Winter, 1967. pp. 76-91.

Wesley, Edgar Bruce, "Let's Abolish History Courses," *Phi Delta Kappan*, Vol. XLIX, No. 1, Sept. 1967.

Whitehead, Alfred North, *The Aims of Education and Other Essays*, The Macmillan Company, New York, 1959.

Wolterstorff, Nicholas, *Curriculum: By What Standard?*, National Union of Christian Schools, Grand Rapids, Michigan, 1966. 16 pp.

Zylstra, Henry, *Testament of Vision*, William B. Eerdmans Publishing Company, Grand Rapids, Michigan, 1958.

Index

aims (see objectives or goals)
analysis
  necessity of, 51-5
  definition of, 51
Aristotle, 163-4
Augustine, 33, 173
authority, 78-80, 199-202

basis, 61-70
  of education, 61-3, 184-6, 199
Belgic Confession, 31
beliefs
  core beliefs, 16, 34-36, 143, 145
  importance of, 16, 23, 25, 31, 32, 177
  relationship to reason, 19
  truth or falsity of, 21-2
  as basic to behavior, 33-36, 65, 143-5, 166
Berkhof, Louis, 32, 34
Bible, as basis of education, 64-70, 82
  teaching of, 56

Calvin, John, 83
Canons of Dort, 73
Change, 61, 71, 84, 88, 112, 142, 153, 163
  as aim of education, 61, 167-8, 171-4
Chesterton, G. K., 64
Clark, Gordon H., 124
Conant, James B., 181
constancy, 142
creativity, 17

Darwin, Charles, 25, 158, 162
democracy, 99, 154, 206
Dewey, John, 16, 57, 86, 117-8, 140-3, 206-7
disciple (the student as), 110
discipline
  as organized subject matter, 37, 39-43, 55, 131, 146-9
  as control of behavior, 78-80, 92, 100, 134, 143, 173-4, 188

education
  need for a philosophy of, 14, 58-63, 82
  relationship to Scripture, 15, 16
  in the church, 19-20, 49, 86, 125-6, 209
  definition of, 49, 57 71, 114-119, 136, 186
  extent of, 57, 116-7, 119, 126
  evaluation of, 59-60, 62-3, 117, 131, 179-188
  ends, 81-3, 132-136, 145-8
  (see also goals, objectives, purposes)
essentialism, 85

faculty psychology, 46
faith
  relationship to reason, 19
  its boundaries, 19-21, 76, 148, 176
  relationship to science, 23, 28, 30
  definition of, 31-2, 177
falsehood, 11, 21, 22 34, 94-6, 162, 185
federal aid to non-public schools, 197-203
foundation(s) of education
  foundation courses 64
  historical 65-6
  philosophical 66-7
  psychological 67-8
  sociological 68
  Biblical 69-70
freedom, 74, 87, 97-107, 152
  definitions of, 98, 100-4, 105
frustration, 170-4

goals (see also ends and objectives) of life, 13, 59-60, 81-113, 149, 153

Heidelberg Catechism, 33, 36, 73, 83, 102, 167
Holy Spirit (active in the learning process), 175-8

in loco parentis, 127, 137, 150, 167

Index

Jaarsma, Cornelius, 46, 47, 48, 73, 91, 136, 138, 142, 147, 157, 163, 166-9
James, William, 164
jargon, 15

knowledge
unity of, 37-45, 82, 149, 154-5
explosion of, 38
importance of, 82, 93, 94, 135, 177
Kuyper, Abraham, 47, 129

learning, 33, 156-178
definition of, 156, 163, 165
connectionist approaches to, 158-160
cognitive approach to, 160-2
Gestalt theory of, 160
emotional dimension of, 168-172
Lewis, C. S., 77, 169
liberal arts, 97-8, 102, 194
logic
limits of, 21
love, 78-80, 86, 91-2, 150, 167, 188, 191

man
in the prelapsarian state 72-5
as sinner, 75
methodology, 59-60, 62, 81, 137-8, 141-4

neutrality, 33, 39, 44, 57, 61, 68, 76, 121, 199, 206, 207

obedience, 92, 102, 135, 150, 165
objectives
of education, 59, 71, 81-113, 141, 149, 153, 167
the ultimate, 81, 83-87, 183
primary, 87-108
secondary, 108-112
objectivity
29, 56, 76

parents
responsibility of, 78-80, 91, 107, 114, 119-130
person
organic unity of, 47-50, 53-4, 138
Pestalozzi, 156, 166
philosophy
of education, 14, 16, 58-63, 82
definition of, 16
Plato, 97, 194, 198
pluralism, 121, 129, 198, 206
pragmatism, 16
professional, definition of, 195
Progressive Education movement, 57, 85, 117, 136, 163
proof
definition of, 29
punishment, 78
purposes of education (see ends, goals or objectives)

quality, 131, 135, 181-8
quantity, 135, 181-8

reason, use of, 19-22, 73-4, 76
reconstructionism, 85
relativity, 121
religion (in public schools), 204-209
resistance to learning, 168-174
Rushdoony, R. J. , 65, 82, 100, 202-3

S-R psychology, 67, 71
Satan, 25, 76-7, 97, 106, 171, 199
schools (types of) 65-6, 120, 197
science, 13, 22-33, 67, 140-1
limitations of, 22-30
relationship to faith 23, 24
scientific method, 26
Scripture, as the Word of God, 16, 17, 29, 31, 82
security, 76-80, 137, 166-7, 182-8
Skinner, B. F., 33, 143, 157, 171
sphere sovereignty (autonomy), 120, 130
rejection of, 126-130
subjects (see also *disciplines*) 69, 133-5, 148-154

Index

teaching
  as art, 139
  as commitment, 145
  as science, 24, 140, 142
  evaluation of, 131-6
  as done by God, 122-3, 169, 172
  as a profession, 191-6
  as a vocation, 191
teaching, learning relationship, 132-6,
  147
theology
  as a science, 26
theory
  relationship to practice, 17, 29 141
truth, 21, 22, 24, 94-5, 102, 162
  testing for, 44-5, 95-6, 182[

unity, 13, 96
  of knowledge, 37-45, 51-2, 55,
  154-5
  of time, 39, 52
  of man, 46-50, 53-4, 88, 155, 159,
  165, 200

validity, 21
values, 28, 137, 149
Van Til, Cornelius, 31, 33
vocation, 191-2, 196

Westminster Catechism, 81, 83
Whitehead, Alfred North, 40
Wolterstorff, Nicholas, 20

Zylstra, Henry, 24, 43-4, 57-8, 87,
  119, 147

Norman De Jong (Ph.D., educational foundations, University of Iowa) is the author of *Teaching for a Change: A Transformational Approach to Education* (P&R, 2001), as well as other books and articles on education and government. He was associate professor of education at Dordt College and, subsequently, professor of education and director of teacher education at Trinity Christian College. He also has served as principal in three schools, and taught at several others.